BRAIN REBOOT

BRAIN REBOOT

NEW TREATMENTS
FOR HEALING DEPRESSION

MICHAEL E. HENRY, MD

Go

hachette
BOOKS

Hachette Go, an imprint of Hachette Books
Hachette Book Group
1290 Avenue of the Americas
New York, NY 10104
HachetteGo.com
Facebook.com/HachetteGo
Instagram.com/HachetteGo

First Edition: November 2022

Hachette Books is a division of Hachette Book Group, Inc.

The Hachette Go and Hachette Books name and logos are trademarks of Hachette Book Group, Inc.

The publisher is not responsible for websites (or their content) that are not owned by the publisher.

Library of Congress Cataloging-in-Publication Data has been applied for.

ISBNs: 978-0-306-92517-7 (hardcover); 978-0-306-92518-4 (ebook)

Printed in the United States of America

LSC-C

Printing 1, 2022

Contents

Introduction:
Don't Give Up Hope!

Many people find themselves feeling engulfed by despair and hope-lessness, which is, basically, the definition of depression.* What-ever brought you to this book, whether it is you or someone close to you who is suffering from depression, know that here you will find its opposite: hope. Even if you have tried medications and therapy and they haven't worked—meaning you have what professionals have deemed treatment-resistant depression—you might not have heard about some of the options you'll learn about here. What's more, myths about these treatments may have caused you or the professionals helping you to overlook them. Much in the field of depression treatment has changed in recent years, and interventions you have not considered might turn out to be key to regaining your mental health and well-being.

Brain Reboot offers practical insight into the treatments that are available when the medications, psychotherapy, and faith-based approaches you may have already tried didn't bring the needed relief from the symptoms of depression. In addition to providing the

---

Author's note: Names and identifying details have been changed, and most examples are composites.

science underlying each treatment, we will discuss the nuts and bolts of deciding whether they are for you and how to access them if you decide to proceed with them. You will learn about what to look for when seeking out a clinic or individual provider. Also, we will discuss the medical conditions that need to be considered and managed prior to and during the treatment, as well as the common side effects people experience with each of the treatments. In the closing chapters of the book, I will provide you with a brief overview of the new technologies that are being deployed in depression, such as genomics, as well as a quick look at other novel treatments in the development pipeline.

Brain Reboot started out as a way to reassure people suffering from severe depression and who had been referred for electroconvulsive therapy (ECT) that old-fashioned shock therapy had been modernized and is safe and highly effective. It is a treatment I have successfully used to help thousands of patients. This large number, in part, reflects the fact that for most of my professional career as a psychiatrist, I have been the director of busy ECT services, first at McLean Hospital and now at Massachusetts General Hospital, where I am also the medical director of the Dauten Family Center for Bipolar Treatment Innovation. However, given the recent advancements in the treatment of refractory or intractable depression (treatment-resistant depression) and other mood disorders, it would be very biased to talk only about ECT. For those with severe mood disorders that do not respond to first-line treatments, two additional powerful interventions are now available: transcranial magnetic stimulation (TMS, also known as rTMS when it is used repetitively) and ketamine. I was first exposed to TMS during my fellowship training at the National Institutes of Mental Health, where my time overlapped with that of Dr. Mark George, one of the leaders behind the development of TMS as a clinical treatment. Over the years, I have had additional training in TMS and have recommended it to my medication patients. Similarly, my experience with ketamine is based on my attempts to use it to bolster the effectiveness of ECT as well as my recommendation of it to my medication refractory depressed patients. In this book, you will learn about these as well as some exciting new potential interventions that show great promise for all sufferers of depression and gain an understanding of these treatments that will help you decide which, if any, would be most appropriate for you.

You will also find a chapter on treatments for the metabolic effects of depression because depression is often associated with deconditioning and weight gain, which can cause long-term negative effects on your health. Recent research has shown that exercise, diet, and improved sleep can have antidepressant effects.[1] I've also included a chapter on psychotherapies because studies have consistently shown that mood disorders, especially depression, improve more when a biological treatment (for example, an antidepressant medication) is combined with psychotherapy.[2]

Most chapters are centered on a clinical case that is typical for that particular treatment and feature a discussion of the science. The purpose of using this format is twofold. First, I wanted to let readers suffering from severe mood disorders know they are not alone, and second, I wanted to make the information more relatable to their individual journey. I disguised patients' identifying details, and most examples are composites. By way of example, let us start with Margie's struggle with depression.

Margie is a forty-six-year-old mother of two daughters who came to our clinic as a last resort. Her nurse practitioner, Paula, had referred her because she "had tried everything and didn't know what else to do." After a brief examination, it was clear that Margie had progressed from feeling blue all the time, dragging herself around, to feeling sheer dread at having to face each day. She was in the depths of what Winston

Churchill, a fellow sufferer, called "the black dog." It was as if a creeping black veil had been hung over the world—and especially over her.

There were days when she could barely get out of bed. The pain of the depression grew ferocious, sometimes crippling her so badly that she had to stop what she was doing and try to breathe. Her husband and her daughters suggested that she get help, but she thought she could beat it by herself. That didn't work.

Paula had tried everything to help her patient, but after months of trying different combinations of medications and different forms of therapy, Margie was only slightly better. Not only did she continue to feel "flat," but in her worst moments, she had thoughts of ending her life. She assured Paula that these were just "silly thoughts" and she didn't intend to actually end her life, but Paula understood that Margie was telling her just how bad it really was: she was still in the depths. During the day she felt like she was wearing lead shoes. Finally, Paula referred Margie to a psychiatrist. The psychiatrist felt that Margie's depression was too deep for TMS, and Margie's family history of addiction made her reluctant to try ketamine. So the psychiatrist recommended a trial of ECT—electroconvulsive therapy.

Horrified, Margie rejected the idea immediately. Snippets from old movies floated through her head of people being tormented, having their brains "fried," and losing every memory of who they were. But after another month of indescribable misery, she agreed to meet with the local ECT doctor. She expressed her concern about having her brain "zapped" and becoming "a vegetable." The ECT doctor explained that the current generation of ECT machines uses a much less intense stimulus over a longer period of time and is specifically tailored to the patient. They discussed the possible memory side effects in detail, and Margie learned that these side effects would be closely monitored and would improve once the treatments stopped. They discussed how usually it is difficult to remember only events that occur around the time of the treatment but that some people have reported forgetting events from their past; however, her ability to learn would not be affected after the treatment ended and might actually improve with the depression out of the way.

She also learned that the brain is in no way damaged with ECT. Certain areas involved in the regulation of mood actually get bigger during a course of treatment, and ECT is thought to protect the brain from the negative effects of depression. Still very anxious, Margie agreed to try it.

On the morning of the first treatment, Margie checked in with the front desk and took a seat in the waiting room, flipping through a magazine without being able to read it. She was called in after what seemed like an eternity but in reality was only ten minutes. She was surprised at how much it was like when her daughter had her wisdom teeth taken out, very bright and medically reassuring—not gloomy and mysterious, as she had feared. The nurse checked her in with a warm but efficient bedside manner. Before she knew it, the psychiatrist had evaluated her and the anesthesiologist had given her a sedative. The next thing she knew, she was a little fuzzy and asked the nurse what was happening. The nurse explained that the procedure was over. The calming manner of the nurse gently reoriented her, and she had some ginger ale. An hour later, her husband drove her home, and she went on with her day under his watchful eye. She couldn't be sure, but she thought she felt a ray of light finding its way through the darkness.

Nine treatments later, the ray had become a full-blown sun. Margie regained her enthusiasm and playful spirit. As she had been advised, her memory became a little shakier with each treatment, but she was able to function just fine on her nontreatment days and found herself laughing at her "senior moments." She remembered how to do everything she needed to do but couldn't recall what she had for dinner on the night before a treatment or what the answer to the final *Jeopardy* question was. She and her husband began to have fun together again, and she beamed when talking about her girls. At a three-month follow-up, her nurse practitioner found that she was taking her anti-depressants regularly and had been able to cut back on the frequency of her counseling sessions as her wellness stabilized.

Margie's story is not unusual. It happens every day. ECT has become much more than a last-ditch effort. Because of its high effectiveness and speed, it has become a primary treatment of choice for many of the millions who suffer from depression and can benefit from it. Like TMS and ketamine, ECT helps people return to a life that isn't dominated by depression.

Depression often starts in the context of significant life stress, and the symptoms can be subtle. People commonly blame themselves and see their symptoms as a personal failure or character flaw rather than an illness. This results in delays in seeking treatment, and over time, these symptoms take an enormous emotional, physical, and financial toll on the person and the people around them. While a significant number of people who receive standard antidepressant medications and therapy improve with treatment, millions of people with depression do not get sufficient symptom relief to enable them to get on with their lives. Throughout the world, depression is a major cause of disability. Because of its tendency to become chronic if not effectively treated, depression can rob people of their ability to do more than exist for years.

Data from the United States in 2017 showed that during the twelve-month period that was studied, 8.9 million adults had depression. Of these, 2.8 million suffered from treatment-resistant depression.[3] Treatment-resistant depression, also known as refractory depression or intractable depression, has been defined in many ways. Generally, it means the person is still depressed after trying at least two standard antidepressant medications at a therapeutic dose for an adequate duration, usually considered to be eight weeks.

After all the time and effort it takes just to figure out that depression is the core problem and it needs treatment, it is easy to become disheartened when initial treatments don't work. People often see treatment nonresponse as confirmation of their brokenness. To make matters worse, a number of people—including at least one major movie star—have been quite public about their disappointment with and opposition to psychiatric treatments. Add all this to the darkness and crushing psychic pain that are part of the illness and you can see why people with depression often give up on treatment and suffer in silence. That is exactly what you must not do! Contrary to public perception, the current psychiatric treatments help many people and are improving constantly.

The treatments we will discuss in this book represent the next generation of antidepressant treatments. They are part of a sea change that began in the late 1980s. Up until this time, depression was thought to be caused by loss associated with unresolved conflicts from childhood. Talk therapy aimed at understanding and resolving those conflicts was a mainstay of treatment. The earliest medications were accidentally discovered as part of attempts to improve on existing antituberculosis medication and existing antipsychotics. The latter became known as the tricyclic antidepressants and came to be used as an add-on to therapy. However, they had a lot of side effects, and patients often found them intolerable. Then fluoxetine, better known as Prozac, came into use, with other newer antidepressants to follow. The current generation of antidepressant medications reflects the pharmaceutical industry's skill at refining medications to reduce side effects. But since these do not offer a new mechanism for addressing depression, there have been no significant gains in effectiveness since Prozac was introduced, until ketamine.

Ketamine, which we will discuss later, offers a totally new mechanism and has shown significant effectiveness in treatment-resistant depression.[4] The use of ketamine for depression has had several benefits for people suffering from depression. First, it offers a treatment for depression that acts rapidly and, most importantly, acts through the glutamate pathway, which is different from the other antidepressant medications available. Second, the recognition of the role this molecular pathway plays in depression has sparked a renewed interest in drug development for mood disorders in general.

The switch away from using only psychotherapy-based treatment toward medications and brain biology also brought about a resurgence in ECT. ECT started as a treatment for schizophrenia in the 1930s, but with the development of modern antipsychotic medications, which offer comparable effectiveness, its use in schizophrenia started to fall in the 1970s. The resurgence in ECT use came as its effectiveness in severe mood disorders became evident. Fortunately, the practice of ECT has been modernized to increase patient comfort and optimize effectiveness. It still remains the most potent treatment for refractory mood disorders.[5] TMS, although new relative to ECT, has had more than twenty-five years of study and refinement. We will discuss in greater detail the recent, exciting advancements in this treatment.

It is immensely rewarding for me as a psychiatrist to see patients with treatment-resistant depression find relief. Each has a unique path to recovery even as each has a unique experience of their illness. I believe that in *Brain Reboot*, you will discover information and stories that will convince you that you have options for depression treatment that have been overlooked.

Part I

Depression 101

Chapter 1

Depression Is a Syndrome, Not Just a Feeling

Many people use the word *depression* casually to describe being down about things that are happening in their life. Those of you suffering from **major depression** know that the word can mean something very different. An episode of depression—or, more accurately, major depression—isn't merely a temporary low mood. Depression is a real illness—an illness of the brain that affects many aspects of everyday functioning. During an episode of major depression your mood is consistently down, your sleep and appetite are disrupted, it is difficult to get motivated or maintain focus, and you prefer to be left alone. After the episode is over, you have to undo its effects on your physical health, and you have to rebuild relationships that withered because you couldn't engage with the people you care about. We will begin with an overview of the different mood disorders that have depression as part of the illness.

Given that the word *depression* is used to describe both a mood and an illness, it is no wonder that people get confused and think that depressed people should be able to "pick themselves up by their boot-straps" or motivate themselves to find their way to a better place. For the person suffering through an episode of major depression, this all-too-common attitude minimizes their struggle, and it unknowingly hurts in at least a couple of ways. First, it implies that they caused their own suffering. **They did not!** Second, it implies that they are too lazy to do anything about it. **They are not!** In fact, the exact opposite is true for the person suffering from major depression. Severe depression can be compared to solitary confinement in a psychological prison, and people suffering from it would give anything to get out. The difference between feeling depressed and an episode of major depression (also known as major depressive disorder or clinical depression) will, I hope, become clearer to you when you read the two case histories described in the following paragraphs.

Raya is a nineteen-year-old college student. Although her freshman year was her first time living away from home, she was making new friends, enjoying her courses, and exercising regularly. She missed her boyfriend and was excited when he called to say he was coming to visit the upcoming weekend. During the course of the weekend, they fought most of the time, and shortly before he left to go home, they broke up. Raya was devastated; she became very withdrawn and had a fitful night's sleep. The next morning, she barely touched her breakfast but did manage to get to her classes. Her friends noticed that she seemed really "depressed" and insisted that she go out with them for dinner. Over dinner Raya told her friends about the breakup and fought to hold back the tears. Her friends were very supportive, and by the end of dinner, she had begun to feel better. Over the next few days, she decided to focus on the positive things in her life and gradually began to feel more like her old self.

In contrast, twenty-two-year-old Salwa was in her last year of col-lege. She was looking forward to life after graduation. She had really good friends, didn't dislike her coursework, and had a great relationship with her partner. She even had a couple of exciting job offers. Around the end of October, Salwa noticed that she felt a little more sluggish than usual, but she wrote it off to the stress of midterm exams and partying too much after they were over. In an effort to get rest, she took a low-key weekend with lots of naps, but she didn't bounce back. Instead, she continued to wake up several times during the night, felt tired and listless throughout the day, and didn't really want to eat. This continued over the next several weeks. When she was around her friends, she had to make an effort to smile but still felt like the color had gone out of her world. She barely made it through finals.

When she went home for the holidays her mother noticed that she did not seem to be herself and asked Salwa what was going on. Her mother listened carefully, and when Salwa finished, her mother told her that it sounded like she was depressed. She explained that her sister and mother—Salwa's aunt and grandmother—had similar episodes where they couldn't really function and needed treatment. Salwa's mother arranged for her to see the family primary care physician, who ruled out medical illnesses and referred her to a psychiatrist. The psychiatrist initially prescribed therapy and exercise, but the symptoms persisted; after a month, she prescribed an antidepressant medication, which gradually lifted Salwa's depression. She graduated on time and with honors.

From the perspective of the person going through it, it can be difficult to distinguish between a normal reaction to an upsetting event and an episode of major depression. Raya's "depression" came on in response to a clear life stressor and resolved with support from her friends and time. Salwa's episode of depression did not have a clear precipitant and in fact came on when things were going quite well for her. Also, her symptoms did not go away with family support, time, exercise, or talk therapy. Sadness, or an inability to fully experience joy, that extends to every part of the person's life and does not go away over time is more likely an episode of major depression. Sadness that is isolated to one part of the person's life, such as a breakup or a friend moving away, and does not affect one's ability to be happy when good things happen is more likely a normal reaction to loss.

Why Can Some People with Depression Still Function Normally?

Major depressive disorder has many different faces. Mild depression slows the person down and makes them feel "fogged in" but still allows them to function. Severe depression can cause overwhelming pain and makes it nearly impossible for the person to get moving. The net effect in virtually all types of major depression is that people are less available to their families, significant others, friends, work colleagues, and children, if they are available at all. During prolonged bouts of severe depression these crucial relationships can wither and die. People lose jobs, are unable to fulfill their role in the family, and find no joy in life, all because of an invisible illness that has attacked their brains. In short, the effects of depression are often life-altering. For people who die by suicide, they are life-ending.

Are There Different Types of Depression?

The short answer is yes. The longer answer is that which type of depression a person has depends on how you define the syndrome of major depression. The ancient Greeks used the word *melancholia*, or "black bile,"[1] to describe a pattern of behavior that was similar to what we now call major depression. Our current classification systems stem from efforts by the then Veterans Administration to classify the mental illnesses they were treating in veterans returning from World War II. This system was largely adopted by the American Psychiatric Association in its diagnostic manual known as the *DSM*, or *Diagnostic and Statistical Manual of Mental Disorders*.[2] In its latest edition, the *DSM-5*, the criteria are based on clinical symptoms described by the patient.[3] The *DSM* system further refines the diagnosis into major depression or bipolar depression. Bipolar depression is used when the person has had an episode of elevated mood, or mania, which consists of euphoria or irritability, increased energy, decreased need for sleep, and increased risk taking and/or pleasure-seeking behavior. For people who have chronic low-grade depression, the *DSM* uses the diagnoses of dysthymia and cyclothymia. The difference between them is that cyclothymia is the diagnosis used when the person has also had periods of low-grade euphoria or irritability.

The reason these distinctions matter is that they can have a significant impact on the treatment you receive. At the start of the third year of my psychiatric residency, one of my first outpatients was a thirty-something-year-old man who had been diagnosed with major depression and alcohol abuse. He had been discharged from the inpatient unit of our hospital after a lengthy stay for depression. When I had met him on the unit prior to discharge, he was unshaven, his clothes were stained and rumpled, and he was lying on a couch. Our conversation was brief, and he gave mostly one-word answers. A couple of weeks later, when I went out to the waiting room to greet him for our first outpatient appointment, I walked right past him. When I called out his name, a well-groomed, sharply dressed young man stood up and walked over to me. I hadn't recognized him, and I couldn't believe the change in his appearance!

When we got into the office, he explained with enthusiasm that he was feeling "great" and that "God had forgiven" him all of his sins. He spoke rapidly as he described his many plans for the future. I quickly recognized the speech, the euphoria, and the increased energy as symptoms of mania. We then proceeded to review the course of his mood symptoms since they first started and realized that he had been using alcohol and other drugs to control the manic side of his symptoms since his teens. This had led his physicians to prescribe antidepressant medications instead of the mood stabilizers that he needed. I realized he was bipolar and prescribed mood stabilizers so he wouldn't be tempted to return to alcohol and other drugs to manage his symptoms. Now that he was on these medications, his mood remained very stable over the next couple of years that he and I worked together.

In fairness to my inpatient colleagues, I treated this patient before psychiatrists realized that antidepressant medications tend not to work in patients with bipolar depression and can even make things worse.[4] **That difference in response to antidepressants may be the reason you are reading this book.** You might have bipolar disorder and not realize it.

Patients like the one previously described are good examples of what is called the bipolar spectrum.[5] The idea behind this concept is that there are variants of bipolar disorder that don't fit the classic criteria of having had at least one full-blown episode of mania, as in type I bipolar disorder. In the evolution of the *DSM* from 3 to 5, this led to the inclusion of the type II bipolar disorder diagnosis.[6] Arguably, since our patient only had a full-blown manic episode while taking an antidepressant and has had several severe depressive episodes over the years, he is best diagnosed as having bipolar II disorder.

At this point it is probably helpful if I quickly summarize the diagnostic criteria for a manic, hypomanic, major depressive, and dysthymic mood episode and cyclothymic disorder.[7]

Mania and Hypomania

The key symptoms of both mania and hypomania are an elevated or irritable mood. In a **manic episode, the change in mood lasts at least seven days unless the patient is hospitalized.** During a **hypomanic episode, the change in mood lasts at least four days and is not severe enough to significantly impair functioning or require hospitalization.** (*Hypo* means "under," so hypomania is a less intense, shorter-lasting mania.) In addition to the change in mood, for both mania and hypomania, the *DSM* requires that three of the seven accompanying symptoms in the following list be present if the mood is elevated and four out of seven if the mood is irritable. **Remember: a key difference between the two is that the hypomanic episode is much less severe and does not substantially impair the person's ability to appear to function fairly normally.** It is this last point that makes it so hard to make the diagnosis before significant damage is done to the person's relationships and/or career. Their behavior is out of character, but they can provide a rationale for it until it blows up on them and leads to disaster. Symptoms of mania and hypomania include:

1. Talkative and/or difficult to interrupt
2. Decreased need for sleep
3. Racing thoughts
4. Easily distracted
5. Increased goal-directed activity
6. Increased self-esteem
7. High-risk behaviors

From this list of symptoms, it is easy to see why the manic symptoms wreak most of the visible damage in the person's life, but it is the depressive symptoms that often lead the person to seek treatment.

Major Depressive Disorder, Dysthymic Mood Episode, and Cyclothymic Disorder

The diagnoses of major depression and dysthymia (from the Greek for "disordered mind") are similar in that depressed mood is the main symptom. Also, both are accompanied by at least some disturbance in sleep, appetite, energy, and concentration, known as neurovegetative symptoms because they're related to the autonomic nervous system that controls certain body functions without our consciously directing it. In addition to a depressed mood, an episode of major depression requires five out of a possible nine of these types of neurovegetative symptoms be present for at least two weeks. Unlike hypomania, which is briefer than mania, dysthymia requires that the patient experience symptoms for two years. In contrast to major depression, only two out of six possible neurovegetative symptoms are required to make the diagnosis.

Lastly, the *DSM* also includes a diagnosis of cyclothymia ("cycling mind"), which is described as having at least two years of mood swings but never with symptoms severe enough or long-lasting enough to merit a diagnosis of hypomania or major depression.

Just to make things more difficult to sort out, the majority of people who develop a mood disorder do so in their teens and twenties. When you consider the different ways mood disorders can affect a person and the number of transitions and challenges the average person faces during this time when they are transitioning into adulthood and its many responsibilities and choices to be made, it is easy to see why people often delay seeking treatment and can easily be misdiagnosed. In an effort to reduce the complexity of distinguishing between the different mood disorders, Table 1.1 presents the main differences between the major mood disorders as defined in *DSM-5*.

Table 1.1: Spectrum of Mood Disorders

	Bipolar I	Bipolar II	Major Depressive Disorder	Dysthymia	Cyclothymia
Mania or Hypomania	Mania	Hypomania	None	None	Never severe enough for diagnosis
Major Depression	Usually but not required	Predominant	One or more episodes	Never severe enough for diagnosis	Never severe enough for diagnosis

Can It Be Something Other Than Major Depression?

As I mentioned, the onset of a person's first mood symptoms often occurs in their teens and early twenties. This is also a time when other conditions that can mimic the symptoms of major depression can begin to impact the person's life. While depression may not be the main symptom, these psychiatric and medical conditions tend to also involve sustained sadness and/or malaise. To make things more complicated, some people can have depression and a second or third co-occurring psychiatric illness. Attention deficit and hyperactivity disorder (ADHD), personality disorders, anxiety disorders, and chronic severe mental illness are common examples of conditions that can be associated with sadness and that can also co-occur with depression.

A general principle for teasing out what is going on is to look at the patient's experiences over time and in different situations. By way of example, one of the more difficult conditions to separate from bipolar disorder is ADHD.[8] Both can have onset of symptoms in childhood, and the inattentiveness, hyperactivity, and impulsivity associated with hypomania can very much look like ADHD. The person with ADHD can also have periods of time where sadness is prominent due to the fallout from their ADHD on their personal and professional lives. It is only when you look at the longitudinal course of the symptoms and see that the hyperactivity and impulsivity only occur when the person is having periods of increased energy, decreased need for sleep, and markedly increased moodiness that the diagnosis of bipolar disorder becomes evident.

Similarly, personality disorders can be difficult to sort out from mood disorders. To make matters worse, some people have both a personality disorder and a mood disorder. Personality disorders are characterized by inflexible and maladaptive patterns of perceiving and relating to people that are consistent across different settings, such as home, school, and workplace. As a result of their difficulties adapting to different situations and getting along with people, they often struggle in life. As a consequence, they can have prolonged periods where they feel irritable, sad, or disappointed. These symptoms often overlap with those of mood disorders, especially bipolar disorder.[9] They also do not respond to medications and can lead to a diagnosis of treatment-resistant depression when the primary issue is the personality disorder. Two personality disorders that can be particularly difficult to sort out are borderline and narcissistic personality disorders.

Borderline personality disorder is characterized by intense and unstable moods and interpersonal relationships, impulsivity, and a sense of emptiness.[10] The mood swings and the self-harming behaviors that people suffering from this disorder use to avoid their overwhelming feelings can resemble the mood lability and risk-taking behaviors seen in bipolar disorder.[11] Likewise, narcissistic personality disorder can be especially hard to tease out from bipolar disorder as the grandiosity associated with bipolar disorder is easily confused with the elevated self-esteem of the narcissist.[12] In addition, the narcissist's maladaptive style usually leads to an internal sense of emptiness and chronic sadness that is easily confused with depression. Their lack of close and supportive relationships makes it hard for other people to recognize when they are in trouble. When an acute stressor occurs, it can trigger significant distress. The person may present as depressed and report symptoms of depression, but when asked, they are able to identify the stressor and usually report that their mood was normal prior to it. Usually, their mood brightens when they are asked about other, more positive aspects of their life. When their mood does not change and the sadness remains consistent, then an additional diagnosis of major depression is warranted.

Acute grief is another life circumstance where people can suffer with symptoms that very much look like an episode of major depression. Grief is usually characterized by sadness over a loss and is often associated with disrupted sleep and diminished appetite. There are two things that can help distinguish grief from major depression. First, the sadness is clearly related to the loss and can lift significantly when something good happens. Second, the person's self-esteem usually remains intact. In major depression, the person often sees themselves as worthless. In grief, the person usually understands they feel bad because of who or what they lost.

The list of medical illnesses that can masquerade as mood disorders is fairly long and beyond the scope of this book. Suffice it to say that if you are suffering through an episode of depression, a visit to your primary care provider as well as your mental health provider is important. Low thyroid hormone levels, or hypothyroidism, and anemia are common, treatable illnesses that can easily be confused with depression.

Since the treatment of a bipolar disorder is very different from the treatment of major depression, you should be monitored by a professional for any signs of hypomania or mania so your treatment can be adjusted appropriately should they appear. Clues that an episode of depression is likely to be part of a bipolar illness before manic symptoms occur are if the patient's mood symptoms started in their teens or even before, if they have a relative with bipolar disorder, or if the patient began using substances like alcohol and illicit drugs at an early age. Accordingly, when an adult presents with an episode of major depression, and any of those features, it should raise the suspicion that this person has bipolar disorder. The diagnosing psychiatrist will be more likely to guide their treatment appropriately as a result.[13]

What Causes Major Depression?

Most physical illnesses can be demonstrated by an X-ray or a biopsy. To date, there has not been a reliable laboratory test for depression and other mood disorders. So how do we know depression is a real illness? Our understanding of depression and other brain-based psychiatric disorders has been limited by the relative inaccessibility of the human brain. It is encased in the bony skull, and once we get through the skull, sampling brain tissue simply to study it is highly unethical. To noninvasively study the brain, neuroscience had to wait for the development of imaging techniques such as computerized axial tomography (CT scanning), positron emission tomography (PET scanning), magnetic resonance imaging (MRI scanning), and electroencephalogram (EEG).

While neuroscience was waiting for these techniques to be developed, psychiatry used the treatments and tools available to understand mood disorders. As a result, depression was at various points explained in terms of unconscious conflicts rooted in the past, inadequate psychological defense mechanisms, a mismatch between the temperament of the child and the primary caregiver, and self-defeating automatic thoughts, to name a few.[14] While I have certainly seen patients with depression for whom these models do a good job of explaining their symptoms, they do not explain the biology of mood disorders.

The earliest insights into what might cause the brain to become depressed came from clinicians who noted side effects of medications that were used to treat other conditions. The blood pressure medications reserpine and propranolol are two examples of drugs that were noted to affect mood.[15] Reserpine reduces the amount of key neurotransmitters in the brain, including serotonin, norepinephrine, and dopamine, that are important in the regulation of mood. In a slightly different mechanism, propranolol blocks norepinephrine from interacting with its receptors in the brain, causing the brain to be unable to fully use the norepinephrine the body produces to maintain a normal mood. The common theme observed was that decreasing the activity of norepinephrine, serotonin, and dopamine in the brain all led to an increased risk of depression.

Conversely, medications that increased the activity of these neurotransmitters improved depression. Iproniazid, the first antidepressant medication to be developed, was initially developed as a drug to treat tuberculosis.[16] Then, clinicians noticed that their depressed patients felt better when they took it. It is thought to work by blocking the breakdown of neurotransmitters, thereby increasing their activity in the brain. Imipramine, the first of the tricyclic antidepressant class, was initially developed as an antipsychotic medication. It failed to treat psychosis but improved people's depression.[17] Its antidepressant effects come from blocking the pumps that limit the amount of interaction neurotransmitters have with their receptors. With the receptors having longer exposure to these important signaling chemicals, the patient's brain is able to pull out of depression. The net effect of both classes of medication is an increase in the activity of these neurotransmitters at their receptors.

The next major forward step in antidepressant medications came with the recent discovery of the antidepressant effects of ketamine, a drug that has been around since the 1950s, when it was used as an anesthetic. The chapter on ketamine describes how the treatment of mood disorders was finally able to turn its attention away from sero-tonin, norepinephrine, and dopamine toward the glutamate system (glutamate is an excitatory neurotransmitter—that is, it is stimulating). The result has been the development of faster-acting medications that work in patients who have treatment-resistant depression.

From the larger perspective of helping drive treatment innovation, these medications contributed to our understanding of depression and mood disorders in three ways. First, they provided evidence that depression was not a character deficiency but a biological illness that could be treated with medicines. Second, animal studies allowed us to understand their effects at the molecular level. That, in turn, helped researchers begin to put together a model for explaining why people become depressed. Third, they became a template from which other structurally similar drugs could be developed. In the United

States, at least four monoamine oxidase inhibitor antidepressants and six tricyclic antidepressants have been used in humans to treat depression as a result of understanding the biology of depression. Each subsequent drug is the result of changes to the chemical structure of the previous drugs and was designed to increase effectiveness and decrease side effects.

It is hard to convey how much of a sea change these medications caused and their importance to patient care. Lives were saved! Unfortunately, until these antidepressants came along, psychoanalysts did not believe that neurotransmitters were the cause of depression. The degree of upheaval caused by the shift from psychoanalytic thinking to neurotransmitters that occurred in the 1980s and 1990s was nothing short of a revolution. When the battle was at its peak, several prominent psychoanalysts were let go on very short notice and then hustled out by security at one of the premier psychiatric teaching facilities in the country. Psychopharmacology became the primary treatment focus. Fortunately, the pendulum has shifted back to the middle such that people realize that a combination of these approaches is usually the most effective. It's gratifying to see how much has changed and how many more people we in the psychiatric field have been able to help.

From Neurotransmitters to Brain Circuits

Although neuroscientists have long been aware that neurotransmitters are part of the circuitry in the brain, the idea of a mood circuit that malfunctioned in depression was also a significant advance. One of the approaches to understanding mood disorders that made this concept more acceptable was the genetic studies that looked at mood disorders in families. Relatives of people with major depression are 3.6 times more likely to have a mood disorder. Studies of twins also provided significant information. In identical twins, 60 percent of the time both twins had mood disorders versus 12 percent of the time when the twins were fraternal (that is, they were not from the same egg and therefore not genetically identical).[18] The finding of an elevated risk for mood disorders in the relatives of people with depression lent strong support to a biological basis for mood disorders.

A large piece of the puzzle in developing our current model of mood disorders came from brain imaging studies. Both had a significant influence on ECT and TMS/rTMS treatments, which we will discuss in later chapters.

Most of the studies used one of three types of scanners: CT, PET, or MRI. Computerized tomography, or CT scanning, was one of the earliest techniques that permitted detailed three-dimensional views of the brain's structure. Dr. Robert Robinson and colleagues at Johns Hopkins and the University of Maryland in the early 1980s made the observation that a stroke in the left frontal region of the brain was associated with an increased risk of depression relative to a stroke in other regions of the brain.[19] Building on these findings, using PET scanning, Dr. Helen Mayberg and colleagues at Johns Hopkins and the University of Toronto in the 1990s were able to show that mood and depression were controlled by several regions in the brain that work together as a circuit.[20] This view of depression has been further refined using MRI scanning. MRI scanners can be used to take very high-resolution pictures of the brain's structure and to look at changes in blood flow. The blood flow technique has been used to develop very detailed maps of brain circuits or dynamic networks. The picture that has emerged from these different ways of imaging the brain of depressed individuals is consistent with the diverse symptoms seen in the clinic.

In short, the verdict is in: depression and mood disorders are circuit-based illnesses of the brain. We tend to think of the brain as special, because it is the source of our thoughts and feelings, but think of it for a moment as just an organ in the body. When an organ is attacked by a serious illness, it requires treatment to restore the person to health. If you knew you had heart disease, you would be very concerned and would treat it very seriously. Most importantly, you would receive a lot of support from the people who care about you. That doesn't happen as often with depression. Depressed people may not have the energy to seek out treatment or discuss their symptoms with the people in their lives.

In today's hectic world, people can easily miss the quiet withdrawal of the depressed person. Also, because of the stigma that is still associated with mental illness, the depressed person may be embarrassed and try to hide their symptoms. The television commercials where people refuse to accept help despite obviously needing it and those that show people carrying a smiley face mask to hold up so people don't see their depression captures these feelings well. Alternatively, as in the case of Salwa, people may not even realize they have depression. Contrast this with our heart disease example above. Heart disease can also sneak up on people without them realizing it. But once they develop symptoms, people often attribute it to working too hard and too much stress. They are generally offered support, not judgment. My hope is that one day, people with depression will be treated with the same compassion that's shown to people with a disease affecting any other organ. Until then, it's vital that as many people as possible know what the early signs of depression are and help the sufferer access the help they need—even if that sufferer is them.

Key Takeaways

- ▶ Unlike feelings of sadness and grief, major depression is an illness that affects not only mood but also the basic functions needed to sustain the physical well-being of the person.
- ▶ People may not realize when an episode of depression is happening. You know you don't feel well but not why.
- ▶ Depression can be a part of bipolar disorder or related to other conditions, or it can be a stand-alone diagnosis.
- ▶ Several lines of evidence show that depression and other mood disorders result from malfunctioning brain circuitry.
- ▶ Treatments that work when the frontline treatments don't are available and constantly improving.

Chapter 2

Sooner Is Better Than Later:
The Importance of Early Treatment

If you suffer from depression, you know it hurts. It negatively affects almost every aspect of your being. It darkens your perception of yourself and robs you of the motivation and self-confidence to be your best self. Important relationships can wither and die because the illness makes it too hard to muster the energy you need to maintain them. Just getting to work is a struggle. Often people can't and wind up unemployed or on disability. Instead of growing and excelling professionally, careers stagnate or worse, when you're depressed you go backward. Your physical health suffers because it is hard to get motivated to exercise. Most importantly, depression is not good for the long-term health of your brain.

While the changes from a single episode of depression can have long-lasting effects, keep in mind, too, that depression tends to be a recurrent illness. If you have one episode of major depression, you have approximately a 50 percent risk of having additional episodes of depression. Three or more episodes and the risk rises to 90 percent or more.[1] In addition, it can take nine months to one year for a person's brain to fully recover from an acute episode of depression.[2] This is important because it is tempting to stop treatment as soon as you are feeling better, but that increases the risk of the depression reemerging and prolonging the episode.

Over time, our view of depression has shifted from thinking of it as a discrete episode with a full recovery in between to the cumulative effects of the longitudinal course of the illness. This has led to a new understanding of the effects of delayed or ineffective treatment on the person's physical and brain health. The longer an episode of depression goes on and the greater number of antidepressant treatments that are ineffective, the more entrenched the depression becomes and the more vulnerable the brain is to future episodes. The fallout from this can be devastating: the collateral damage to self-esteem, relationships, physical health, and career over subsequent episodes tends to be cumulative.

I know the statistics on depression recurrence can be discouraging; if you have depression, you may be aware of these numbers already. Fortunately, *effective* treatment has been shown to lower the risk of recurrence.[3] The challenge is to set aside stigma, break out of any denial, and get help *now*. If your current depression treatment is not working well for you, do not hesitate to pursue other treatment options.[4] This chapter will focus on why **it is important to begin treatment as soon as you recognize you are depressed and, once you are better, develop a plan to stay well**.

When You Treat the Depression, Doesn't That Fix Everything Else?

In a word, no. Effective treatment of mood disorders requires attention to the many parts of a person's life that are negatively affected by the illness. As you well know, when you are suffering with depression, it is difficult to initiate and sustain the effort needed to accomplish basic hygiene and self-care, never mind work on personal development. Consequently, your self-image gets pretty beaten up, and it becomes even harder to get going. As you can imagine, it is difficult to study the damage depression does to a person's everyday life. One common way to do this is to measure quality of life.[5] Quality of life scales ask people about their level of satisfaction with their relationships, work, ability to function, economic status, leisure time activities, and overall sense of well-being. Since these scales are based on the person's perception of their situation, they provide a way to measure the person's self-image and, indirectly, self-esteem.

In a study of people with depression seeking treatment at an out-patient clinic of a community hospital, Dr. Waguih IsHak and his team at UCLA found that quality of life scores for the people with depression were essentially half those of the control group.[6] Similarly, Dr. Keming Gao and colleagues further examined this issue in a different group of subjects with unipolar and bipolar depression.[7] They found that when the subjects were not depressed, their quality of life scores were at the lower end of the "normalcy spectrum." When the subjects had mild depressive symptoms, they reported a statistically significant reduction in quality of life. These findings are worth noting since a significant number of patients treated for depression report chronic mild symptoms of depression. They also highlight the many spheres of the person's life that are affected by depression and, most importantly, that dissatisfaction and distress cause an increase in the level of depression. It's a vicious cycle.

One area that has a large impact on mood and self-esteem is social support. People struggling with depression tend to have fewer close, supportive relationships and smaller social networks. It is not clear which comes first. Studies indicate that loneliness increases a person's risk for depression, while great support (as perceived by the person) protects against the onset of depression.[8] Unfortunately, depression causes decreased self-esteem, loss of interest in daily activities, and decreased motivation, which results in withdrawal from one's family and friends. From a cognitive behavioral theory perspective, the individual's negative automatic thoughts become increasingly entrenched, and they go into dark places more easily and for longer periods of time. The Study of Depression and Anxiety from the Netherlands examined 2,981 subjects and found that people with unipolar depression had smaller social networks, engaged in fewer social activities, and had less social support and more loneliness than individuals without psychiatric illness.[9] As you might predict, individuals with the relatively common combination of depression and anxiety had even more difficulties with their social functioning. So, if you find yourself feeling lonely and isolated during or after an episode of depression, know that this is not a measure of who you are. It is a symptom of the illness and something that is important to work on with your therapist.

I'm Kind of Shy: Are Social Connections Really That Important?

If you are normally shy, introverted, or socially uncomfortable, you will want to decide the level of social connection that is healthy for you and address any challenges you are having achieving it. The reason I am emphasizing this is that isolation combined with the immobility and pessimism that accompanies depression creates a negative feedback loop that can cause a downward spiral. For some people this spiral leads to suicide. Stronger social connections can actually save lives. Dr. Julianne Holt-Lunstad and colleagues reviewed 148 studies on the effect of social relationships on mortality.[10] Across these studies they found that stronger social relationships were associated with a 50 percent increase in survival rates. In contrast, unsupportive social relationships increase the risk of premature death at levels comparable to smoking, excessive alcohol consumption, and obesity. The take-home message from all these studies is that **having or rebuilding a supportive social network is vitally important for the whole person to get well**.

Remember Salwa from Chapter 1? To illustrate this concept more concretely, let's revisit her. She is now twenty-five years old. After graduating from college, she and her partner moved to Minneapolis and began working in jobs they both enjoyed. Through work and each other they had a solid group of friends, and Salwa continued to be in contact with her close friends from home and college. About a year after moving, Salwa felt well enough to go off her antidepressant medication and scaled back on her therapy sessions. Things continued to go well for the next two years until the fall of the third year.

At first Salwa noticed that she was having trouble sleeping and it was just a little more difficult to get started in the morning. Although she had many good things happening in her life, she smiled but didn't really mean it. She found herself preferring quiet evenings at home instead of meeting up with her friends. Her partner commented that she seemed quieter than her usual self. She apologized and made an effort to be more interactive.

Initially, she was able to be more present with her partner and friends but quickly faded back into being quiet. As she declined more invitations to get together, she found that her friends stopped inviting her to do things. She also noticed that her partner began doing more things with friends that didn't include her.

Listening to her on the phone, her mother suspected she had slid into another episode of depression and urged her to seek treatment. Initially, Salwa resisted, but when she realized that people seemed to be pulling away and her job performance was suffering, she agreed. After about a month of treatment, Salwa began to feel better and sought to reengage with the world. She was shattered when her partner decided to end their relationship to begin dating someone he had met while she had been depressed and withdrawn. She also found that her friends sounded sympathetic when she told them what had happened, but few had the time to meet up and truly be supportive. She felt better mood-wise but often felt lonely and betrayed. It took about a year for her to grieve the loss of her relationship with her partner. Rebuilding her social network was more challenging since a lot of her friends were also her ex's friends, and she had been very hurt by how they had moved on while she was depressed. With persistent effort, she was able to develop a group of friends she feels close to and who are likely to be supportive if she gets depressed again.

Depression Really Did a Number on My Career

As you may know from personal experience, depression can have a significantly negative impact on your career. Even the most supportive boss will find it difficult to stay enthusiastic about your performance when you are struggling with depression. When you have recurrent episodes of depression, there will be periods of time when you are not your usual self at work. During an episode you are likely more withdrawn and less interactive than usual. You may miss meetings and make simple mistakes that you don't usually make when you are feeling better. Even if they are not openly discussed, these things get noticed and become important when decisions about raises, bonuses, and layoffs are being made. The patients I have seen over the years who have struggled in their careers because of their depression have come up with some creative ways to survive. Most primarily did it by cutting costs to the bone, but some also switched to less intense work or to temporary or freelance jobs that allow them to not work when they are not well.

Often, less income and a sense of frustration over what they could have accomplished accompany these professional adjustments. Consistent with my clinical experience, Barbara Biasi and her colleagues studied the effects of mental illness on income in Denmark.[11] They found that unipolar depression reduced income by 20 percent after diagnosis. Similarly, bipolar disorder decreased income by 25 percent after diagnosis and increased the risk of dropping into the bottom 10 percent income bracket by 120 percent. One note of optimism is their work on the positive effects of treatment on limiting the damage to income. They looked at the effects of treatment with lithium on bipolar disorder and found that treatment with lithium reduced the decrease in earnings by a third. To put this in context, lithium helps a great many people with bipolar disorder, but a significant number do not benefit or can't tolerate it. As more effective treatments are developed, hopefully, the economic as well as the social cost of the illness to the individual and society can be further reduced and eventually eliminated. If you are disappointed by depression's effect on you professionally, there is hope thanks to advances in treatment, so read on.

How Did I Get So Out of Shape?

The effects of depression on the individual, their career, and their social network clearly indicate the need for a rapid and multipronged approach to treatment. The physical changes that can occur as a result of depression add to that urgency. One of the hallmarks of depression is appetite disturbance: people often under- or overeat. While some people may think of weight loss due to decreased appetite as a desirable symptom of depression, it is not. Unplanned weight loss has significant consequences on your body and long-term health, since it is mostly a loss of protein and muscle mass.[12] This combined with the inactivity associated with severe depression leads to a loss of strength in core muscle groups. In the young adult, this can lead to a loss of stamina, or deconditioning, that takes hard work to recover.[13] In older adults, depression-induced weight loss has similar effects on muscles and strength, but because they are usually starting from a less conditioned state, the loss can have a greater effect on their mobility. They become more vulnerable to falls and broken bones. Even if they do not fracture a bone when they fall, the resulting anxiety over future falls may cause them to walk more slowly and cautiously, which can actually make them more vulnerable to falling, and/or it may make them too fearful to live independently. They also lack the nutritional reserve to support normal healing from their injuries. In severe cases, sustained periods of minimal nutrition can lead to abnormal heart rhythms and even heart failure.

Alternatively, instead of a decreased appetite, depressed people can have an increase in appetite. To make matters worse, a lot of the medications we use to treat depression can cause an increase in appetite and slow down your metabolism.[14] One social media post that I saw recently put it something like this: "They put me on meds for my depression. When I started to gain weight, they told me to intermittently starve and do high-intensity workouts! I couldn't do it and gained thirty pounds." Even when the medications effectively treat the depression, their metabolic side effects can cause significant problems for the person's health and self-esteem.

As you know, depressed people tend to be more inert during a depressive episode than when they are not depressed. This combined with the changes in appetite and the effects of the medications can cause people to have significant weight gain.[15] One area of the body where the adipose or fatty tissue tends to accumulate is the abdomen. Abdominal fat plays a role in regulating the body's response to insulin and can trigger an increase in inflammatory molecules in the brain as well as the body.[16] This affects learning and memory and—you guessed it—mood. We will discuss the current thinking about how this contributes to depression in a later chapter, but the take-home message is that over the long term, weight gain and the resulting chronically elevated inflammation can lead to a decrease in blood flow to the brain and damage key parts of the mood circuit, which then worsens the depression.

Does Exercise Really Treat Depression?

I hate to admit it, but all of those people hawking exercise machines on TV are right about one thing: exercise is really good for you, especially when you are depressed. We will talk in more detail about the mechanism by which exercise helps depression in a later chapter, but let me quickly touch on the highlights. Regular exercise causes the release of growth factors that increase the strength of positive connections in the mood circuit. It also increases the release of proteins from the peripheral fat that reduce inflammation and other negative effects of obesity. Lastly, it raises serotonin levels in the brain.[17] When a person stops exercising, the levels of these beneficial molecules drop. If you have depression, this sets off a molecular cascade that makes your mood even worse. In addition, the deconditioning that occurs fairly rapidly when you stop exercising makes it harder to exercise sufficiently to quickly reverse these changes. In older patients, being sedentary contributes to an increased risk of falls and a loss of mobility and independence. When you are older, it is even more difficult to rebuild after an episode of depression. The need for rapid and comprehensive treatment is even more urgent.

Does Depression Have to Get Worse as You Get Older?

Over time, the social, psychological, and physical stress caused by depression take a toll on the brain itself, which in turn worsens the depression. The goal of addressing these issues is to minimize their effect on brain health and functioning.

To have a nondepressed mood requires successful integration of several brain functions and several brain regions. High-resolution brain scans have found differences in the structure and functioning of the brains of people with mood disorders when compared to healthy subjects: functional brain scans that image the activity of different brain regions have shown decreased regulation of the mood circuit, and structural brain scans have shown corresponding decreases in the volume of the structures thought to mediate those functions. To simplify things greatly, brain regions that negatively interpret the environment (for example, seeing problems in a situation but not potential solutions or positive aspects of it) tend to be overactive. Meanwhile, brain regions that integrate and moderate these negative inputs, allowing the person to give context to difficulties and imagine how to address them, tend to be underactive.[18] To better illustrate these points, we will look at the effects of mood disorders on the brain imaging findings from two different brain regions: the amygdala and the prefrontal cortex.

The amygdala is an important part of the mood circuit. Its role in the brain is to translate information that comes in from the periphery and determine whether it should be perceived as something negative or dangerous. Are you truly in danger, or are you overreacting to a criticism a coworker made about the quality of your work? Your amygdala helps you decide.

Research indicates that during an episode of depression, parts of the amygdala associated with negative stimuli are more active.[19] With the amygdala's innate bias toward the negative and the pessimism seen in the depressed state, this observation is not surprising. However, it is worth noting that the amygdala does not integrate the signals from many stimuli that need to be processed by the brain. An area of the prefrontal cortex, otherwise known as the dorsolateral prefrontal cortex or DLPFC, is a part of the brain that sorts and synthesizes input from many brain regions and then decides on a course of action.[20] Given its central role in human behavior, this region has been highly studied using both structural and functional imaging techniques. High-resolution functional MRI scans have been used to compare the brains of people with unipolar and bipolar depression to those of healthy control subjects. The result is that the prefrontal cortex has consistently been found to be underactive when the person is suffering through an episode of major depression and to normalize with effective treatment.[21]

Combining the activity of these two brain regions during a depressive episode offers a greatly stripped-down model of depression. The amygdala, which is important in detecting threats and other negative stimuli, is working overtime and overwhelming the underactive prefrontal cortex, whose job it is to counterbalance the amygdala with positive mechanisms.[22] The net effect is that the mood network is telling the person they feel depressed.

While this model seems to work well, the brain is significantly more complex than I'm describing, and several other brain regions have been identified as playing a significant role in mood disorders. One of those regions is the hippocampus, which is involved in memory and learning. It is thought to work as a positive counterweight to negative input of the amygdala when the brain is determining whether a memory is positive or negative.[23] The hippocampus is also interesting because it is one of the few brain regions that retains the property of plasticity. Plasticity is the ability of a brain region to grow new connections and change its structure in response to functional demand. Several studies have found that depression is associated with diminished plasticity and decreased hippocampal volume, which is consistent with decreased positive input to the DLPFC. This is exacerbated by the social isolation and increased inflammation of depression, which reduce the number of positive inputs into the brain and further reduce plasticity, respectively. The good news is that antidepressant treatments, including ECT, ketamine, and TMS/rTMS, increase hippocampal activity and volume.[24]

The next chapter provides more detail about treatment and also addresses what to do when your current treatment isn't working. Part II will introduce you to three very powerful treatments that are used when the first-line options don't work. Together, they have saved many lives and helped many more people start rebuilding after a severe episode of depression.

Key Takeaways

▶ Depression has significant effects on the whole person.
  ■ The social isolation that results from depression can have long-term effects on a person's overall well-being.
  ■ The difficulties with attention and other effects of depression have negative impacts on career advancement and income.
  ■ Decreased activity and changes in weight during an episode of depression can lead to changes in your physiology that cause chronic illnesses.
▶ The physical changes that occur in the body as a result of depression affect brain health, especially executive functioning and perception (such as whether you perceive a memory to be negative or positive).
▶ Getting effective treatment sooner rather than later is critical to your long-term health and well-being.

Chapter 3

How Do You Treat Depression and What If It Doesn't Work?

Once you realize you are suffering from major depression, the next step is to decide how you want to treat it. As you learned, the consequences of not treating depression can be significant, so even if your depression seems mild, I strongly suggest you get help for it. You might already know you have major depression and are treating it with antidepressants and interventions (such as exercise) but are unsure of whether your current treatment is adequate and will continue to work well. Maybe you recognize that you have treatment-resistant depression. Knowing what your options are may make it easier to trust that no matter what happens, you will be able to access effective treatment.

If you have mild depression, or concern for a loved one who is depressed, you might want to know about non-medication-based treatment options as well. There are several that show some benefit in treating depression. Let's look at those, along with how to access them, before we move on to antidepressant medications; in later chapters, we will address ECT, ketamine, and TMS/rTMS.

Where Do You Begin When You Suspect
You Have Depression?

As you may already know, the hardest part of treatment for depression often is reaching out to make an appointment with your primary care provider or a mental health professional. People are often embarrassed by their illness and don't want to pull back the curtain and allow someone to see how bad things have gotten. Other people have had so many people urging them to seek help, they are sick of talking about it. Maybe you thought you had left depression in the past only to have it show up again, and you no longer have access to the health professional or professionals who treated you originally. When my patients tell me they don't want to start seeing a new therapist because they don't want to rehash their story, I usually tell them about wakes. In the culture I grew up in, when someone died, there were calling hours, otherwise known as a wake, the day or two before the funeral. While wakes have a reputation as being a time for telling funny stories about the dead person, what they do very effectively is provide a place for their family to begin to talk about their loss and their grief. It is the retelling of your story and feeling understood by an empathic listener that is the beginning of the healing journey, so tell your story to a professional who cares and who wants to help—that's the first step.

What Should I Expect When Working with a Provider?

The purpose of the first few meetings with you is for the professional to get a clear picture of your current symptoms and your past psychiatric and medical history so they can help you. When you meet with them, the more you have organized your information beforehand, the more productive the meeting will be. Make sure you can describe your current symptoms, when they began, and whether there was anything new or stressful going on in your life when the symptoms started. If you have been using alcohol or recreational drugs, be honest about that, as it will assist your doctor or mental health provider in developing a better sense of what you're experiencing and why. Remember the example you read earlier of the man with bipolar disorder who was self-medicating with drugs and alcohol to manage hypomania symptoms? Knowing about this habit could lead to questions about why the patient is drinking or using drugs and bring to light symptoms that point to a particular diagnosis.

At your initial appointment, it will also be helpful if you can describe any prior episodes of similar symptoms, as well as any past medication trials and whether they were helpful or not. If you cannot remember your past medications, your pharmacist may be able to help you piece this together. The health care provider will also want to know whether there is a family history of mood or other psychiatric disorders. They almost certainly will ask other questions, but if you have the facts about your mental health history at hand when you walk into the office, you will find the meeting will be less stressful. Most of all, no matter how uncomfortable it may be to talk frankly about your symptoms and history of depression, remember that your health care provider is there to help you, not judge you. The more information you offer, the easier it will be to get the treatment or treatment adjustment you need.

One of the first decisions your provider has to make before deciding on which treatments to use is what your diagnosis is. With mood symptoms, such as depression, a key distinction is whether you are suffering from an acute reaction to a particular event in your life or whether you have a mood disorder, such as major depression, that is likely to benefit from medication. For people with a mood disorder, the next question is whether the depression is part of a bipolar illness. By definition, in bipolar disorder, the person has a history of mania. In contrast, in unipolar depression, the person never has mania. An estimated 3 to 9 percent of patients who visit their primary care provider for depression have undiagnosed bipolar depression.[1] As you learned, bipolar depression responds differently to traditional antidepressant medications, so it's important to know whether the patient has ever exhibited mania. In the STEP-BD study, a large treatment study for bipolar disorder sponsored by the National Institutes of Mental Health, the antidepressant bupropion was found to not be any better than a placebo in treating bipolar depression.[2] Earlier data on the use of tricyclic antidepressants in the treatment of bipolar depression suggests that they may make the episode worse by inducing rapid cycling or a mixed state.[3] Rapid cycling is when a person has four or more mood episodes in a year. A mixed state is when the person has symptoms of depression and mania at the same time.[4] While this can be difficult to conceptualize, you can think of it as feeling sad but also very activated and agitated. Clues that suggest a person may have bipolar depression include having a family member who has bipolar disorder, an early age of onset (childhood or teens), or a lack of response to previous antidepressant trials.

Once you and your mental health provider have settled on a working diagnosis, the next step is to figure out a treatment plan. This will focus on which treatment(s) to use and in which setting (inpatient versus outpatient). A key consideration when you partner with your health care provider to formulate a treatment plan is the severity of your current symptoms. Someone who feels blue and more fatigued than usual but is able to go to work and take care of their other responsibilities can be treated as an outpatient. If you are very sad all day, unable to get out of bed, and actively suicidal, you are in trouble and need intensive professional help to keep you alive and begin your recovery. You also need antidepressant medication or ECT, ketamine, or TMS/rTMS to get you out of your suicidal state. The person with the milder depression has more time to explore different treatment options and can try less intensive treatments first.

What Role Should Psychotherapy Play in Depression?

If your depression is mild to moderate in severity and not part of a bipolar disorder, you may opt to treat the episode with psychotherapy, exercise, or a combination of treatments (many of which you'll learn about later in this book). Let's start with a brief look at some of the psychotherapies that you might find helpful, recognizing that if you have moderate to severe major depression, you will almost certainly need to take medications regardless of whether you undergo psychotherapy.

Cognitive behavioral therapy, or CBT, is a very structured form of psychotherapy that focuses on the automatic, reflexive thoughts and the negative cascade that follows when the person feels something bad has happened. Rather than focusing on the patient's feelings, the cognitive component of CBT uses the objective side of the brain to stop and change that cascade. The goal is to realistically assess a situation rather than automatically reinforce negative conclusions. The cognitive approach helps you avoid adding more fuel to an already sad or depressed mood. The behavioral component focuses on changing the behaviors that worsen the depression. CBT usually involves a more interactive approach along with worksheets and homework that help the person become aware of their automatic mental processes. If the thought of homework is unappealing, know this: CBT works! CBT has been extensively studied with randomized clinical trials that demonstrate its effectiveness.[5] CBT adapted for bipolar disorder has been shown to reduce the number of relapses, improve social functioning, and reduce hospital admissions.[6]

Interpersonal therapy, or IPT, views depression from the context of the person's relationships and how they affect moods. With respect to depression, the core hypothesis of this school of thought is that the depressed individual doubts that people truly care about them. Although they may receive reassurance from the significant people in their environment, they do not believe it. This results in a need for reassurance that is excessive and drives people away, confirming the depressed person's negative self-image and leaving them socially isolated. IPT focuses on helping the person identify the pattern of difficulties they are having in their relationships and strengthen the person's skills for dealing with those issues.[7]

Psychodynamic approaches focus on helping the person uncover the root of why they are having trouble and what they want to change. Psychodynamic psychotherapy tends to be longer in duration to allow the person to explore these issues in greater depth, and the therapist is less directive than in CBT and IPT. The objective is to help the person build the life they want to lead rather than the one their therapist thinks they should live. A significant number of people find this approach helpful, but others want concrete advice specific to their situation.

There are many other approaches to therapy. If you will let me oversimplify greatly, these other approaches can be useful as well. When faced with all these options, choosing the one that's right for you can seem impossible, especially when you are feeling depressed. The key point I want to convey is that it is not as difficult as it seems. For therapy to be helpful, there are a few basic ingredients that are essential regardless of the underlying theory behind the approach.

Find the Right Therapist for You

A key ingredient is to **find a therapist who you feel listens and understands** your struggles. Studies have shown that the greater the connection between the person and the therapist, the greater the improvement.[8] This is all the more reason to make sure you are feeling heard in the therapy. Human interaction is complex, and there may be many reasons why you may not feel like that is happening. That's OK. If you're having a problem with your therapist and you feel up to it, try discussing it with them. That may resolve the issue for you and allow effective therapy to proceed. Working through the difficulties that occur in getting the therapy started may allow you to better understand patterns that impede other relationships in your life. This may be beneficial to you in the long term, but don't lose sight of your need to get help now. If you are not benefiting, you should consider switching therapists.

Be Sure the Therapist's Approach Is Working for You

Another important ingredient for a successful therapy is that you feel like the therapist is actively working to help you get better. When therapy goes well right from the start, people often wonder aloud why they didn't start it sooner. However, there can be hiccups. Over the years, I have heard a number of people complain that their therapist doesn't say much and they have to do all the work in the sessions. Most likely the therapist is following a classical psychodynamic approach. Many people find this approach helpful, and the differences in how people respond to it highlight how one size does not fit all in therapy. You should not hesitate to discuss things with your therapist if you feel the therapy is not helping you.

Be Clear on Whether You Are Getting the Guidance You Need

For therapy to be successful, you need to feel you are receiving guidance that is tailored to your needs. If you feel your therapist is not understanding the situation or their input is not helping, you should not hesitate to raise this with your therapist. The discussion that often follows this kind of feedback can greatly clarify things and be quite productive.

This list of psychotherapies is not intended to be exhaustive. The point is that there is a range of therapies, and if you are not getting better, don't hesitate to discuss it with your therapist or, if need be, change therapists.

Regardless of the type of therapy you undergo, there are some tools that CBT therapists use that will help most people with depression. They usually focus on sleep hygiene and exercise. Difficulty falling asleep or initial insomnia is common in depression. Over time people will find that their sleep becomes very erratic and they are often up into the middle of the night and in bed until midday. As a result they are usually exhausted and upset about how little they are getting done. This makes them feel worse about themselves and feeds into their negative self-talk. It is a common enough problem that a specific type of CBT, called CBT-I (the "I" is for insomnia), has been developed. We will discuss both exercise and sleep in the later chapter on metabolic treatments. But to give you a brief preview of what's called sleep hygiene: the therapist advises the patient to keep to a set sleep schedule, whereby they go to bed and wake up at the same time every day. In addition, they will focus on helping you eliminate behaviors that make it harder to fall asleep and remain asleep. These usually include not having caffeinated beverages after a certain cut-off in the afternoon and not looking at computer or TV screens for at least an hour before bedtime. The light emitted by these screens contains a significant amount of blue light. The blue light tricks you into thinking it is daytime and causes the brain to break down the chemicals it makes to cause you to fall asleep.

Another behavioral change a CBT therapist will usually advocate for is regular exercise, for reasons you read about earlier. While everybody agrees they should exercise, even nondepressed people have a hard time getting regular exercise. When you are depressed, it is that much harder but also that much more important. Studies that have looked at exercise in depression have found it to have a significant antidepressant effect.[9] In mild to moderate depression, studies have found it to be as effective as antidepressant medication.[10]

How Do I Decide About Medications?
Do I Have to Take Them?

If you tell people that you are considering antidepressant medication, you are likely to get a number of opinions. Critics of the pharmaceutical industry and psychiatry have argued that antidepressants aren't any better than sugar pills, or placebos, in treating depression. However, **for the Food and Drug Administration (FDA) to approve a drug for use in humans, they require at least two large-scale trials where the drug proves itself to be more effective than placebo.** People have noticed that some people have an antidepressant response to the placebo in these studies and have used this to argue that antidepressant medications don't offer much benefit. This is not true and overlooks a few key points. First, and most important, **the placebo did not do as well as the active drug or the active drug would not have been approved.** Second, a clinical trial visit is not the same as a visit to your prescriber or therapist. During a clinical trial, you are attended to by a number of people whose job it is to make you comfortable and make sure you want to come back to complete the trial. For the depressed patient, the experience is usually different. They have one-on-one meetings with their providers and limited interactions in between. Although most providers are highly motivated for their patients to do well, it is not the same amount of attention and encouragement as the patient would get in a clinical trial. Probably just as important, as part of a clinical trial, you are expecting to receive the latest wonder drug, so there is a hopefulness that the treatment will work, and even if it does not, you still have very smart people thinking about how to understand your illness. Lastly, you have made a contribution to science and may feel better about yourself for contributing.

There are a number of antidepressant medications approved by the FDA. When and which medication you are prescribed depends a lot on where you start when seeking treatment for depression. Primary care providers usually have at least one or two antidepressant medications they are comfortable prescribing because of their experience with them, so they may start you with one of those. Others routinely refer patients to psychiatrists or other mental health clinicians for treatment. Psychologists or counselors may do this as well. Note that you may see the term *psychopharmacologist* instead of *psychiatrist*. This simply means the psychiatrist specializes in prescribing medications.

As we discussed, the first step in treatment with medications is for you and your health care provider to decide that you have a condition that is likely to benefit from medication. This is where you should also consider family history. Mood disorders have a strong genetic component, so if any of your family members have had similar episodes of depression and medication was helpful to them, the same is likely true for you. What works for one family member will often work for another because of shared genetics.

The next step is to decide which symptoms you are going to target. If your mood disorder includes an episode of mania or hypomania, it is likely that you and your health care professional will want to include a mood stabilizer or one of the newer generation of antipsychotic medications (or both). Otherwise, for depression, most physicians will start with whichever selective serotonin reuptake inhibitor, or SSRI, they prefer. This approach is reasonable if you haven't taken these medications in the past and have no knowledge of whether medications have worked for relatives with depression, as the available data shows that the different classes of antidepressant medications have comparable antidepressant effects.[11] Know that there are also serotonin norepinephrine reuptake inhibitors (SNRIs), atypical antidepressants, older tricyclic antidepressants (TCAs), and monoamine oxidase inhibitors (MAOIs), any of which you might be prescribed.

If you have been treated with medications in the past, then your past experience with antidepressants can be very helpful. Questions that should be asked include: Were there medications that did not work and medications that did? If you're no longer on a medication, why did you stop? Medications that worked in the past are likely to work again. However, medications that have "pooped out" are unlikely to work and are usually only tried again if other medications don't work and there are no other good options. When you consider the negative effects of depression on a person's health, social network, and career, a strong argument can be made for trying ECT, TMS/rTMS, or ketamine instead of going back and retrying a medication that stopped working.

Nonetheless, knowing which medications did not work for you in the past can help your health care professional choose the right one for you. For a medication to work, enough of it has to get to the brain over a long enough period for it to have time to induce positive changes in the mood circuit. Some people have problems remembering to take medications and the drug never builds up to a therapeutic level. **Using a daily pill box or setting reminders on your phone can significantly help you take your medication or medications consistently.** Alternatively, you might have problems with your GI tract that affect absorption (irritable bowel syndrome, for example) or you might take the medicine with foods that interfere with absorption. Thyroid medication, which can have significant mood effects, is often poorly absorbed when taken with other medications. One of the more striking examples of the effect of food on drug absorption I have encountered clinically was when one of my patients switched her breakfast from toast to oatmeal. The way I found out about that change was that her medications stopped working and the usual adjustments did not work either. I asked if she had changed anything in her diet, and when she told me about her new breakfast habit, I suggested she change back to her usual breakfast to see what happened. She did, and she gradually felt much better on her usual medications.

Even when a medicine is well absorbed, how much of a dose of medication actually gets to the brain can vary widely from person to person. One of the key determinants of this is the rate at which it is cleared from the body. When you swallow a pill, the drug goes from the small intestine into the bloodstream and through the liver. The liver is the organ in the body that inactivates most medications. As a result of medications going first through the liver and then to the brain and the rest of the body via the bloodstream, a significant amount of the medication is inactivated and never reaches the brain. This process is known as "first pass metabolism." Depending on the amount of medication your liver deactivates, you might need to increase your dosage.

What About the Genetic Testing I've Been Hearing About?

One of the benefits of the rapid advances in genetic testing has been the ability to determine how efficient people are in breaking down drugs based on their genes. There is a class of proteins, known as the cytochrome P450 proteins, that handle the initial breakdown of a large number of medications in the body. For each type of cytochrome P450 protein, people can either be extensive, intermediate, or poor metabolizers. Extensive metabolizers break down medications more quickly than average and need higher doses of medication to reach a therapeutic drug level. Poor metabolizers break down drugs more slowly and will have higher blood levels of the medication. Since side effects tend to occur at peak blood levels, these are the people who have trouble tolerating even small doses of medications. The intermediate metabolizers are, as the name indicates, the average person whose medication levels are usually in between the two extremes. A genomic panel to determine what kind of metabolizer you are can sometimes be helpful if you have been prescribed an antidepressant, given it eight weeks to work, and found its effectiveness inadequate.

How Do I Choose Among the Different Medication Options?

The good news is that you don't have to do it alone. Your prescriber should make a recommendation and be able to explain to you their rationale behind it. Your therapist should also be able to talk through and support you in making the decision. Since the different classes of antidepressants have comparable antidepressant potency for most people, the choice usually centers on a couple of things.

The most important consideration when choosing an antidepressant is the person's general health conditions and the safety profile of the medication. A good example of the safety is the difference between SSRIs and TCAs. TCAs have significant effects on blood pressure and slow electrical conduction in the heart. As a result, they must be used with care in patients with cardiac conditions. SSRIs have far fewer cardiac-related side effects and were a significant advance in the safety of antidepressants.[12] Given that the two classes of medications have comparable antidepressant effectiveness, most clinicians recommend SSRIs for patients with heart disease and do not prescribe TCAs unless other antidepressants have been tried and failed to alleviate the depression.

As I said, SSRIs are also often chosen as the first medication. That's because they have mild side effects and are usually well tolerated by most people. This stands in contrast to another strategy: choosing antidepressants based on side effects. Although this practice is common, it should be avoided. This strategy tries to improve the person's symptoms using a medication's side effects. For example, if difficulty sleeping is part of the symptom complex, then use a sedating antidepressant. While logical, this strategy often does not work. Once the depression is treated, the person no longer has insomnia, but they often still have the sedation from the medication. This side effect can lead to the patient stopping the medication and experiencing a relapse of their depressive symptoms. The inability to tolerate a medication's side effects and inconsistently taking them are among the leading reasons why people don't get better after starting a medication.

How Do I Start the Medication?

When going on antidepressants, it is usually advisable to begin with a low dose and work up to the standard dose fairly quickly. This approach minimizes side effects, which tends to help with your willingness to comply with the prescription, but does not ignore your suffering and need to feel better. Factoring in the obstacles to compliance is important because 30 percent of people prescribed antidepressants do not refill the medication, and medications don't work if they stay on the pharmacy shelf.[13] If the medication does cause side effects, often the body adjusts and the patient improves with time. A general rule is to wait two weeks after a patient has begun taking a medicine at a full dose before considering a change due to side effects. If they are intolerable, it's usually best to switch drugs. It would also be advisable to check the person's drug metabolism by doing a genomic panel. If there are no improvements in the depressive symptoms by two weeks, Dr. Andrew Nierenberg and his team at Massachusetts General Hospital found that it is best to switch or to augment the antidepressant (by adding a second medication, which I'll discuss shortly).[14] If there is some improvement but still a significant amount of depressive symptoms, then it is reasonable to give the medication more time. As we discussed earlier, the brain circuits that control mood and the associated vegetative symptoms are complex and interwoven. A change in one aspect of the circuitry causes a chain reaction, and it takes time to reset the rest of the circuitry. While one to two months is usually enough time for the changes to occur, for some patients, it can take up to four months for the full antidepressant response to manifest itself.

My Antidepressant Didn't Work. Now What?

The next question, and this may be the reason you picked up this book, is what to do when the first medication doesn't work. As we discussed previously, hopefully, you have found a therapist who you feel can be helpful, have been able to exercise more regularly, and have had your friends rally around you. If, after all that work, you still find your antidepressant has not adequately treated your depression, there are some general principles to guide you.

The first question is whether to increase the dose of the medication, switch, or augment with an additional drug. Dr. Maurizio Fava and his group, also at Massachusetts General Hospital, compared increasing the dose of fluoxetine (Prozac) to augmenting the original dose of fluoxetine with either lithium or the older tricyclic antidepressant desipramine (Norpramin). Although a number of people responded to each treatment approach, none was statistically better than the others.[15] This study predates the genetic testing that is available today, so today, in addition to the approaches outlined above, it would be reasonable to use testing to guide the treatment choice when someone doesn't respond to their initial antidepressant.

Second, if you are going to switch medications, it makes sense to increase the number of neurotransmitters targeted. For example, you might switch from a selective serotonin medication (SSRI), such as sertraline, to a serotonin and norepinephrine reuptake inhibitor (SSNI), such as duloxetine.

The third option, augmenting with a second medication, presents a number of choices. If you choose to add a second antidepressant, then the strategy again is to broaden the spectrum of neurotransmitter systems that are targeted. Traditional antidepressants can be thought of as increasing the activity of serotonin, norepinephrine, or dopamine, or some combination of them. For example, escitalopram is a pure serotonin reuptake inhibitor. If that is the medication that has not had the desired antidepressant effect, then adding bupropion, which enhances norepinephrine and dopamine activity, is a logical choice that is often quite effective.

One of the original augmentation strategies is to add lithium to the antidepressant, even in the absence of any bipolar history.[16] The rationale for this is rooted in the early diagnostic approaches to mood disorders. When the categories of mood disorders were first described in the early 1900s, any condition with recurrent mood symptoms was considered bipolar disorder. Viewed from this vantage point, augmenting antidepressants with lithium makes a lot of sense. And it often works!

Thyroid augmentation is another approach that has been frequently used. This approach stems from the finding that depressed mood and lack of energy are common symptoms of thyroid disease. Boosting the person's thyroid hormone levels has been shown to be effective, with one important caveat. The majority of the positive studies were done with the less common form of thyroid replacement, T3. Due to its cardiac side effects and the fact that it is inactivated five times more quickly than T4,[17] it is not used often. T4, which is converted in the body to T3 and has a better safety profile, is the standard treatment for uncomplicated thyroid disease. When treating depression and co-occurring hypothyroidism, the standard approach is to augment with T4.[18]

Probably the most commonly used approach today is to augment with one of the newer, or second-generation, antipsychotics. These are the medications you will see advertised often on television. The first-generation antipsychotics acted primarily by blocking dopamine. The second-generation antipsychotics act by blocking both serotonin and dopamine. When these newer medications first began to be used, people noticed they also seemed to have positive effects on mood.[19] Then, when the Eli Lilly company was testing the effectiveness of olanzapine in bipolar depression, the FDA requested that it add a fluoxetine-olanzapine group to the study design. The medication combination was more effective than the placebo and olanzapine alone in treating depression and led to the FDA approving the combination as a treatment for bipolar depression. Pretty much every new antipsychotic that has followed has been tested as an augmentation agent in treatment-resistant depression and as a treatment for bipolar depression and mania.

This list of medications is not intended to be exhaustive, and your prescriber may have other augmentation strategies they prefer. The main idea is when you are picking a strategy, you want to broaden the mechanism of action through a combined approach. Also, you want to minimize the number of medications used, since each medication comes with its own set of potential side effects.

Bipolar depression presents a different challenge. Whereas with unipolar depression there are a number of different classes of medications that have been shown to be effective, there are few medications that have shown themselves to be effective in bipolar depression. The main choices available include lithium, the antiepileptic medications lamotrigine and divalproex, and some of the second-generation antipsychotic medications discussed previously. The traditional antidepressant medications have shown limited antidepressant effects in people with bipolar disorder. One notable exception is fluoxetine in combination with olanzapine.[20] However, when these medications are used in combination, the patient should be monitored for signs of switching into mania or other signs of increased cycling. Note that ECT has also been shown to be quite effective in treating acute episodes of depression and in long-term maintenance treatment of bipolar disorder.[21] If you are suffering from a bipolar depression, there are many nuances to successful treatment, and you should consider seeking out a psychiatrist who specializes in it.

Chapter 8, on ECT treatment, offers more detail on treatment-resistant depression; see pages 120–122.

In summary, effective treatment for an episode of depression starts with a clear picture of your symptoms. There are a number of conditions that can present with a depressed mood, including the long-term effects of trauma, recreational substances, and physical illness. Once it is clear that you are in a major depressive episode, you can pursue psychotherapy, which can be very helpful by itself in mild to moderate cases. In more severe cases, the combination of medications and therapy has consistently been shown to be the most effective treatment option. In treating unipolar major depression, most classes of antidepressant medications have comparable efficacy. The choice of which medication to start with is usually based on its safety and side effect profile; however, remember that attempts to treat symptoms using the medication's side effects are usually not effective, as the side effects will remain after the symptoms improve or resolve over the course of treatment. The effectiveness and side effects of an antidepressant medication are influenced by its absorption and clearance. Genetic testing can help clarify the situation when someone's response to medications leaves them with significant symptoms or intolerable side effects. If you have not responded adequately to an antidepressant medication, in addition to reevaluating the diagnosis, you and your prescriber have options that include increasing the dose, switching medications, or augmenting with additional medications. When those approaches don't work, the treatments discussed in the remainder of this book are often quite successful and can be life changing.

Key Takeaways

- ▶ Effective treatment starts with a clear understanding of the target symptoms.
- ▶ Antidepressants are more effective than placebos in the treatment of major depression.
- ▶ The efficiency with which a medication is absorbed and eliminated can have a significant impact on its effectiveness.
- ▶ Recently developed genetic testing can be quite helpful for sorting out the contribution of the drug's rate of clearance when medications don't work as expected.
- ▶ Psychotherapy, especially cognitive behavioral therapy, has proven effectiveness in treating depression.
  - ■ In mild to moderate depression, it may be the only treatment needed.
  - ■ In more severe depressions, a combination of medication and therapy has been shown to be more effective than medications alone.
- ▶ When the first antidepressant medication is not successful, strategies for improving the response include increasing the dose, switching medications, or augmenting with additional medications.
- ▶ Bipolar depression requires a completely different medication approach than unipolar depression.

Part II

The Reboot: Introducing Ketamine, TMS, and ECT

Chapter 4

Ketamine:
How an Old Anesthetic Became an Antidepressant

I once heard a senior clinician describe his patient's past medication trials as "everything from A to Z—Anafranil to Zoloft." His shorthand description was not too far from the truth. Over the course of several years, he and his patient had systematically tried the majority of the available antidepressant medications. What was disappointing was the realization that these medications worked through very similar mechanisms. In effect, they had essentially tried the same treatments over and over again. Psychiatry was in need of new treatment options. Ironically, it turned to the past and the old anesthetic ketamine. In this chapter, we will discuss how ketamine was repurposed into a psychiatric treatment. Let us begin with Keisha's experience with ketamine.

Keisha is a forty-three-year-old woman who was in the process of separating from her husband when she heard about a new type of antidepressant that was being studied at the university hospital where she worked. She had struggled on and off with depression since her twenties but had been doing well until her escitalopram (Lexapro) stopped working about ten months before. She had tried supplementing it with a second antidepressant, and when that didn't work, she moved to a third antidepressant. Each change brought more side effects but not relief. As time passed, she got less and less done at home and was barely able to keep up with her two children and their activities. She felt chronically guilty for all the little things she didn't get to or forgot to do for them. She was too exhausted to be a partner to her husband, and they began to fight about "stupid little things." She had thought about electroconvulsive therapy (ECT) but was concerned about childcare during her treatment and recovery. Her husband had used up his paid time off just covering things she usually did for the kids. Neither of their families lived nearby, and no one could afford the time needed to come and stay with her to take her to ECT. She was becoming more and more desperate, even beginning to think everyone would be better off without her.

One day, she was on the elevator at work and saw a flier for a trial of a new antidepressant medication, ketamine. Desperate, she decided to go ahead and try it. After her second dose, she began to feel like a cloud had lifted, and she was able to be more present at home. She smiled for the first time in months.

Ketamine: A Game Changer

The discovery of ketamine as an antidepressant has been a game changer in the treatment of severe depression for several reasons. It works in a significant number of people who have not responded to the established antidepressants, such as fluoxetine (Prozac), and its antidepressant effects can occur within hours, not weeks. Also, its success has convinced research funding agencies and pharmaceutical companies that there are still new approaches to treating depression to be discovered. Ketamine has launched a new generation of antidepressant research. In many ways, this medication was uniquely positioned to move quickly from discovery to clinical practice. It had been used as an anesthetic since the 1970s, and its safety in humans was well established.[1]

Still, many of my patients who are curious about ketamine are worried about taking it themselves; after all, many of them think of it as either a horse tranquilizer or a recreational drug. I often discuss the scientific reasoning behind ketamine's transformation into a depression treatment with my patients who want to hear it. They often find what I say reassuring, and it helps them in their decision-making about treatment. I'll share this information with you, as well as the nuts and bolts of how ketamine works as an antidepressant. Although this section may get a little technical, it is designed to provide you with a framework for understanding why ketamine is worth trying for your depression even after you have not responded to other medications.

Ketamine for Depression?

When you have suffered through the side effects of multiple medication trials for your depression, it is easy to feel like a "guinea pig" or that your doctor is "experimenting" with your medications. Ketamine, with its storied past and lack of FDA approval for depression, is particularly vulnerable to these concerns. But the use of ketamine for depression is actually rooted in solid science. Let me take you through its history to show you why I believe that.

The history of ketamine starts with another drug that is still well known today: phencyclidine, or PCP. In the mid- to late 1950s, the Park Davis pharmaceutical company developed PCP as an anesthetic agent for surgery. Initially, PCP was well received, but with wider use, some patients developed an extended period of confusion after surgery and others became addicted to it. In an effort to find a similar but safer anesthetic drug, ketamine was synthesized in 1962 at Park Davis.[2]

Ketamine (Ketalar) was first approved by the FDA for use in humans as an anesthetic in 1970. The advantages of ketamine as an anesthetic agent are significant. It causes the person's consciousness to disconnect from reality while raising their blood pressure and not decreasing their drive to breathe. This makes it very useful in emergency situations. Ketamine also provides pain relief that extends beyond its sedative effects, a property that is quite useful during recovery from surgery. Unfortunately, at anesthetic doses it also has a tendency to cause hallucinations and agitation, and so it fell out of favor as a first-line anesthetic.[3]

Ironically, it was the side effects of ketamine, the hallucinations and other dissociative effects, that led to the resurgence it is experiencing today. At their worst, in vulnerable individuals, the hallucinatory side effects resemble the core symptoms of schizophrenia, a serious chronic mental illness. In an effort to better understand this illness, researchers took advantage of these temporary side effects to study the changes in the brain that occur with hallucinations. These studies pointed to the neurotransmitter glutamate, the main chemical in the brain that activates neurons, as the cause of these symptoms. The speed with which ketamine produced its effects on the activity of glutamate in the brain also established its usefulness as a tool for studying the activity of the glutamate system.[4]

Both patients and psychiatrists have long been frustrated by the amount of time traditional antidepressants take to work. John Krystal and his colleagues at Yale University hypothesized that the key problem causing depression might "reside" in the parts of the brain that primarily use glutamate and gamma amino butyric acid (GABA) rather than the other chemical messengers, such as serotonin, through which the traditional antidepressants appear to act. They had done some of the work using ketamine as a probe of glutamate in psychosis and proposed to try it in depression. Their results were surprisingly positive. In their words: "To the amazement of our patients and ourselves, we found that ketamine produced rapid, profound, and surprisingly durable antidepressant effects." They also found that "the initial euphoria produced by ketamine was not part of its antidepressant effect."[5]

The key follow-up study that led to ketamine's widespread use as an antidepressant in intractable depression was published in 2006 by Dr. Carlos Zarate from the National Institute of Mental Health. In this study, 71 percent of subjects had a significant reduction in depressive symptoms, or antidepressant response, and 29 percent reported resolution of the majority of their symptoms or remission (a much stricter standard) of their symptoms on the day following the ketamine infusion.[6] The clinical trial definition of treatment response is a drop in the depression rating scale by half or more. To achieve remission means that almost all of the symptoms have resolved. The people who enroll in such a study generally have failed several medication trials and their symptoms are well entrenched (and therefore, hard to completely resolve).

Unfortunately, due solely to the costs associated with bringing a new drug to the clinic, large-scale studies proving ketamine's effectiveness in depression have not been done. To get around this problem and still develop new drugs based on the actions of ketamine, companies are doing trials on the different components of ketamine to see if they have antidepressant properties by themselves. For example, Janssen Pharmaceuticals has achieved regulatory approval for esketamine, one of the two mirror-image constituents of ketamine.[7] The other mirror image of ketamine, arketamine, is also currently undergoing clinical studies to determine whether it has antidepressant effects.[8]

There's a lot more detail on this subject I could share, but what you need to know is that there are three versions of this drug: esketamine, arketamine, and the combination of the two, ketamine. Esketamine has already been approved as a treatment for depression. Arketamine is currently going through the paces toward FDA approval, and ketamine is too old to be profitably developed as a drug for depression. In addition, different medications that work on the same circuitry are also being actively explored.

Ketamine and esketamine are used in treatment-resistant depressed patients. In double-blind multicenter trials of treatment-resistant depression, esketamine was more effective than control medication when added to standard antidepressant medications.[9] In a separate study, ketamine showed a 64 percent response rate versus 28 percent for the control medication.[10]

You may be wondering, if ketamine itself is not FDA approved for the treatment of depression, why ketamine is still used in a lot of clinics and whether esketamine is "better" than ketamine for treating depression. The answer to the first question is due partly to timing and partly to finances. Ketamine was already available for "off-label" use in the clinic while esketamine was only available in clinical trials. "Off-label" means that the medication has not been approved by the FDA to treat that particular disease—which means that insurance companies usually don't cover the use in treatment, but people can pay out of pocket. Also, with any new treatment, insurance companies usually have a lag between approval and when they routinely cover the medication. This has also been true for esketamine, and patients often wind up paying out of pocket. Since the cost of the required monitoring for ketamine and esketamine is essentially the same, the cost of the medications made it less expensive to use ketamine. The other reason some clinicians still offer ketamine is because they feel it is a more potent antidepressant than esketamine. This is still a topic of heated debate in the scientific community, but the initial data appears to favor intravenous ketamine as being more potent than esketamine, which is given via the nose, or intranasally.

In an effort to more systematically answer this question, Dr. Anees Bahji and his team in Ontario, Canada, in collaboration with Dr. Zarate the National Institute of Mental Health in the United States, reviewed the reported studies examining ketamine and esketamine in the treatment of depression. They found a total of twenty-four studies, with a total of 1,877 subjects, that were scientifically rigorous enough to fit their predetermined inclusion criteria.[11]

The interpretation of the results is nuanced. Some of the studies with esketamine were done early in the process of building the application for FDA approval when the company was trying to figure out dosing and how to optimize the study design. Studies with ketamine and esketamine cannot be done with the standard comparator sugar pill, or placebo, because the medication is sedating, which means the trial subjects can tell that they have received the placebo and not the actual drug. Therefore, studies of ketamine and esketamine used inactive comparator medications that were also sedating. When data from across the twenty-four studies was looked at for antidepressant effect, relative to that of a control medication, people treated with ketamine had a positive antidepressant response three times more often, whereas in those treated with esketamine, the response rate was just under one and a half (1.38). Similarly, the remission rates were 3.7 times greater with ketamine versus 1.5 times greater with esketamine. In the analysis done by the Canadian and American teams, ketamine was associated with a greater decrease in suicidality than esketamine. In addition, based on the number of subjects who dropped out of these studies, it appears that ketamine was better tolerated than esketamine.

Note: the majority of studies included in the analysis mentioned previously were not head-to-head comparisons. **The one reported study that directly compared the two medications found that esketamine did *not* do worse than ketamine** in reducing depressive symptoms and there were no significant problems with tolerability to either treatment. **The bottom line is that both medications are much more effective than the traditional antidepressant medications for refractory depression. Getting relief as soon as possible is much more important than any differences between the two medications.**

Ketamine Does Many Things

Ketamine is an anesthetic, treats depression, reduces the perception of pain, and can cause hallucinations. This broad range of effects reflects the number of systems in the brain and body that ketamine acts on.[12] It is likely that ketamine's action at the glutamate receptor starts the antidepressant cascade, and then some of its other actions boost and/or sustain the initial antidepressant response. Ketamine has at least four additional actions that may contribute to its antidepressant effects:

1. It changes the communication between brain regions involved in the regulation of mood. For example, brain regions that send negative information to the prefrontal cortex, which leads to increased depression, have their connectivity decreased.
2. It promotes the release of growth factors that change the hardwiring of the mood circuitry.
3. It reduces inflammation. Inflammation is the body's immune response to infection and other types of tissue damage. You only have to think of how miserable you felt with your last bad head cold to understand how inflammation can lead to depression. Usually, once the infection is cleared, the inflammation reduces and the body and your mood quickly recover. However, some illnesses, such as diabetes, cause chronic low-grade inflammation, and these illnesses are associated with an increased risk of depression. Similarly, drugs that activate the immune system to treat chronic infections, such as interferon, which is used to treat chronic hepatitis C, often induce symptoms of depression as a side effect.

   As you might expect, the chemicals that mediate the inflammatory response also tend to be elevated in the blood of depressed individuals.

Accordingly, medications that reduce inflammation have been proposed as potential antidepressants.[13] Although the effects of ketamine on inflammatory proteins in the blood in depressed individuals have been somewhat difficult to sort out, ketamine anesthesia has been shown to lower these pro-inflammatory proteins in both cardiac surgery and cesarean section (C-section).[14]

4. It interacts with opiate receptors to improve mood and reduce suicidality.

You may have seen the pharmaceutical ads that talk about the pain of depression. As you know, depression makes physical pain worse. In fact, prior to the opiate misuse epidemic, several drugs that worked directly on the opiate system were under study for use as antidepressants. Ketamine is known to provide significant pain relief and is used extensively in surgery and chronic pain syndromes for precisely this effect.[15] One surprising finding was ketamine's effect on the opiate system also contributes to its antisuicide properties.[16]

In short, ketamine and esketamine's actions at multiple sites in the brain seem to work together to give them antidepressant effects that far exceed those of traditional antidepressants in refractory depression. While there are some risks and common side effects of ketamine and esketamine (which we'll discuss in Chapter 5), ketamine is a safe drug with more than fifty years of clinical experience, and esketamine has not shown itself to be significantly different from a safety perspective in the studies done to date.

Another unspoken outcome of the discovery of ketamine's antidepressant properties has been a renewed willingness to explore the possible therapeutic effects of other hallucinogens. This has already been a tremendous catalyst for new discoveries about the causes of depression and potential novel treatments, offering even more hope for people with depression.

In fact, one of those medications—a combination of the cough suppressant medication dextromethorphan and the antidepressant bupropion—has just been approved by the FDA for the treatment of major depression. Like ketamine, the drug acts through the NMDA receptor and in clinical trials also exhibited a rapid antidepressant response. Its big advantage is that it can be taken at home on a daily basis. I have included a brief description of this new treatment option on page 209.

Key Takeaways

- ▶ The discovery of ketamine's antidepressant effects has brought relief to many people suffering from severe, previously intractable depression. When prescribed by skilled clinicians, it has shown to be well tolerated and safe.
- ▶ The evidence to date indicates that ketamine and esketamine work primarily through the glutamate system.
- ▶ Ketamine and esketamine also act, in part, by remodeling the brain. They cause the release of growth factors that increase the volume (and activity) of certain brain regions and change the intensity of the connections between regions within the mood circuit.
- ▶ Ketamine's effects on inflammation and the opiate system in the brain appear to add to its antidepressant effects.

Chapter 5

I Want to Try Ketamine:
What Do I Do?

If you have tried to get treatment with ketamine, you know that many centers have long waiting lists and can be expensive. Esketamine (Spiriva) is FDA approved to augment antidepressant medications and is covered by an increasing number of insurances, making it more affordable. Still, waits of weeks to months are not uncommon (this is the case in Massachusetts, where I practice). Fortunately, things are improving as insurances and clinicians get more experience with these medications and their benefits. To better illustrate how these medications are used in the clinic, let us start with a discussion of Sally's treatment with esketamine.

Sally is a fifty-five-year-old mother of two adult children who lives with her boyfriend of fifteen years in a small town outside of Boston. She had struggled on and off with depression since her late teens. This current episode of depression took over her life about twelve years prior for no apparent reason. After trying several combinations of medications, she had almost given up when she heard about esketamine, one of the chemicals in ketamine, in a support group she attends monthly. She was desperate but also worried about ketamine's reputation as a street drug. Cautiously, she discussed it with her prescribing nurse practitioner, who reassured her that it is safe to try. She was not completely convinced but also knew "she had to do something." She called the clinic her prescriber had recommended and booked an appointment with the psychiatrist for a screening interview.

When she arrived, she was warmly greeted by the receptionist and given some insurance paperwork to fill out. The doctor came out and took her into an interview room. They went over her recent history, focusing on how this episode of depression started and was impacting her quality of life and ability to function. They also talked about the first time her mood symptoms occurred in her late teens and the fact that they have intermittently recurred throughout her life. She listed the various medications she had tried and the reasons they were discontinued. She found herself feeling even sadder than usual when she realized how much time the illness had robbed from her and her family. She naturally transitioned into describing her mother's battle with depression and the times she was absent from the family during Sally's childhood. Sally also remembered that one of her mother's cousins had died by suicide, something she had forgotten and something the family never talked about. The hour went by quickly, and Sally felt drained at the end of it. Overall, she felt the interview went well, and she became more comfortable with esketamine as the doctor described what she could expect from the treatment.

On the evening of her first appointment, Sally checked in a few minutes early at the esketamine clinic and waited anxiously. She quickly completed the questions about her symptoms and other paperwork. The nurse came out to get her and brought her back to a small curtained-off area with a stretcher. She was told to make herself comfortable and lie down on the stretcher. The nurse quickly hooked her up to a heart monitor and took her blood pressure. An anesthesiologist came by, introduced herself, and asked some questions about Sally's general health and past medical conditions. She then told Sally that she would be monitoring her physical response to the esketamine. The psychiatrist came by to check on her, ask about her depression symptoms, and answer any last-minute questions. The nurse confirmed the dose of esketamine the psychiatrist had prescribed and verified Sally's name and date of birth to ensure they had the right patient. They asked Sally if she was ready to begin. When she said yes, the psychiatrist asked her to start by blowing her nose. The nurse then handed her the device for delivering the medication. She inserted it into her right nostril until she felt the device touch the middle of her nose. She closed off her other nostril, started to breathe in, and pushed the plunger to deliver the medication. After the medication was delivered, she was instructed to sniff a few times to ensure the medication stayed put in her nose. She was then instructed to switch to the other nostril and repeat. Since the starting dose required her to use two devices, she repeated this process five minutes later.

After the medication dosing was completed, Sally lay back, put on her headset, turned on the soft music she had loaded on her phone, and closed her eyes. Gradually, Sally felt herself starting to feel a little fuzzy and then felt as if she were in a different reality. The music became more intense, and she began to see vivid, dreamlike images with bold colors. She had no perception of time but knew that she was starting to regain consciousness when she became aware of people moving about and talking in the neighboring cubicle. Gradually, she felt herself getting more connected to her own surroundings and feeling more awake. The experience had lasted a little more than an hour, but she only figured that out after she looked at the clock. About a half hour later, the nurse checked her vital signs, and they were back to her baseline.

After a glass of ginger ale, Sally felt awake enough to return home, and her boyfriend came into the cubicle to fetch her. She felt herself wobble a little bit as she made her way out of the clinic and into the car. The ride home was brief. When they got home, her boyfriend helped her inside, and she went straight to bed. The next morning when she woke, she noticed that she felt much lighter. She didn't feel the heavy sadness she had been feeling for the past several months. The next day, Sally still felt much better but noticed that her mood had slipped back a little. Fortunately, the next treatment would be later that evening. Three weeks later, after her eighth treatment, she was feeling consistently better and ready to transition to the clinic's maintenance program.

Sally's experience is not uncommon in at least two respects: the long struggle over years with multiple failed medication trials and the speed of her response. It is a testament to the number of people who suffer with treatment-resistant depression that ketamine, and now esketamine, centers have become quite commonplace. It has been estimated that the number of ketamine clinics in the United States increased from sixty to three hundred between 2015 and 2018.[1] What makes this especially remarkable is that during this time, insurance generally did not cover the treatment, and people have been paying thousands of dollars out of pocket for a course of treatment. As we discussed previously, ketamine has FDA approval only for lab use as an anesthetic, so use in psychiatric disorders is considered "off-label." Off-label use of drugs is commonplace in psychiatric illnesses, but when those treatments are expensive, they are usually not paid for by insurance companies. This has been the case with ketamine.

Let me answer the most frequently asked questions about treatment.

Will Ketamine or Esketamine Work for Me?

To date both ketamine and esketamine have only been studied in people with some degree of nonresponse to the first-line antidepressant medications, such as Prozac. Those studies that added ketamine and esketamine to the person's ongoing antidepressant medication have shown both of them to be rapid acting, potent antidepressant treatments in both major depression and bipolar depression.[2] While the dream of many mental health professionals is to have tests that precisely guide diagnosis and treatment, they do not yet exist. What we do know is that if you have the clinical symptoms of major depression— sad mood; inability to enjoy life; disturbances to sleep, energy level, appetite, or concentration; and, for some people, thoughts of death or suicide—then you have symptoms that can respond to ketamine and esketamine.

When Do I Try Ketamine/Esketamine in My Course of Treatment?

This will depend on the severity of your symptoms and the approach your health care team has to ketamine (or esketamine). If your symptoms are quite disabling and/or you are having a lot of active suicidal feelings and thoughts, then your clinician will likely be thinking about trying ketamine (or esketamine) or one of the other treatments discussed in this book sooner rather than later. If medication after medication has failed you, that will also likely prompt a recommendation for ketamine. The other determinant is whether your clinician has seen people get better with ketamine. There is nothing more gratifying than having a patient who is suffering badly with depression get better quickly. A good result invariably opens the clinician's eyes to the potential of the treatment in a way that no scientific study can. **Most importantly, please don't forget that you can ask your clinician if a trial of ketamine or esketamine makes sense for you.**

How Effective Are Ketamine
and Esketamine?

While we do not have predictors of response, we do know that patients with medication-resistant depression have a 1.3 to 3 times greater chance of responding to esketamine and ketamine than they do to inactive, or placebo, treatment.[3]

Are Ketamine and Esketamine Safe?

Ketamine has been used as an anesthetic in people for more than fifty years with an excellent safety record. As we discussed previously, esketamine is one of the chemicals in ketamine, and based on the information provided for the rigorous FDA approval process, it appears to be equally safe.[4] Ketamine has many desirable properties as an anesthetic. It produces a mental state that has been described as "dissociative anesthesia": said another way, surgery patients under ketamine did not feel the procedure being done, but unlike with most other anesthetics, and very importantly, they kept breathing.[5] In addition, because of the analgesic effects of ketamine, they had significant and extended pain control.[6] Ketamine was the most commonly used battlefield anesthetic during the Vietnam War specifically because it does not suppress breathing and supports blood pressure.[7] It is also used with infants and children. In short, ketamine is not only safe to use but has therapeutic effects that have been found to be beneficial in at least two very vulnerable groups of people: soldiers, who had severe combat wounds with associated blood loss, and children, who are more physically fragile than most adults.

Most people tolerate ketamine anesthesia, as well as ketamine and esketamine for depression, quite well and only experience minor side effects, if any. Keep in mind that the doses of ketamine used to treat depression are less than the doses used for general anesthesia, further increasing the safety of the treatment.

Isn't Ketamine a Drug of Abuse? Will I Get Addicted?

The dissociative effects of ketamine can produce a pleasant high in some people. It also enhances the activity of dopamine in the brain, a characteristic shared by many pleasurable substances, including chocolate. I am not trying to minimize the risk of misuse or addiction, but it is important to realize that carefully screening patients for a history of addiction and monitoring for signs of misuse has allowed many people to safely benefit from the antidepressant effects of ketamine and esketamine.[8]

To give you a more quantitative picture, Dr. Ewa Wajs and colleagues reported on the long-term safety data for esketamine.[9] In this yearlong study, 802 subjects were enrolled, 364 patients were dosed for six months, and 136 were dosed for twelve months. To monitor for the possibility of drug use during the study, urine drug screens were obtained every eight weeks. Of the 802 patients, 7 had drug screens that were positive for addictive drugs. Overall, the rate of positive screens was only 0.0146 per person year, or 1.46 percent.

What Side Effects Should I Expect?

Side effects reported with ketamine and esketamine can be grouped into three basic categories: cardiovascular, systemic, and brain effects.

Cardiovascular Side Effects

The cardiovascular side effects of ketamine can include increased heart rate, increased blood pressure, and abnormal heart rhythms. Again, in order to provide context, esketamine was associated with an increase in blood pressure in 17 percent of subjects versus 2 percent for the placebo group, and an increase in heart rate in 2 percent versus 0.5 percent. These side effects reflect the stimulant-like effects of ketamine. Paradoxically, and much less frequently, ketamine can also cause a slow heart rate and low blood pressure.[10]

These effects are the main reason why a thorough review of any heart or vascular problems you have had is an important part of the pre-screening process before using ketamine or esketamine. Even when your history is negative, you should be monitored during and for a couple of hours after the administration of ketamine. A small but significant number of people have "silent" disturbances in their cardiac rhythm and blood vessels, especially those supplying the heart.[11] These problems are considered silent because they are mild enough that they do not cause symptoms under normal conditions. But when the system is stressed, such as when ketamine triggers an increase in heart rate and blood pressure, the heart tissues' demand of blood flow and oxygen can exceed the cardiovascular system's ability to deliver them. This phenomenon has been reported by physicians using ketamine in the emergency room but was not seen in the esketamine studies that led to FDA approval.[12]

The cardiac effects of ketamine can also be a problem when you have structural weakness in your blood vessels. An aneurysm is a weakness in the wall of the blood vessel that makes the vessel prone to rupture when blood pressure increases. Similarly, a malformation of the blood vessels where the small arteries flow directly into the veins, without the capillaries to buffer the pressure on the arterial side, can also lead to severe bleeding. Since these conditions are very uncommon,[13] complications from them are also rare. To avoid these risks, you should be screened for any past history of heart or blood vessel issues and have emergency access to more intensive levels of medical care when using ketamine or esketamine. **But I want to stress again that these conditions are not common and a good pretreatment workup should uncover any issues or concerns.**

Systemic Side Effects

The common systemic side effects that are seen with antidepressant doses of ketamine include nausea and vomiting, increased liver enzymes in the bloodstream, and jaundice. Subjects in the esketamine studies with moderate to severe liver disease had higher levels of drug in their blood, suggesting that they may need a lower dose than usual.[14]

Urinary tract disturbances—such as blood in the urine and irritation of the bladder, known as cystitis—occurred in 2 percent of subjects treated with esketamine versus 1 percent treated with placebo.

Brain Effects

Over the course of treatment, the starting dose of ketamine may need to be raised to achieve antidepressant effects. At the therapeutic dose, people usually experience a "trip" or dissociative episode. For most people this is a pleasant, sometimes even mystical experience that some have described as life changing. However, for some people, it can reawaken past traumatic events or be associated with a feeling of being trapped or helpless. A supportive approach that reassures the person and then encourages them to work through the feelings can be very healing, even more so than if only the depression were treated. During these episodes, patients have sometimes reported feelings of agitation, fear, panic, unpleasant dissociative effects (that is, a sense of being detached from one's body), hallucinations, nightmares, and vivid dreams or dreamlike states. Patients usually feel sedated during and for a period of time after treatment.

Other nervous system–based side effects reported include insomnia (mostly on the night of treatment), alterations in taste, slurred speech, double vision, muscle twitches, tremors, loss of coordination, and repetitive, uncontrolled eye movements, known as nystagmus. These, too, are usually temporary and resolve with time and supportive measures. Since esketamine did go through clinical trials to obtain FDA approval, we do have some data on how often these side effects show up in people undergoing treatment for their depression. I've chosen a few of the most common to give you an idea of how often they occur.[15]

Table 5.1: Most Common Side Effects

	Esketamine	Placebo
Dissociation	61%	5%
Nausea	28%	9%
Sedation	23%	9%
Vertigo (dizziness)	23%	3%
Anxiety/agitation	13%	6%
Increased blood pressure	10%	3%
Vomiting	9%	4%
Insomnia	8%	7%

How Do I Find a Treatment Center?

If you and your health care team feel that ketamine or esketamine is a good thing for you to try, the next step is to find a provider or clinic that has expertise in administering these medications to patients. The easiest way to do this is to ask your psychiatric and/or primary care provider. If they have a practitioner they like, then it is reasonable to proceed with that treatment facility. If they do not, then start with online resources. There are a couple devoted exclusively to ketamine. Johnson and Johnson, the maker of esketamine, also has a website that lists clinics that offer the treatments. Since just getting out of bed can be too hard when you're depressed, you may want to enlist the help of a family member, friend, or significant other with this research.

If you live in an area with limited resources for treating mental illness, you may want to consider getting a second opinion before proceeding with ketamine or esketamine. Over the years, I have seen depressed patients treated by many different types of providers. All of them are well intentioned, but some can be reaching beyond their expertise to help a person in need. If you are not currently seeing a therapist or other provider who is psychiatrically trained, and you just aren't getting better, you should consider having a comprehensive evaluation by a psychiatrist before seeking treatment with ketamine or esketamine. This will help you clarify your diagnosis, identify any other psychiatric conditions that may be impacting your response to treatment, and rule out medical conditions that can mimic psychiatric conditions, such as low thyroid hormone. Your primary care provider can usually help you find someone.

If your primary care office and other people whom you trust enough to talk with about your depression do not have a recommendation, or you tried who they recommended and it wasn't a good fit, there are other options available. Before moving on to where to find other providers, let us talk about how to increase your chances of successfully connecting with a provider.

First, think about positive encounters you have had with health care providers in the past. Did you wait for them to ask you questions, or did you look things up on the internet and come in with a list of questions, or did you fall somewhere in between? Use whichever approach works for you. No matter how much or little research you did, some providers may not respond favorably to your questions. If you find yourself in this situation, don't hesitate to ask them what amount of research they prefer you to do and see if you can get comfortable with their response.

Another thing to think about when choosing a provider is how they communicate information to you. Is it presented in a way that is understandable and not rushed? Do they take the time to answer your questions? Lastly, do they seem like a warm person, interested in helping you? If you do not feel an immediate connection with them, it may be worth going back for a second visit. All people have bad days, and you may have a very different experience the second time.

Other questions to ask a potential new provider of depression treatment include the following:

1. How much will you charge me for consultation and treatment?
   This is more a question for the front desk staff than the provider. I hate to have to talk about money, but people have had to file for

bankruptcy due to large medical bills. There's no sense investing your time looking into a clinician whose services and treatment you won't be able to afford.

2. Do you treat people in my age group?
3. Do you treat people who are [name any group that you identify with, such as LGBTQ]?
4. Do you treat mood disorders? Specifically, are you comfortable with complicated or treatment-resistant cases?
5. Do you focus on medications only?
    Many psychological conflicts and grief can masquerade as depression. You want someone who has a working knowledge of the different psychotherapies.
6. Do you know about ketamine/esketamine? Do you administer it?
7. Do you know about rTMS?
8. Do you know about ECT?

If you decide that this provider will not work, there are usually other options for finding an affordable one. The US Department of Health and Human Services has set up a national helpline under the Substance Abuse and Mental Health Services Administration that provides confidential referrals to local treatment resources. The Depression and Bipolar Support Alliance is a "peer-directed national organization" that has support groups and other helpful online resources. As always, there are several more online sites that can be helpful, and the most important thing is to find resources and providers that you feel comfortable working with and who help you feel better.

You should think of the initial encounters with any clinician as a two-way interview. You are there to see if you want to work with them, and whether they are likely to be helpful to you, while they are also trying to decide if they can be helpful to you. Two questions may help you sort this out. First, do you like this person's style? Some providers are very efficient and get right to the point. Others seem more accessible as people and take a moment to exchange pleasantries. If you are like me, the first type can be anxiety-provoking and sometimes cause you to forget to ask important questions. I usually prefer the less-driven approach when choosing a provider. Second, does this person really know about your problem? Many practitioners have a good working knowledge of mood disorders, but the expert asks about the small details and can tell you when something doesn't make sense. They just *get it.* Try to find someone who instills confidence in you with their depth of knowledge.

What Should I Look for in a Treatment Center?

As with ECT and rTMS, the most important consideration when choosing to work with a specific ketamine provider is that you feel comfortable working with them. The staff should seem organized and knowledgeable. The provider should take a thorough history and give you time to ask your questions. Yet they should be busy enough that there is a little bit of a wait list. Studies have shown that patients undergoing complex surgeries could improve their chances of surviving by selecting surgeons who perform the surgery most frequently. While ketamine is not surgery, the finding that practice makes perfect seems to hold true across medicine. You want to go to a center that has been doing it for a while and is busy.

The incredible demand and a general shortage of mental health professionals has led to a great deal of variation in the range of expertise individual clinics offer. The treatment described in the opening of this chapter is typical of an academic medical center. Things may be different in community settings. The minimum capabilities a ketamine/eskatamine clinic needs to have are:

- the ability to deliver the drug and then monitor the patient, including vital signs, for a couple of hours after dosing the drug
- the capability to handle any adverse effects of the medicine—given that most people coming for treatment are suffering from severe illness

and that there is a range of responses that occur when people take ketamine, ketamine centers should have the capability to deal with both
medical and psychiatric emergencies

- a way to effectively monitor the person's depression over time to make
  sure it is safely improving and, if it is not, the ability to arrange for
  appropriate, more intensive treatment

Another attribute that a treatment center should have is the ability
to manage the psychiatric and medical side effects of ketamine and
esketamine. Ketamine and esketamine have been used safely in many
patients, but centers need to be prepared for the times when patients
have serious side effects.

What If My Suicidal Thoughts Get Worse
While I'm Getting Treatment?

Suicidal thoughts are common in people suffering with depression.
They usually do not mean that you want to die; more commonly,
they mean you want the intense psychological pain you are in to stop.
Usually, people can manage these thoughts when they are reassured
the depression and pain will be addressed. However, there are other
people whose depression has taken them to a place where they feel
they need to act on these thoughts. If they have only a minimal or
partial response to the treatment, they can start to feel desperate. The
situation can become dangerous when they have enough energy to
act on their impulses before the despair has lifted. The treatment center should have the expertise to carefully monitor and manage these
symptoms.

What About Medical Emergencies?

Another important question to ask is how the treatment center han-
dles medical emergencies. I want to emphasize that **both esketamine
and ketamine have a high degree of safety** and that serious medical

consequences are rare. However, they do increase blood pressure and heart rate and these effects may unmask previously silent cardiac or vascular disease. In rare cases this can lead to an abnormal heart rhythm, heart attack, or stroke. Again, the treatment center should have the capability to handle these types of emergencies and have access to more intensive levels of care. **From a financial perspective, you should check with your insurance plan to make sure that the medical facility that backs up the treatment center is covered by your insurance.** You do not want to have a side effect to esketamine or ketamine and a large hospital bill on top of it.

How Is Treatment Administered?

It depends. Since ketamine has not been FDA approved for the treatment of mood disorders and therefore is not covered by most insurance, people have gotten creative in finding ways to afford it. The most common way it is administered is intravenously. However, people have also had compounding pharmacies make nasal sprays, much like the nasal spray cold medicines that you inhale through your nose. Other providers have tried to have people put the ketamine under their tongue and let it be absorbed rather than swallowed. Others have tried administering it in a suppository form. The goal of all these approaches is to avoid having the drug go through the intestines and the liver, which is what happens when it is swallowed. The reason for this is that when ketamine is taken by mouth and swallowed, only 20 to 25 percent of the medication reaches the bloodstream, compared to the 100 percent of intravenous delivery. In contrast, esketamine is only approved to be given by inhalation through the nose.

Another important consideration with either of these medications is which of the traditional antidepressants to pair it with. The FDA approved esketamine for use as an adjunct to standard antidepressants. Some of the insurance companies that cover ketamine also apply this standard to treatment with ketamine.

Will I Need to Take Time Off for This Treatment?

In most cases the answer is no. Most centers administer the treatment in the evening. Usually people go home and go to sleep after treatment. The next morning, the medication is out of their system, and they are good to go about their normal day. However, some people report a side effect of insomnia on the night of treatment. If you find that you are unable to sleep after a treatment, it is a good idea to take the next day off from your responsibilities that require sustained focus, such as work, driving, and childcare.

The same goes for other side effects. If you find they persist into the next day, adjust your schedule to give yourself time to recover. Also, be sure to mention them to your esketamine provider, as there may be medication they can give you to counter these symptoms.

Should I Be Treated with Ketamine or Esketamine?

Keep in mind that esketamine is thought by some to be the active ingredient in ketamine. There is very little data comparing the two medications, and the only head-to-head comparison found that esketamine was not less potent than ketamine. The study was not designed to prove either of them was better but to show one was not less potent than the other. This is based on complicated statistics that I will spare you.

In terms of your treatment, your depression is costing you a lot every day. Therefore, you should take whichever of the two medications is offered near you, at a cost you can afford. Your insurance will likely prefer esketamine, but some plans prefer ketamine because the cost of the medication is cheaper.

What Does Treatment Feel Like? What If It's Unpleasant?

As I said, the majority of people who get ketamine or esketamine describe a sense of floating and being disconnected from their bodies while being semiawake. Most experience this as a neutral or even pleasant experience. Other people find it to be uncomfortable and get mildly anxious. A small number of people will have marked anxiety and agitation, and fewer will have paranoid delusions and/or hallucinations. Most of the time these side effects can be handled with a dose of a benzodiazepine, such as lorazepam, which are often used for acute anxiety. The possibility of experiencing anxiety severe enough to require medication is another reason you want to make sure your clinic has skilled personnel and a plan to treat any agitation you might experience.

I Feel Better. Now What?

One of the more frustrating parts of depression and other psychiatric illnesses is that they tend to recur. In general, once you are better you usually need to continue the same treatment at the same doses to stay better. With esketamine, the recommended maintenance schedule after the initial four-week induction with twice-weekly treatment is once weekly for four weeks and then once every other week, unless the person's mood drops and then the maintenance schedule goes back to weekly to recapture the mood. With ketamine, the available data is more limited, but making adjustments to the individual's needs somewhere between weekly and monthly seems to be the accepted practice. When the person's depressive symptoms have been absent for an extended period of time, it is reasonable to either gradually increase the interval between treatments or decrease the dose.

Note that the FDA approved esketamine as an adjunct to standard antidepressant medications. Fortunately, medications are not the only treatments that have antidepressant effects. CBT and exercise have also been shown to have antidepressant effects. If you are already in therapy and exercising regularly, please keep them up. If not, as you begin to feel better from the ketamine or esketamine, it makes sense to see if you can add these treatments into your regimen.

What Does Treatment Cost?

Ketamine and esketamine have two components to their cost. The first is the cost of the drug. In the case of ketamine, this is usually pretty minimal. Esketamine, being the newer drug, is more expensive but is usually covered by insurance except for any copayment. The second component is the cost of administering the medication and monitoring the patient until they are ready to go home. By way of a ballpark figure, at the time of writing the total cost for a single ketamine infusion in Boston is around $600. That figure will vary by site and depends on several factors, including the clinic's fixed costs (staff salaries, rent, and so on). The good news is that since esketamine is FDA approved, insurance companies are starting to cover it. Some are even starting to cover ketamine infusions. Before starting out, it is often helpful to reach out to the customer service department of your health insurance company to see if the provider you are planning to see is covered by its network. If not, you should ask for a list of providers near you who are covered. If these providers have a long waiting list, you should ask the insurance company for other options. For example, they may agree to cover an out-of-network provider who can take you sooner. Most insurers require that they review and authorize esketamine treatment before you begin it. If they deny treatment, even after an appeal by your clinician, you can call their customer service line and ask them what other options they have for you to get this treatment. Never underestimate the power of polite persistence.

The discovery of ketamine's antidepressant properties represents one of the most important breakthroughs in psychiatric treatment. I have seen patients get genuine relief from ketamine and esketamine after years of struggling with depression despite trying multiple medications and pushing through significant side effects. In the hands of skilled clinicians, ketamine and esketamine are safe and effective. More importantly, they can be lifesaving for the suicidal patient as well as life changing for people struggling with chronic depression.

Key Takeaways

▶ Esketamine and ketamine are rapid-acting, effective anti-depressant medications that work through different pathways from those of traditional antidepressant medications. They often work when the others do not.

▶ The FDA has approved esketamine as an add-on to traditional antidepressant medications.

▶ Ketamine's patent protection has expired, making it too expensive to seek FDA approval, but its effectiveness in treatment-resistant depression is well supported by the scientific literature.

▶ When considering getting treatment from a provider, ask how they handle medical emergencies. Although serious side effects are uncommon, the clinic should have the medical expertise to handle an emergency. If more intensive treatment is needed, make sure they can send you to a hospital that takes your insurance.

▶ Check with your insurance company about how to get the treatment covered. If your insurance company refuses to cover your treatment, either you or your advocate should reach out to them. Polite persistence is sometimes quite effective.

▶ Although everyone is unique, most people are able to get their treatment in the evening and wake up fully functional the next day. Most people do not need to put their life on hold for treatment.

Chapter 6

Transcranial Magnetic Stimulation
Using Magnets to Treat Depression

Transcranial magnetic stimulation has emerged as a highly effective treatment for depression as well as obsessive-compulsive disorder and smoking cessation. Over its relatively short life span, it has progressed from being a research technique for probing the function of different brain regions to a highly effective clinical treatment. To give you a better idea of when the treatment is used and what it is like, we will start with Tom and his battle with depression.

Tom is a fifty-two-year-old man who has had recurring episodes of depression every few years since his thirties. These episodes have usually responded to an adjustment of his antidepressant medications and time. Tom also had seen a number of therapists over the years. His current episode began about a year ago after his divorce was finalized. Although he had a small group of supportive friends and his grown children kept in touch regularly, he felt down most of the time. He couldn't enjoy anything good that happened and even contemplated killing himself to end this miserable state he was in. His psychiatrist adjusted his medications, and the "cocktail" of three different antidepressants helped somewhat, but the insomnia and lethargy they caused seemed to make things worse instead of better. Tom was faithfully seeing his current therapist, whom he felt was a good fit because they had been able to work through a number of issues from his past. Still, he wasn't able to shake the black cloud that hung over him wherever he went.

Tom's psychiatrist recommended he try ECT, but he didn't have anyone who could pick him up and get him home after the treatment, nor could he take the time off from work needed. He felt that he had used up a lot of goodwill with his boss when he was going through his divorce and had needed extra time off and a more flexible schedule; he was worried she would use this as an excuse to replace him with someone younger who had lower salary requirements.

His psychiatrist then recommended a trial of transcranial magnetic stimulation (TMS or rTMS, with the *r* standing for "repetitive"). Although the treatment would require a significant time commitment, he could get it done first thing in the morning and then go in and work a full day. Tom agreed to give it a try. At first the treatment was a little uncomfortable. The magnetic coil used to deliver the treatment pressed slightly on the left side of his head as the team moved it into position. Once they were satisfied with the position, the treatment began. There was a clicking sound that was muted by the earplugs they gave him to protect his hearing. He also felt a twitching sensation on his scalp. However, he quickly got used to the treatment and almost enjoyed coming in every day for it.

After a couple of weeks, the black cloud began to lift. Tom noticed that everyday life did not require as much effort. He was surprised about five weeks in when he went on a weekend camping trip with his oldest son and was able to really enjoy it. After six weeks, Tom was feeling much better and was able to stop treatment. He still had to repair his relationship with his boss and find a new "normal" as a single person living alone, but his medications had been streamlined, and he had more energy and was confident he could do it.

What Is rTMS and How Was It Discovered?

Transcranial magnetic stimulation was first developed as a way to stimulate specific areas of the brain to probe their function. Researchers then discovered that if they repeatedly applied the stimulus, they could change the activity of the targeted brain region. A treatment in which TMS is applied repetitively became known as rTMS, and in current use, the two terms are used interchangeably.

In a relatively short period of time, repetitive TMS has gone from being a tool for understanding the brain to a full-fledged treatment for depression, obsessive-compulsive disorder, and smoking cessation. Yet it is highly likely that rTMS is only in its infancy, as the equipment, stimulus settings, and parts of the brain targeted by rTMS are areas of active research. As this research continues, the potency and range of future applications of rTMS will almost certainly continue to grow. In this section, I will provide you with a brief history of how TMS went from an idea to receiving the FDA's clearance as a treatment for depression. I will also share the recent advances that have occurred and how they may be applicable to your treatment.

Transcranial magnetic stimulation is based on the physics of electromagnets. An electromagnet is a coil of wire that becomes a magnet only when electricity is flowing through the coil. One property of electromagnets is that when an electromagnetic coil is placed next to a second coil and an electrical current is pulsed through the first coil it causes current to flow in the second coil. **The key insight came when people realized that since the brain uses electrical impulses**

to communicate within its circuits, it could be thought of as the second electromagnetic coil and be influenced by the first.

TMS was initially developed in 1985 by Dr. Anthony Barker and his colleagues in the United Kingdom. It was first approved for use in treatment-resistant depression in 2002 in Canada and in 2008 in the United States.[1] This gap between its initial development and approval for clinical use reflects, in part, the fact that it was developed as a means for studying regional brain function. It also reflects the fact that it "grew up" during a time of resurgence of electroconvulsive therapy, or ECT. People were trying to understand how ECT worked when treating depression. The leading theory was that the seizure induced during ECT was necessary for people to get better.[2] TMS does not usually cause seizures, so TMS practitioners could not use the ECT experience to determine where to put the magnet, how intense a stimulus to deliver and for how long, or how many treatments to deliver. In short, they had to overcome old biases and start from the ground up to turn TMS into a treatment for psychiatric illnesses. Eventually, people figured out how to use sustained stimulation to cause longer-lasting effects on brain circuitry to treat depression and other brain-based illnesses.

How Do We Know rTMS Works?

The FDA has cleared rTMS for the treatment of depression. Doing so required data from large-scale clinical trials showing that the potential benefits outweigh the risks associated with the treatment. Prior to 2004, while the treatment methodology was still being worked out, rTMS was tried out in a number of small single-site studies.[3] While the combined results from these studies suggested that rTMS was an effective treatment for depression, some of them used different treatment approaches, and some failed to show an antidepressant response. Also, since the FDA generally does not accept the results of small studies as the basis for clearing a treatment for use in humans, large-scale trials spread across multiple clinical centers were needed before rTMS could be used in routine clinical practice.

The results from two multicenter rTMS trials were reported in 2007. The divergence in their results illustrates the challenges that were faced by this emerging technology. The first study, reported in October by Dr. Uwe Herwig and colleagues, treated 127 depressed subjects across seven clinics in Germany.[4] To keep the treatment as naturalistic as possible, the study participants received both antidepressant medications and rTMS. Study participants were divided into an active treatment group and a control group. The active treatment group received pulses that increased the activity in the left front part of the brain (the left prefrontal cortex). They had rTMS for fifteen consecutive working days. The control group received inactive rTMS, or sham rTMS, over the same time period. This study did not find any difference in antidepressant response between those subjects treated with active rTMS and those treated with sham rTMS.

While the results of that research were disappointing, shortly thereafter, in December 2007, a second study was reported. Fortunately, this study, a large multisite trial of rTMS run by the Neuronetics corporation, was successful. Between January 2004 and August 2005, 301 subjects with treatment-resistant depression across twenty-three study sites were treated with either rTMS or sham rTMS. Similar to the German study, the active rTMS group had the coil placed over the left prefrontal cortex, and the pulses were applied at a frequency that stimulated the underlying brain tissue. A key difference between the two studies was that in this group, participants received treatment five days per week over six weeks, followed by treatment two days per week for three weeks. By the six-week mark, the active treatment group had essentially twice the rate of remission from symptoms as the simulated, or sham, group.[5] This trial firmly established the effectiveness of rTMS for treating depression and was one of the key reasons the FDA devices division approved the Neuronetics device for use in the United States in 2008.

While this study met the FDA's standards and established rTMS as a legitimate treatment for depression, there was still a lot to be learned about the use of rTMS in the clinic. With this in mind, the National Institute of Mental Health sponsored the optimization of TMS or OPT-TMS study. This study was conducted across four university hospital rTMS centers. It was designed to determine the best way to deliver rTMS treatment by defining the optimal stimulus duration and intensity, or dose of rTMS, for active treatment. Out of 190, 154 participants completed the study. The odds of going into remission were four times greater, or approximately 30 percent, in the active treatment group.[6]

There's more good news. Since rTMS received clearance from the FDA to augment antidepressant medications in the treatment of depression, our knowledge of how to use the treatment most effectively has grown substantially. In 2012, Dr. Linda Carpenter and colleagues reported the results of 307 patients treated in "real-world clinical practice settings" with rTMS.[7] Those who participated in the study completed rating scales to assess their mood during their course of rTMS. After six weeks of treatment, approximately 52 percent of patients had responded to it and 31 percent saw their depression go into remission. These numbers are impressive by any stretch; they are even more so when you compare these results to the STAR*D study funded by the National Institute of Mental Health, which found remission rates in people who had failed with two prior medications to be between 12 and 20 percent depending on the antidepressant medication used.[8]

This study also confirmed some important findings from earlier studies: first, younger patients tended to respond better than patients who were fifty-five years and older, and second, the more medications the patient failed prior to trying rTMS, the less likely they were to respond to the rTMS. This result has also been shown to be true for antidepressant medications, ketamine, and ECT.

One notable question that remains is whether certain antidepressants are better than others when combined with rTMS. The studies that controlled for medications have used venlafaxine (Effexor) or mirtazapine (Remeron) for their broad-spectrum antidepressant activity. The results were somewhat disappointing. However, it is conceivable that other antidepressant medications may work better when combined with rTMS based on their effects on the brain's electrical rhythms. We're still exploring the effectiveness of rTMS for people using specific antidepressants; I'll talk more about that in just a bit.

Why Do People Try Multiple Antidepressant Medications Before Trying rTMS?

Believe it or not, it is common for people to have suffered with depression for months and even years before they come for rTMS. In part, that's because they may not have heard about it, or it may not be available in the community where they live. Also, depression is sneaky. It often comes on in the middle of life stress, and people usually think that is the reason why they don't feel well. They simply don't realize they have depression until after the suffering has gone on for too long. In Tom's case, he had previously battled depression and recognized the symptoms, so he did not have a delay in starting medications. But similar to a number of people, he did try to work things through in psychotherapy before trying rTMS.

A second factor that often delays people from seeking treatment with rTMS is that among clinicians, there is a bias toward medication over procedural interventions. Years ago, the shift from psychoanalysis as the primary treatment for depression to antidepressant medications was almost a street brawl. Ultimately, the medications became the primary treatment for depression because they are much more affordable than psychoanalysis and work for a majority of people. The result is that there are more than twenty antidepressant medications available and huge amounts of marketing dollars that have gone into creating the impression that each drug offers unique advantages. In reality, the medications are more similar than different, and as we've discussed earlier, only about two-thirds of people with depression respond to them. Also, as with ECT and ketamine, some people may not be aware of rTMS or that it is a viable option for them. If they are aware of it, they may have looked into it before TMS received FDA approval, when the treatment had a high out-of-pocket cost.

The bias against procedures also reflects the inconvenience of having to go to an office to get the treatment. It also probably reflects that some people associate it with ECT and its need for general anesthesia.

How Can the Same Treatment Work for Obsessive-Compulsive Disorder and Smoking?

All forms of rTMS work by using a fluctuating magnetic field to change the activity of parts of the brain that are exposed to the field. However, where the magnetic field is applied determines which circuits are changed and which symptoms are treated. In depression, the coil is placed on the side of the head just above the temple to target the posterior lateral portion of the front lobe of the brain, where the dorsolateral prefrontal cortex is located. Most often the stimulus is applied to the left side of the brain, but some treatments stimulate the right side. In obsessive-compulsive disorder, the coil is placed near the front part of the brain, by the orbitofrontal cortex (which is above the eyes) and near where a deeper structure, the anterior cingulate cortex, is located. In the smoking cessation trials, the lateral portion of the front part of the brain (the lateral prefrontal cortex) and a structure known as the insula were targeted. In other words, different parts of the frontal lobe of the brain, or more specifically parts of the prefrontal cortex, are targeted when treating these three diseases. This reflects the multiple roles this brain region has in organizing behavior. The fact that rTMS targets a different part of the prefrontal cortex for each disease highlights its functional complexity.

What Does the Latest Research Show?

As rTMS is a relatively new treatment, there are many areas to explore to optimize the treatment. One of these is the shape and size of the coils that are used. You may recall a common demonstration that science teachers like to do with magnets: they put a magnet under a flat surface and sprinkle iron filings on top to demonstrate that the filings will line up with the outline of the magnetic field produced. The shape of the field reflects the shape of the magnet. Likewise, the amount of filings that line up with the field reflects the strength of the magnet and their distance from it. The same is true of rTMS coils: the shape of the coil determines the shape of the field produced and the size of the region stimulated.[9] The strength of the magnetic field produced in the coil determines the depth and intensity with which the brain tissue is stimulated. The coils used in the early trials of rTMS only stimulated the superficial surface of the brain (about three-quarters of an inch).[10]

To address this limitation, a new type of coil known as an H-coil has been developed. Its shape and the strength of the magnetic field produced allow the stimulus to reach deeper structures in the brain, not just the surface tissue.[11] This new coil design was tested in a clinical trial of 212 participants with depression across twenty medical centers. The participants received either active deep rTMS or placebo (sham rTMS) five days per week for four weeks, followed by twice-weekly maintenance treatment for twelve weeks, a total of sixteen weeks of treatment. At the end of treatment, 40 percent of the participants had responded to deep rTMS and 29 percent had remission of their symptoms; those who received the placebo had a 26 percent response rate and 22 percent remission rate.[12] In short, these response and remission rates are encouraging, but they also highlight that this type of rTMS is still a work in progress.

There are other coil designs under development. These include coils that stimulate multiple regions at the same time or sequentially.[13] Both the deep coil design and the multisite coil design reflect recognition of the fact that depression is a disease of brain circuits and not just one region.

Another area that is actively being explored is the stimulus used to treat the patient. The effect of rTMS on brain tissue depends on the frequency of the stimulus applied. Pulses that are applied at a frequency of one per second (1 Hz) inhibit the neurons, reducing activity, while pulses applied at ten hertz or faster tend to excite them, increasing activity. Potentially, this allows for very precise treatment, such that inhibitory pulses can be applied to overactive brain circuitry, while excitatory pulses can be applied to underactive parts of the circuit. In current clinical practice, rTMS uses the excitatory pulses at ten hertz to the left prefrontal cortex to treat depression. A treatment session typically takes thirty minutes.

A new set of stimulus parameters called intermittent theta burst stimulation (iTBS, or just TBS) works even faster. Theta burst brain wave activity is a pattern used by the brain itself to change emotional memory circuitry to reflect new learning. The brain will use short bursts of intense activity (50 Hz) followed by slower activity at the theta (5 Hz) frequency to form new associations. In theta burst rTMS stimulation, this pattern of activation is mimicked by a TMS machine. What is exciting about this approach is that unlike conventional rTMS, theta burst rTMS can be delivered in just three minutes per treatment session.[14] And some laboratories have been exploring whether giving multiple treatment sessions in one day can greatly reduce the six weeks of treatment needed for the current practice of rTMS.

Data on the effectiveness of rTMS and, more recently, TBS in reducing symptoms associated with PTSD (post-traumatic stress disorder) is emerging. In contrast to depression, studies using TBS for PTSD stimulated the right prefrontal cortex and saw improvements in social and occupational functioning. Once again, research shows that targeting different brain regions yields different results.[15]

Do We Know What rTMS Does to the Brain?

We know that rTMS uses magnetic fields to change the activity of the brain tissue it stimulates.[16] However, we still have much to learn about how rTMS affects the mood circuitry. Fortunately, today's high-resolution brain scanners permit us to look at how different regions function within the brain's circuitry, which helps us with our understanding of rTMS and how it's affecting the brain. Remember that rTMS is applied to the scalp over the frontal part of the brain, the prefrontal cortex. This area plays an important role in the brain's mood circuit. In one study, fifty people with treatment-resistant depression treated with rTMS underwent functional magnetic resonance imaging before and after treatment. The imaging, which shows how the brain is operating, revealed that effective rTMS normalizes the functional connections of other more distant parts of the mood circuit.[17]

In closing, repetitive transcranial magnetic stimulation, rTMS, is a safe and effective treatment that has come a long way in a short time and continues to be refined for greater effectiveness to treat depression and other brain-related challenges such as PTSD. One of the key advantages of rTMS is that it permits specific brain regions to be targeted. As our understanding of the brain circuitry involved in different illnesses evolves, the usefulness of this treatment should continue to expand, offering hope to an even wider variety of patients who are currently known to be good candidates for rTMS.

Key Takeaways

- ▶ rTMS as it is currently used in clinical practice is an effective treatment for medication-resistant depression, and it is only getting better.
- ▶ Advances in the types of pulses delivered, such as theta burst stimulation, offer the promise of much shorter treatment courses. Brain imaging studies show that TMS brings about significant changes and normalization of the mood circuit in the brain.
- ▶ Clinically, rTMS often allows people to streamline their medications and reduce side effects during the course of treatment. Since it does not require general anesthesia and does not affect your memory, you can get the treatment and still go about your everyday life with little interruption.
- ▶ The response rate for rTMS is around 50 to 60 percent in people who have failed their previous medication treatments.
- ▶ rTMS has been shown to be effective for other mental health challenges, such as obsessive-compulsive disorder and addiction to smoking. The current data on PTSD is quite promising.
- ▶ rTMS and TBS, unlike ECT, do not require anesthesia and do not induce a seizure to treat depression.

Chapter 7

Starting rTMS Treatment

The practice of TMS is evolving relatively quickly, and the types of rTMS available can vary widely from one community to the next. The good news is that the different types of rTMS practiced today have all been shown to be safe and effective treatments. Martha, whose treatment is described below, received a course of rTMS using a standard coil and pulse sequence. If she had seen a different provider, she might have received treatment with a deep coil or an intermittent theta burst pulse sequence. The available clinical data has not yet shown one approach to be better than the others. With that in mind, let us begin our discussion of treatment with rTMS with Martha's case.

Martha, a forty-five-year-old married woman, reported that her current episode of depression began about two years ago, shortly before Thanksgiving. She remembered it because she usually hosts the holiday for her family and enjoys it quite a bit. That year was distinctly different, and although she pulled it off, she really found it to be a struggle. When asked, she could not come up with any significant life stressors that might have contributed to her depressed mood. Instead, she was clear that this episode was very similar to her previous episodes of depression, except it seemed to be lasting longer.

After the holidays, she had resumed individual therapy and began seeing a psychiatrist, who restarted her previous SSRI antidepressant medication, sertraline. After a few weeks her mood lifted somewhat, but she still felt "flat"—as she put it, "like the color had been washed out of my world." After a couple of months without any further improvement, her doctor switched Martha to a different class of antidepressant, the SNRI venlafaxine. Again, Martha noticed some additional improvement but was still sad most of the time. Even though she had some very positive things happening to her and her family, she really could not enjoy life; she no longer went hiking with her family, got together with friends, or did the little things for others that she used to enjoy so much. Then, her psychiatrist tried boosting the venlafaxine with several different medications, including lithium, bupropion, lamotrigine, and thyroid hormone, but none significantly lifted her mood any further.

Martha's teenage daughter read about rTMS on the internet while looking for ways to help her mother feel better. At her daughter's urging, Martha raised the idea of rTMS with her psychiatrist. The psychiatrist was aware of it but had not yet sent any of his patients for TMS. He agreed that Martha should at least get a consultation and called the TMS clinic at the university hospital in a nearby city to make a referral. On the morning of her consultation at the clinic, Martha was nervous but hopeful that this new technique could help her get back to living instead of just struggling to survive.

When she arrived, she checked in and took a seat in the waiting room. After a very brief wait, she was called back into the office and met the TMS psychiatrist. The psychiatrist smiled warmly, asked if she was comfortable, and then proceeded to take her history. The psychiatrist confirmed the diagnosis of a unipolar depression that was partially responsive to medications. She made sure that Martha did not have any history of seizures and did not have any metal implants, including aneurysm clips, stents, and jewelry that could not be removed, in her head. She also verified that Martha had never had a cochlear implant, vagal nerve stimulator, or deep brain stimulator, explaining that any of these could interfere with the TMS. The psychiatrist also asked Martha several questions about suicidal thoughts and any past suicidal behavior. Martha was relieved to report that suicidal thinking had never been a part of her depression.[1]

Once the history taking was completed, the psychiatrist asked Martha if she had any questions. Yes, she said, Martha was a candidate for a trial of rTMS, and the response rate is around 50 to 60 percent for cases like hers, with about 40 percent achieving full remission of symptoms. The treatment schedule would be five sessions per week, each session would take about forty-five minutes, and she could go about her usual day afterward. The first session would be the longest since they would need to customize the treatment parameters for Martha, as they do this for every individual.

Martha decided to try TMS and chose the noontime slot so she could get the treatment during her lunch hour and not miss too much work. After she arrived at the clinic and checked in, she was brought back into the treatment area by a technician. In the treatment room, Martha sat in a comfortable reclining chair with a console behind it. The psychiatrist came in and checked on how she was feeling and whether there was any change in her depressive symptoms. After that, the technician placed a thin white cap on her head and the psychiatrist told her that they would get started. The psychiatrist explained that the first step was to determine the motor threshold and that she should expect her hand to twitch. Martha was given earplugs to protect her hearing and a spacer was placed on the bridge of her nose. The technician ran a comb-like device across her scalp, and then she felt the coil being positioned. After a short while, it came to rest gently but firmly on the middle of her head.

The psychiatrist informed her that they were going to get started, and Martha then heard a very brief click followed by several more in a slow and rhythmic pace. She then noticed that her hand began to twitch in response to the clicks. After a few more minutes of clicks, the psychiatrist told her that they were ready to begin her treatment. The technician helped her remove the cap, and the coil was moved forward and secured in place over the front of the left side of her head. The machine began to click in rapid succession, and Martha felt as if there was a woodpecker tapping on her head.

After a short while, she got used to the sensation and allowed her mind to wander. She was brought back to reality by the technician lifting the coil and telling her that they were done and they would see her tomorrow. She left the office, drove back to work, and finished her day.

Martha completed the six-week course of treatment and, by the end, felt that she had rejoined the land of the living. She stayed on the venlafaxine and reduced the frequency she was seeing her therapist to once a month.

Martha's case is a TMS success story on many levels. She was fortunate in that her psychiatrist was able to quickly refer her to a university clinic that performed rTMS, she felt comfortable with the staff, and she had an excellent response to the treatment. Hopefully, your referral and treatment will also go as smoothly. To help with that, let us discuss some common questions that patients ask about the treatment.

Will the Treatment Help My Depression?

Once the rTMS clinician agrees that you have a diagnosis that is likely to respond to rTMS and that you do not have a medical contraindication to the treatment, the next step is for you to provide informed consent and proceed with the treatment. A recent study comparing rTMS

to iTBS reported an antidepressant response in 47 and 49 percent of
the depressed subjects, respectively.[2] These response rates are actually
quite good when you consider that these subjects had not responded to
other antidepressant treatments.

How Do I Find an rTMS Provider?

Much like ketamine (and, as you'll see, ECT), once Martha and her psychiatrist decided that TMS was a reasonable next step in her treatment,
the issue became finding a provider who performed TMS. Often your
psychiatrist or mental health professional will have a colleague whom
they have worked with in the past to whom they can refer you. In this
case the psychiatrist did not but was able to network through colleagues
to find someone. If this is not an option for you, then asking your primary care provider and reaching out to local support groups for people
with depression is often helpful and can give you insight into the patient
experience. Lastly, there is the internet. Some of the companies that
manufacture the TMS machines have websites that list practitioners in
the different states. If you are having difficulty finding a practitioner, a
combination of two or more of these approaches may work best for you.

What Happens During the Initial Consultation?

Once you have identified a TMS practitioner, you should book an initial consultation with their office. For most people the purpose of the
initial consultation is twofold. First, they want to get the advice of the
doctor as to whether TMS is a good treatment for them, and second,
they want to see if this person (and their team) is someone they want to
work with. (See Appendix A for questions to ask a potential provider.)

The process is similar for the practitioner. They want to understand the person's illness and whether it is **likely to respond to rTMS.
At present, that means unipolar major depression, obsessive-
compulsive disorder, and smoking cessation, the three indications**

for rTMS cleared by the FDA. The diagnosis of depression can be unclear sometimes, as people may have concurrent or comorbid conditions such as anxiety, substance use, and/or the long-term effects of childhood trauma. While each of these conditions can be associated with prolonged bouts of sadness, they may not be an episode of major depression and may require a completely different treatment approach.

Are There Preexisting Conditions That Affect My Potential for Treatment?

If you have a condition or implant that makes it dangerous to place a high-field electromagnetic coil near your head and pulse a current through it, you may not be able to have rTMS treatment. Additionally, since the treatment directly stimulates the underlying brain tissue, any brain illness or injury to the brain's tissue can create an irritable area that makes the person vulnerable to seizures. Accordingly, patients with a history of seizures, family history of epilepsy, or conditions such as a past stroke, brain tumor, or traumatic brain injury are at risk for triggering a generalized seizure during rTMS. Generalized, or grand mal, seizures can potentially lead to severe injury; therefore, TMS practitioners do their best to avoid treating patients who have these conditions. Fortunately, in **individuals *without* such conditions**, the risk of seizure from rTMS has been estimated to be **fewer than one seizure per sixty thousand treatment** sessions.[3]

Another potential risk associated with rTMS is if **metallic implants that should not be removed are dislodged by the application of the magnetic field**, running the risk of potentially disastrous consequences. **Examples of these are medical devices such as cochlear implants, aneurysm clips, stents to keep arteries open, vagal nerve stimulators, or deep brain stimulators**, to name some of the most common. Jewelry with iron or nickel inside will also be drawn to the magnet and can cause serious harm depending on its starting location.

There are some medications that can affect your response to rTMS. For most medications, this does not seem to be the case. There are two important exceptions: **benzodiazepines and stimulants**. Benzodiazepines such as lorazepam (**Ativan**), clonazepam (**Klonopin**), diazepam (**Valium**), and alprazolam (**Xanax**) are sedative medications. These types of medications have been shown in two large-scale studies to reduce the overall response rate to rTMS.[4] This has led to the suggestion that clinicians consider reducing the dose of these medications during a course of rTMS.[5] However, dosage reduction must be done with care, as too rapid a decrease in either sedatives or their cousins anticonvulsant medications has been associated with an increased risk of unintended seizures. The sedatives and, to a lesser extent, the anticonvulsants are also used clinically to detoxify patients from heavy alcohol use. So, it is not surprising that heavy binge drinking, with its large fluctuations in blood alcohol levels, is associated with an increased risk of seizures. (As a side note, heavy binge drinking can cause many of the symptoms of depression, and if you are struggling with this problem, it may make sense to seek treatment for problem drinking before considering a change to your treatment for depression.)

Interestingly, stimulants, such as **amphetamine** (Adderall, Vyvanse), **methylphenidate** (Concerta, Ritalin), **modafinil** (Provigil), and **armodafinil** (Nuvigil) were shown to increase the response rate to rTMS.[6] You might think that adding any one of these medications to treatment would be a good idea. Unfortunately, given the potential for addiction, it is not clear that adding stimulants when there is not another diagnosis, such as attention deficit hyperactivity disorder, is a good idea.

What Are Common Side Effects?

The risks of rTMS and the newer iTBS can be divided into two groups: uncomfortable but not life-threatening ones and serious or potentially life-threatening adverse effects.

Less Serious Side Effects.

The most common non-life-threatening adverse effect associated with rTMS is headache. As you probably know, there are many types of headaches, from tension headaches to migraines. The direct effects of the magnetic field on the muscles in the scalp can cause muscle tension headaches, and patients are given earplugs to help prevent that side effect. The available data indicates that the TMS machines' sound does not harm the patient's hearing, but at a minimum, it is uncomfortable: patients often report feeling a "tingly" feeling on their scalp during the treatment.

If headaches become a problem for you during treatment, your practitioner may advise you to take acetaminophen or another non-steroidal anti-inflammatory medication prior to treatment. If you are prone to migraines, your provider may advise you to pre-treat with your migraine medications or bring rescue medications, such as sumatriptan, to the treatment center with you to take after treatment.

Other side effects include dizziness, fatigue, insomnia, anxiety, and back or neck pain. Vomiting, tinnitus (ringing in the ears), and "unrelated" accidents are very rare side effects.[7]

Serious Side Effects.

The most common serious potential side effect is the **risk of seizure**, but the safety precautions in place today make the risk of a patient experiencing a seizure during rTMS miniscule **(0.003 percent per treatment)**.[8]

Other rare (less than 1 percent) but potentially serious side effects reported in treatment studies include a heart attack or myocardial infarction, agitation that required hospitalization, and worsening depression and suicidal ideation.[9] Syncope, or passing out, was reported in one study and is a rare side effect.[10]

Another potential serious side effect is triggering mania. This would strongly suggest that the person has an underlying bipolar disorder and would be a good reason why the antidepressant medications had not worked. Bipolar depression usually requires different medications, such as lithium and other mood stabilizers.

Long-Term Side Effects

Generally, the side effects of rTMS occur during the course of therapy and end when the treatment ends. Some people have reported ringing in their ears that persists for a short period of time after treatment. There are no reported instances of this being permanent.

What Is the Treatment Like?

While Martha's and Tom's stories give you a sense of the treatment, here is a full picture of what you can expect on the day of each treatment.

After you check in at the clinic, you will be led back to the area where the treatment is delivered. You will be asked to remove any jewelry and other objects that can interact with the magnetic field. You will be provided with earplugs for your comfort and to protect your hearing.

At the first session, once you are seated in the chair, you will be fitted for proper placement of the coil. The main objective of your first session is to determine the motor threshold. When your rTMS practitioner is determining the motor threshold, the coil is placed over the part of the brain that controls movement of the hand. The goal is to find the weakest magnetic field, or lowest settings on the machine, that will cause your thumb to twitch. To accomplish this, you will feel them moving the magnet around on your head and you will hear a series of clicks. Almost immediately after some of these clicks, you will feel your thumb and index finger twitch. They will continue adjusting the settings until the motor threshold is determined. The motor threshold is defined as the level of stimulation where you consistently respond to the click with a twitch. Often, the rTMS practitioner will then move the magnet slightly and determine once again the motor threshold in adjacent areas. Your treaters will then use the motor threshold to ensure that the TMS treatment settings have been optimized for you.

Once the practitioner is confident that they have identified the correct position and your motor threshold, they will move the magnet forward until it sits over the part of your scalp that corresponds to the left dorsolateral prefrontal cortex. There are a couple of different ways to do this to ensure the proper positioning. When rTMS was first used, practitioners would move the magnet five centimeters (about two inches) forward from where the motor cortex is located, usually just above the temple. While this has worked reasonably well and was used in some of the clinical trials that established the efficacy of rTMS in depression, other approaches have evolved in an attempt to improve the treatment response. The most elaborate approach is to get an MRI scan of the brain and use a computer to guide placement based on the scan; currently, this is usually only used in research studies. The in-between approach is to use a computer to guide placement based on external anatomic landmarks, such as the bridge of the nose, the ears, or the top of the skull. Once the area for treatment has been identified, the team will position the magnetic coil in the same spot for each subsequent treatment.

The next decision that needs to be made in order to start your treatment is which type of stimulus to use. With regular rTMS, which is applied to the left side of the front of the head, the dorsolateral prefrontal cortex, the stimulus is usually set at 120 percent of motor threshold and applied at ten cycles per second (Hz).

As we discussed in Chapter 6, a new type of rTMS known as theta burst stimulation (iTBS) has recently been developed. This approach simulates the pattern of brain waves used during memory formation and learning of complex concepts. Since memory centers are important components of the mood circuit, it makes sense that this approach can treat depression. During a TBS treatment session, this pattern of theta burst stimulation is repeated until a total of six hundred pulses is applied. As you learned, this takes a little over three minutes compared to the twenty to forty minutes required for a standard rTMS treatment session.[11] One particularly interesting possible application of the shorter treatment time for theta burst is whether multiple treatments can be given in a day. If studies prove this to be successful, the time to antidepressant response would be shortened and the number of trips into the clinic for treatment reduced. However, the current accepted knowledge is that both rTMS and theta burst stimulation appear to be equally effective. Therefore, treatment recommendations will depend on the TMS practitioner's experience and preference.

How Long Does Treatment Take?

Martha completed a six-week course of treatment—as did Tom from Chapter 6—and this reflects the standard schedule of treatment for both rTMS and theta burst magnetic stimulation, which is thirty individual sessions. Usually, this means treatment five days per week for six weeks. Different centers may vary this schedule and total number of treatments slightly, depending on their experiences and the individual's response to treatment. At some centers, they will reverify the motor threshold every week or some other interval during the course of the treatment. At other centers, they are comfortable keeping the settings constant unless there is a suspicion that the motor threshold has changed. For example, the provider might adjust the motor threshold in a person who was getting better and then stopped improving. Other reasons would include a change in anticonvulsant or sedative-hypnotic medications that the patient is taking or a change in the person's pattern of alcohol consumption.

Your rTMS practitioner may have other conditions and changes in medications that they consider to be a risk. Therefore, you should let them know if there are any changes in your health or medications.

What Happens After the rTMS Course Is Done?

As mentioned in the previous section, a course of rTMS is usually thirty treatments over six weeks. If the person's symptoms are in remission, most practitioners would monitor the patient and treat only if they exhibited any signs of relapse. If you have an especially robust and effective response to the treatment, your team may decide to discontinue the treatment before the full thirty treatments. Some centers also taper over a small number of treatments: for example, at Massachusetts General Hospital's program, there is usually a six-treatment taper.

At this point it is not clear that ongoing or "maintenance" rTMS treatments offer any advantage over careful clinical monitoring and treating any relapses in mood. If there is only partial improvement, there may be adjustments in medications and a recalibration of the motor threshold, and the treatment is usually continued. If you do not respond to the initial course, your team will need to determine whether additional treatments are warranted or you should be referred for another treatment modality, such as ketamine or ECT.

But Does It Last?

There is data to suggest that rTMS's effects last for a significant amount of time following the treatment. Although rTMS is thought to produce this effect by inducing long-lasting changes in the mood circuitry, it is also possible that other factors can create prolonged improvement—including how rTMS works in conjunction with antidepressant medication. In the existing clinical trials, rTMS treatment was added to the patient's antidepressant medication. For antidepressant medications to work, they require consistent access to the brain for an extended period of time. People over sixty-five years of age, for example, may require up to sixteen weeks to respond to an antidepressant; rTMS may permit them to stay on the medicine long enough for it to work. Most likely, the rTMS and medications affect the mood circuitry in a way that is additive and beneficial.

The new approaches to rTMS and the technologies that are being developed to study the brain will surely provide additional insight into the mechanism of action. In the meantime, rTMS has been shown to be effective and well tolerated—and that means that people get well and stay well.

Does Insurance Cover rTMS Treatment?

During your consultation, you will want to talk with your provider's office about payment and insurance. rTMS does not require general anesthesia and therefore does not need to be performed in a hospital setting (nor does recovering from the treatment consume most of the day). As the machines have become more available and insurance companies have become more convinced of the utility of rTMS in depression, the cost to the patient has become less prohibitive. Martha's course of treatment was mostly covered by her insurance, except for a small copayment, which is a huge improvement over the roughly $15,000 out-of-pocket cost for a course of rTMS that some people had to pay in the past.

Key Takeaways

- ▶ rTMS is an effective treatment for depression and is continuing to improve.
- ▶ rTMS and TBS do not negatively affect your ability to function, even on the day of treatment.
- ▶ Since rTMS and TBS do not use anesthesia and do not affect cognition, treatment can be fit around the person's work/home schedule and does not require taking a leave from work.
- ▶ Insurance companies are increasingly covering the treatment, thereby lowering the person's cost of treatment.
- ▶ rTMS is not safe for people with certain medical devices that cannot be removed.
- ▶ Side effects to rTMS tend to be minor and are usually responsive to minor adjustments in the treatment. Be sure to mention any side effects to your treatment team.
- ▶ People with a history of seizures or who have certain heart conditions should not undergo rTMS. Your cardiologist should be able to provide you with guidance.
- ▶ If the most recent data holds up—that is, if it's confirmed by more studies—iTBS will drastically reduce the amount of time required for treatment.

Chapter 8

ECT:
Do They Still Do That?

J ust the mention of electroconvulsive therapy, or ECT, evokes frightening images from the various movies in which it has been portrayed. ECT as it is practiced today is a very modern and safe medical procedure that bears no resemblance to what people have seen on screen. To paint you a more realistic picture of what the treatment is like today, let's take the case of Bob.

Bob, a forty-nine-year-old married father of two, first started to have problems with his moods and alcohol abuse in his mid-teens. After he flunked out of college because of excessive drinking, his parents were able to convince him to go into an alcohol detox and rehab facility. During his stay at the facility, his depression became quite obvious to the treatment team. Further exploration led to the realization that he suffered from bipolar disorder. He was treated with lithium and other medications with good results for a number of years.

Bob had been working as a crane operator on the construction site of a new office building. The general manager of the company he was working for came by for an inspection. During his tour of the site, the general manager and Bob's direct supervisor passed underneath the area where Bob was moving heavy concrete slabs overhead. Bob had a slight tremor from the lithium, and this combined with his anxiety about "the big boss" being on site caused him to accidently hit a lever that released the slab he was moving. Fortunately, he missed both men by a few feet, but he was immediately terminated. He quickly scheduled an appointment with his psychiatrist during which he insisted he come off the lithium that had cost him his job and probably his career. After a couple of weeks off lithium, as the reality of his job loss hit him, he sank into a deep suicidal depression. He was admitted to his local hospital's inpatient psychiatric unit for treatment.

On the unit, he sank further into depression and became immobilized and catatonic. He was quickly referred for ECT. He tolerated the treatments well, and his mood brightened considerably. After the sixth treatment, as I passed him sitting in the hallway of the inpatient unit, he stopped me. He said, "I want to thank you for getting me back from wherever it is I was. I don't know where I was, but it was horrible." After four more treatments, he was in complete remission and decided to go back on his lithium, which again stabilized his mood.

What Is ECT, Exactly?

Electroconvulsive therapy (ECT) uses brief pulses of electricity to induce a controlled seizure in an unconscious patient who is under short-acting general anesthesia. The treatment can be either unilateral, meaning that the two electrodes used to deliver the stimulus are placed on one side of the head, or bilateral, where they are placed on both sides. Unilateral ECT is generally quite effective for depression and has fewer memory side effects than bilateral ECT. Ultra-brief unilateral refers to the width of the pulses that are applied during the treatment. The shorter pulse width (ultra-brief) is associated with fewer memory side effects. Bilateral ECT is used when unilateral ECT is ineffective or when the person has severe suicidality, mania, prominent psychotic symptoms, or catatonia. A typical acute course of treatment consists of six to ten treatments given over three to four weeks. Continuation and maintenance ECT are the same treatment given on a less frequent schedule, usually weekly to monthly. They are given after the person is feeling better to prevent relapse. **Currently, ECT is primarily used in treatment-resistant depression and other severe psychiatric disorders, such as catatonia**, that prevent people from functioning on even a basic level, shorten their lives by causing them to neglect their overall health, and increase their risk of death by suicide.[1]

This chapter is not going to try to "sell" you on ECT. Instead, it is intended to give you a practical overview to the history of ECT and show you what the treatment looks like today. As we discuss what state-of-the-art ECT is, we will also confront the stereotypes and myths that prevent people from getting the help they need from this highly effective and safe treatment. My goal is to arm you with the facts so that you can make your own decisions.

Isn't ECT Just Old-Fashioned Shock Therapy?

Yes and no; ECT as practiced today is the procedure that has evolved from shock therapy that started in the 1930s, but it has been modernized and is much improved.[2] Patients receive a brief anesthetic to make the procedure safe and comfortable, and the electrical stimulus delivered is much less intense than that used in the 1930s and '40s. Nonetheless, people commonly react with fear when their doctor recommends a course of ECT treatment.

Here's a good example of the visceral reaction that people have when the subject of ECT comes up: When one of my neighbors found out that I was director of the ECT service at McLean Hospital, he just shook his head and said, "I thought they stopped doing that to people." After I explained to him that the machines were much improved and the use of anesthesia made it a very safe, modern, and effective treatment, he still shook his head. When I asked him what about the treatment triggered that reaction, he said that he had this dark image of "shock therapy" from the movies and that he thought it "fried people's brains."

This was in sharp contrast to a conversation I had with a case manager that I worked with in the early 1990s. She and I were talking about sending one of our patients for ECT, and then ECT in general. She disclosed to me that her mother had ECT in the late 1950s when she was growing up. She said that because the anesthesia had been pretty primitive, her mother didn't like the treatment. But she did it because it was the only thing that kept her stable enough to function as a mother. She was grateful that ECT had allowed her family to stay together. She was also glad to hear that improvements in anesthesia had greatly improved the patient's experience and that changes in the machines and the stimulus they delivered had significantly reduced the memory loss and other side effects of the treatment.

What these two people illustrate are two very different reactions to ECT. Those who only know about ECT from what they have seen in movies and the media often have a highly negative opinion of ECT. Those who have had the treatment or seen its benefits in other people close to them have a much more favorable one.

How Did ECT Get Started?

ECT evolved from convulsive therapy for schizophrenia to electroconvulsive therapy that is used primarily for depression and other mood disorders. Although electricity had been proposed as a treatment for psychiatric illness in earlier times, the history of modern electroconvulsive therapy begins in the 1930s. The Hungarian neurologist Ladislas von Meduna was working with the brains of deceased patients at the Hungarian Psychiatric Research Institute in Budapest. He observed that the brains of people with schizophrenia had fewer of the structural support cells, known as glia, than did the brains of people without schizophrenia. Conversely, he noticed that people who had seizure disorders had an increased number of these support cells. He reasoned that he could correct this deficiency in the schizophrenic patients by inducing seizures in them, increasing their number of glial cells to a normal level and thereby "curing" them. Although this idea was incorrect, when he tried the treatment in the clinic, the patients improved significantly.[3]

The first convulsive therapy was performed on a thirty-three-year-old man who was suffering from catatonia and who had been psychotic, mute, and withdrawn for four years. He required feeding through a tube in the stomach. As Dr. Max Fink describes in his book *Electroconvulsive Therapy*, "On January 23, 1934, Meduna injected camphor-in-oil into an arm muscle, and 'after 45 minutes of anxious and fearful waiting the patient suddenly had a classical epileptic attack that lasted 60 seconds.' Meduna repeated the injections at three- to four-day intervals and '. . . two days after the fifth injection, on February 10 in the morning, for the first time in four years, he got out of his bed, began to talk, requested breakfast, dressed himself without help, was interested in everything around him, and asked about his disease and how long he had been in the hospital. When we told him he spent 4 years at the hospital, he did not believe it.'"[4]

Because of patient discomfort and variability in the time between administration of camphor and the seizure, camphor was replaced by Metrazol (cardiazol). Metrazol is a drug that had been shown to safely and more quickly induce seizures in animals. It worked well and became the standard drug for inducing convulsive therapy. However, Metrazol was a difficult drug to tolerate, and the search continued for a more tolerable way to reliably induce seizures. In 1938, the Italian psychiatrist and neurologist Ugo Cerletti and his assistant Dr. Lucio Bini replaced Metrazol with electricity to induce the seizure. "In 1938 a 39-year-old man, found wandering the streets of Rome, was admitted to the institute. He spoke in neologisms of being telepathically influenced, he was passive in his behavior, and his affect was flat. A year earlier in Milan he had received eight Cardiazol treatments with apparent success. He received an electrically induced seizure and immediately thereafter spoke coherently. After 11 applications he recovered and remained well at the time of his discharge in June 1938. At follow-up 1 year later, he was working at his former job."[5]

How Has ECT Changed over Time?

Convulsive therapy, administered using either chemically or electrically induced seizures, was an enormous leap forward in the treatment of severe psychotic illnesses. Since it was first developed in the 1930s, the actual procedure has changed significantly. Back then, there was no anesthesia to reduce the person's anxiety or physical manifestations of the seizure, and the devices delivered an unrefined electrical stimulus. Electricity travels in waves and the stimulus delivered by the early ECT machines used the entire wave to induce the seizure. The machines used today deliver the electrical charge in short pulses that use only part of the wave. The result is a more efficient, targeted stimulus that exerts a therapeutic effect with a lower amount of overall electrical charge being delivered to the brain. An important benefit of this approach is a significant reduction in the memory loss with ECT without losing the therapeutic benefits.

Another advancement in ECT that has reduced the cognitive side effects is the dosing of the electricity based on the seizure threshold. A person's seizure threshold is the minimum amount of electricity needed to induce a generalized brain seizure. Studies have shown that the antidepressant response depends on the dose of electricity being significantly above seizure threshold.[6] This is especially true for unilateral ECT.

As we discussed previously, today, ECT is used primarily to treat mood disorders, usually depression, but also mania and catatonia. As you can imagine, when a new treatment that has very powerful therapeutic effects is developed, especially when few other effective treatments are available, researchers test it to see if it works for different illnesses. In the case of ECT these included schizophrenia, severe depression, bipolar disorder (both the manic and depressive phases of the illness), and Parkinson's disease. ECT has been shown to have efficacy in each of these conditions, which is not surprising given the number of brain circuits whose activity is modified during a course of ECT.[7]

Fortunately, the rest of psychiatry has not stood still either. New medications and other types of treatment are continually being developed. Accordingly, the role of ECT in psychiatric treatment needs to be continuously reassessed.

How Has the Use of ECT Changed?

Unless the person's illness is life-threatening, like malignant catatonia, most people agree that ECT should be considered only after first-line treatment has been tried. Consider what has happened to the treatment of schizophrenia over time. As described, convulsive therapy was initially conceived as a treatment for schizophrenia. In the two years that followed his initial report on his use of ECT, Dr. von Meduna performed convulsive therapy in 110 patients with schizophrenia and achieved significant improvement in 53 of them.[8] So clearly, ECT is effective in treating this illness, yet it is used infrequently to treat schizophrenia today. What happened? Fortunately, as frequently happens in modern evidence-based medicine, something better came along.

In the 1950s the antipsychotic Thorazine was developed and several other antipsychotic medications followed. These drugs are generally effective in controlling what are called the positive symptoms of schizophrenia—that is, the hallucinations and delusions. In head-to-head comparisons, the medications worked as well as ECT for short-term treatment and better in patients who needed chronic treatment. These studies did point to a role for ECT in boosting the effects of the medications in treatment-resistant cases, which is how ECT is mostly used in schizophrenic patients today.[9]

The other major shift that occurred in the use of ECT was a shift away from seeing it as a treatment for schizophrenia toward seeing it as a way to address treatment-resistant depression. In the 1960s and 1970s, ECT developed a negative public image due to its association with another treatment known as insulin "shock therapy," as well as negative portrayals in movies and the media. This combined with the development of better medications for treating psychiatric illnesses led to a significant reduction in the use of ECT in the United States during the 1960s and 1970s.[10]

In the 1980s, the use of ECT to treat severe psychiatric illnesses began to rebound. There was a shift away from the use of ECT for patients with psychotic illnesses, who were typically men living in public institutions, to use in patients with depression and other mood disorders (often middle- and upper-class older women, who are more often treated in private community hospitals). This shift to treating primarily mood disorders with ECT reflected an increasing awareness of the brain chemistry basis of depression and other mood disorders as well as improvements in ECT technique.[11] This shift continued as people realized that antidepressant medications were often ineffective or only partially effective in treating depressive symptoms. With the introduction of ketamine and the continued refinement of rTMS, the use of ECT will likely continue to evolve.

However, the important questions that you need answered are: When should it be used or, more importantly, not used? Is there a best practice for electroconvulsive therapy? What are the risks if you have ECT?

When Is ECT Used Today?

The decision to prescribe a course of ECT rests on two questions. First, does the person have an illness that is likely to respond to this type of treatment? If yes, then does the person's clinical situation indicate that ECT should be used? The primary use for ECT today is in the treatment of mood disorders. Most often this is for **depression**. Conversely, **mania**, which can be thought of as the opposite of depression and, as you learned, is characterized by an elevated, euphoric, or irritable mood usually accompanied by behavioral changes, such as excessive risk taking, increased energy, and a decreased need for sleep, is also responsive to ECT.

As discussed earlier, **psychotic illnesses** were the first illnesses treated with ECT, and it remains a useful tool in their treatment when the person cannot tolerate or does not fully respond to medications. **Catatonia**, which can range in presentation from a frozen posturing to an agitated state with frequent repetitive movements and mannerisms, is also usually responsive to ECT. This includes a very severe variant known as lethal catatonia as well as the similar-appearing **neuroleptic malignant syndrome**, which can occur after treatment with antipsychotic medications. The incidence of catatonia, especially autoimmune-induced catatonia, has been increasing. We will go into this in greater detail later in our discussion of special populations because this illness often affects adolescent patients. **Parkinson's disease**, which results from the loss of dopamine-producing neurons in the brain, has a high incidence of difficult-to-treat depression, and in the late stages of the illness periods of getting frozen. In these cases, ECT can be helpful with both the mood and the move-ment difficulties.[12]

In most cases, the patient's diagnosis is relatively clear. The next question to ask is whether the symptom severity, especially suicidality, or lack of reasonable treatment alternatives makes a trial of ECT the logical choice for the next treatment. One of the main reasons for pro-ceeding to treatment with ECT is that the patient has **not responded to the usual psychotherapies and medications** used to treat the condition.

As the number of psychotherapies and FDA-approved antide-pressant medications expand, the definition of treatment resistance changes. In the early 1980s, treatment-resistant depression usually meant the person had failed a trial of two different tricyclic antidepres-sants. A good example of this would be failing trials of nortriptyline (Pamelor) and imipramine (Tofranil); nortriptyline acts on the norepi-nephrine system, while imipramine acted on both the norepinephrine and serotonin systems. This is an oversimplification, since the tricyclic antidepressants act on other neurotransmitter systems as well. But the main idea remains: you don't try several drugs that do essentially the same thing when other options are available.[13]

In the past, another important consideration for determining that a patient was treatment resistant was the duration and adequacy of the dose of the medications. Adequate dosing of these medications was not a small problem. Common side effects include dry mouth, dry skin, and constipation. Further complicating the issue was that except for nortrip-tyline, the blood level needed for an antidepressant effect from each of these medications had not been defined (and still hasn't been). So get-ting depressed people to take a large enough dose for the two to sixteen weeks it takes to feel better from these medications was challenging.

Things got much better for patients and more complicated for their clinicians with the approval of fluoxetine, or Prozac, in the late 1980s.

Fluoxetine had comparable antidepressant effects to tricyclic antide-pressants and caused significantly fewer side effects in head-to-head comparisons.[14] Fluoxetine was wildly successful, with sales reaching $350 million within a year of its introduction and ultimately reaching $2.6 billion per year.[15] The majority of antidepressants that followed fluoxetine, until the approval of esketamine, largely work through a similar mechanism of action as fluoxetine but have different (some-times better) side-effect profiles.[16]

In recognition of the similarities and differences of the antidepres-sant medications, a staging system for treatment-resistant depression was proposed much like the staging systems for various types of can-cers. An example of one such system proposed by Drs. Michael Thase and John Rush is summarized in Table 8.1.[17]

Whether consciously or unconsciously, most clinicians base their decision to recommend ECT on a similar paradigm. With the excep-tion of psychotic depression and severe suicide risk, most clinicians do not use ECT as a first-line treatment. Instead, they will try an antide-pressant medication with psychotherapy, and if that is not successful, they will either augment or replace the antidepressant with a second medication. It is then that ECT often enters the decision tree, for sev-eral reasons. First, most patients get very discouraged after a second failed medication and may not be willing to try a third. The sense

Table 8.1: Stages of Treatment-Resistant Depression

Stage of Resistance	Treatment Failed
I	One antidepressant
II	Two different classes of antidepressants
III	Stage II plus failed a tricyclic antidepressant
IV	Stage III plus failed a monoamine oxidase inhibitor (MAOI)
V	Bilateral ECT

of despair that builds with these medication failures can increase the risk of acting on suicidal thoughts that are often present in depressive illness. Hopelessness has been shown to be one of the things that moves people from suicidal ideation to suicidal acts.[18] Perhaps the most important consideration in deciding when to use ECT is the effect of depression on the brain. Depression causes people to not pay attention to nutrition and to stop exercising as well as decreases their social connectedness, none of which is good for the brain. There is also evidence that depression may increase risk for dementia.[19] Recognition of these risks from inadequately treated depression has led many clinicians to advocate for moving to ECT sooner rather than after exhaustive and heroic medication trials.

Medication intolerance is the second reason why people are referred for ECT. Some people are terrified of taking "psychiatric drugs" and are psychologically intolerant to the medication.[20] Others try the medications but develop side effects that make it difficult or impossible to keep taking them. One highly motivated patient I treated responded to the fifth antidepressant we tried. Unfortunately, she had to stop the medication when it caused severe constipation and almost stopped her bowels from working altogether. She required hospitalization to get her digestive tract back in order and almost required surgery. After that experience, she chose to undergo ECT and experienced a dramatic improvement in her depression. She continues on maintenance ECT as of this writing. This patient is a good example of how sensitive the brain and the body can be to the effects of medication.

If you are having a hard time tolerating your antidepressants, keep in mind that different people with depression can have very different reactions to the same drug. People can have difficulty tolerating a medication because of how their brain reacts to it. Let me illustrate this further using fluoxetine, or Prozac, as an example. Some people find fluoxetine to be a wonderful antidepressant. Their mood goes from

ECT: *Do They Still Do That?*   123

constant sadness to feeling good. Their anxiety drops significantly, and they feel at peace as they go about their day. In his somewhat controversial book *Listening to Prozac*, Dr. Peter Kramer describes similar responses in several of his patients and argues that Prozac has the ability to change the human character.[21] My take on it is that he is describing how life changing it can be when we successfully treat depression and anxiety and allow the real person to come out. Now contrast this with the person who is also suffering from depression and anxiety but who takes one dose of fluoxetine and feels restless and agitated or, worse, suicidal. Then there is the person whose depression improves but they find themselves unable to do anything because the drug seems to have made them apathetic and disinterested. As one research subject once explained to me, "I used to be sad and worry all the time; now I don't . . . but I have to get off this drug because I'm too laid-back, my bills aren't getting paid, my dishes aren't getting done, and I'm doing poorly in a course I'm taking." In the examples here, fluoxetine is eliciting three different types of responses in people suffering with depression. This mostly reflects underlying differences in the mood circuitry in their brains.

The range of responses seen may also reflect differences in how they absorb or metabolize the drug. Another common reason why you may be having difficulty tolerating medications is that they have built up to high levels in your blood and brain. This is a result of your metabolism processing medications more slowly than the typical person. Psychiatrists are fond of mixing multiple medications when the first drug doesn't quite get the patient better. It is called "rational polypharmacy." These combinations lead to some people having one of the medications build up to much higher levels than usual.

Because of the risk of medication buildup and the proliferation of antidepressant medications in the 1990s, researchers did a detailed exploration of the enzymes in the liver and their effects on drug clearance from the body. We now recognize that there are six different enzymes that metabolize most of the psychiatric medications in use today. For any one of these, a person can be a poor metabolizer, an extensive metabolizer, or an ultra-rapid metabolizer.[22] The person who is a poor metabolizer will have a higher concentration of the medication in their blood than a person who is an extensive or ultra-rapid metabolizer. The higher the concentration, the greater the side effects and the less likely a person is to tolerate the drug. Fortunately, as you learned earlier, **genetic testing can be performed to guide drug choice and avoid this problem**, but it has not yet reached the point where it can inform us about the likely response of brain circuits.

Two other reasons for proceeding to ECT when the patient is depressed are **past response** and **patient preference**. People who have been through several medication trials and suffered through extended bouts of depression are often anxious to get back to ECT. They are acutely aware of how much depression steals from them and how quickly ECT gets them out of it. One patient who I treated years ago could not get off the couch on the inpatient psychiatric unit where he was being treated. After a month of extensive medication trials and difficult side effects without benefit, he was referred to ECT. He had a dramatic response and was back to his old self after eight unilateral ultra-brief treatments. After a few months, when his mood began to slip, despite the fact that he was religious about taking his medications, he quickly came back in for some additional treatments and then proceeded with maintenance ECT treatment. Another patient had an episode of depression shortly before retiring. After several unsuccessful medication trials, he had a good response to ECT. He completed the course of treatment and went back to work before retiring a couple of years later. About a year into a very enjoyable retirement, he became depressed again. This time he insisted on going back to ECT and then started on a course of maintenance ECT. A few years later, he spoke about his experience at a patient and family conference. He credited ECT with saving his retirement. He spoke quite eloquently about how when he was depressed the world was black and he was barely able to take care of himself. With maintenance ECT, he had been able to travel, maintain an active garden, read extensively, and enjoy his relationships with his wife, children, and grandchildren.

In a similar but different vein, some people have seen the effectiveness of ECT firsthand in one of their relatives. Since depression has a significant genetic component, if a relative gets depressed they often recognize, for example, that they have the same illness as did their aunt who benefited from ECT. When they get depressed, they are often advocates for starting ECT sooner than usual. In one extreme case of this, I was consulted by a patient who refused medications and wanted to proceed straight to ECT. When I asked why she wanted ECT before trying medications, she explained that her aunt had severe depression. Her aunt had suffered for quite a while and had tried multiple medications without benefit. Finally, after her aunt had attempted suicide, her psychiatrist recommended ECT. After treatment, she was a completely different, happy person. My patient felt that since her illness was very similar to her aunt's, she did not want to wait to feel better. She also didn't want to go through all the side effects from medication that her aunt had gone through.

ECT and Special Populations

In addition to these mainstream uses of ECT, there are some special populations that should be included in this discussion.

Pregnant Women

Society and the media tend to portray pregnancy as a time when women are generally very happy. While this seems to be true for most women, there are some, especially those with preexisting mood disorders, who find that the changes and fluctuations in hormone levels that occur during and immediately after pregnancy cause them to have significant mood symptoms.

It has been estimated that 10 to 16 percent of women suffer from depression during their pregnancy.[23] Antidepressant use in pregnancy has been associated with small but increased risks of miscarriage, congenital heart malformations, preterm birth, and breathing difficulties in the infant. Conversely, depression during pregnancy can make it difficult to get proper nutrition, take routine medications like prenatal vitamins, get regular exercise, and maintain social supports, all of which can have a profound impact on the baby's health. In addition, suicidal ideation appears to be increased in pregnant women with depression.[24] Therefore, although there are no risk-free options for pregnant women with depression and other psychiatric illnesses, there is a clear need for treatment.

Postpregnancy, the most serious condition is a postpartum depression with psychotic features. This very tormented state can cause delusions that lead to the death of the infant unless the infant is protected and the mother treated.

ECT has several advantages in pregnant women: it is relatively quick acting, the exposure to the anesthetic agents is brief, and it has been shown to be safe in all three trimesters of pregnancy, when done with appropriate monitoring.[25]

When mood symptoms emerge during the pregnancy, they can generally be safely treated with ECT. The baby has a very brief exposure to the sedative medication, but the muscle relaxant does not cross the placenta to get to the baby. However, there are a few considerations that should be kept in mind.[26] As the baby grows, it pushes down on the woman's intestinal tract. This increases the risk that fluids from the stomach can be regurgitated and get into the lungs. After the baby reaches twenty-nine weeks gestational age, the anesthesia team may want to take additional steps to prevent this from happening. In our practice, we also have the obstetrical service check the baby's heart rate before and after each treatment. When prescribed by the obstetrician, ultrasounds of the baby are performed—at a minimum before the start of treatment and after the last acute treatment.

Postpartum depression is also very responsive to ECT, although there is a medication, allopregnanolone, that has been approved by the FDA for this indication. For patients who do not have access to this treatment or for whom it is not successful, ECT remains a highly effective option.

Children and Adolescents

Generally, when children and adolescents are referred for ECT, they are quite ill. Mood disorders that are severe and start before adulthood are usually bipolar disorder or a mix of psychosis and mood symptoms, known as schizoaffective disorder. Psychotic illnesses that start before adulthood are also often severe. Antipsychotic medications usually provide some relief but may not induce a full remission. These patients get referred for ECT when they are acutely suicidal or at risk for assaultive behavior. Psychotic illnesses are chronic in nature, but ECT is usually effective in reducing the acute symptoms and reducing the suicidality.[27] There are some small studies that suggest that ECT given at the start of the illness can reduce its severity over the course of the person's lifetime.[28]

Catatonia

Catatonia is a psychiatric illness that afflicts adults but also children and adolescents. While traditionally it has been thought of as a subtype of schizophrenia or a severe mood disorder, there appears to be an increasing incidence of autoimmune catatonia. In the most common variant of this illness, the immune system generates antibodies to the brain's N-methyl-D-aspartate (NMDA) receptor. This is the same receptor where ketamine is thought to act.[29]

Clinically, catatonia is characterized by a severely shut-down mental state and abnormal movements, either being frozen physically or frenetically moving about without an obvious purpose. In the most severe form of catatonia, malignant catatonia, the person's muscles can start to break down, leading to other vital organs shutting down—which, if not reversed, can lead to death. Catatonia can be caused by schizophrenia, severe mood disorders, and medical illnesses. When it is caused by a medical illness, the symptoms are usually the downstream effect of autoimmune antibodies disabling key receptors in the brain. Should someone you love be afflicted with catatonia, it is important to ensure that the medical evaluation looks for these potential medical causes of catatonia.

The first line of treatment for catatonia today is usually high doses of the benzodiazepine medication lorazepam. A single dose of this medication can be quite impressive: the symptoms melt and the person reemerges. One patient I treated years ago was standing frozen in her hospital room, not communicating. The nurse called me to evaluate her, and from across the room, it was obvious she was in a catatonic state. We gave her a dose of lorazepam, and within a half hour she was relaxed, spoke with us about how she was feeling, and accepted some food and fluids. She was put on a standing regimen of lorazepam and eventually was able to be discharged from the hospital. ECT is useful in catatonia when the lorazepam does not work.

In those individuals whose catatonia is caused by an autoimmune disease, the neurology team should be involved. They have medications that can suppress the immune system and turn off the attack. In cases of autoimmune catatonia, treatment teams may use ECT to reduce the amount of time the person spends immobilized by the illness. This can reduce the intensity of the medical care the person requires and reduce the amount of rehabilitation that needs to be done by the person once they are better.

How Is ECT Done?

We will discuss this in greater detail in the next chapter, but here are the basics. Most ECT treatments today are performed in a hospital and involve five parts to each ECT treatment: the check-in, the anesthesia, the treatment, the recovery, and the discharge. Check-in, recovery, and discharge are usually handled by nursing staff. In most places I've worked doing ECT, these nurses volunteer to be assigned to the treatment and are very invested in the patients doing well. The anesthesia used is very brief and administered by a trained anesthetist. While the person is asleep, the ECT practitioner administers the treatment, which usually takes only one to four minutes. The treatment involves an ECT machine, which is likely to be from one of two main manufacturers. They are very similar in how they deliver the treatment and over time have shown themselves to be very reliable. Once the treatment is over, the anesthetist makes sure the person is medically stable and then the nurses take over the recovery.

Obviously, I have greatly simplified things, but what you should take away is that when you have ECT you will be treated by a team of professionals working together to help you get better safely.

What Are the Risks?
Doesn't ECT Fry Your Brain?

The most common side effects of ECT are the memory problems that it causes. This is mostly limited to the period around the treatments, but it can also affect past memories. To elaborate further, people's ability to remember new things starts to rebound a couple of weeks after they stop treatment, or if they are doing maintenance treatment, after the treatments are usually spaced out beyond two weeks. ECT's effect on past memories is variable. Some people report losing important memories while others do not report significant memory problems. For most people the relief from the pain of the depression and the ability to make new memories makes the ECT beneficial. For those individuals who do forget significant events from their past, I recommend looking at photo albums and visiting places where the memories were made. I had one patient who had forgotten a significant event from his past. About two months after stopping ECT, he went back to the place where the event happened and was looking through a photo album when his memory of the event was restored, including the small details.

The available scientific evidence indicates that it is caused by an increase in the size of the memory circuit and the remodeling that goes along with it. There is no evidence that ECT causes brain damage, yet this is one of the most persistent and scary pieces of misinformation about ECT. The possibility was first raised in the early years of ECT when it was still being refined. Specifically, the electrical stimulus used the entire electrical wave, the dose of electricity was not titrated to the person's specific needs, and there was no anesthesia to minimize the risks to the patient. This led to significantly more severe memory difficulties than described previously, and a subset of mental health professionals argued that the memory side effects reflected underlying brain damage. To this day there are still groups that make this claim.[30] They point to articles published in the 1940s that looked at the brains of people who had died from other medical illnesses.[31] The authors attributed changes they saw in these brains to ECT rather than the illnesses that caused the person's death.

More recent reports of ECT using modern, sophisticated techniques to examine the brain are available. At least two notable cases have been reported. The first was that of a man who suffered from chronic mood and psychotic symptoms for most of his adult life and received 422 ECT treatments. He died approximately one month after his last treatment. Despite this unusually large number of treatments, the autopsy showed there was no evidence of brain damage.[32] Similarly, Jason Scalia and colleagues reported on the case of a ninety-two-year-old woman with late-onset depression who received ninety-one ECT treatments during the last twenty-two years of her life.[33] Her autopsy revealed only age-related changes; there was no evidence of gross or microscopic damage from the ECT. The authors noted that she had achieved a perfect score on a cognitive test, the Mini-Mental Status Examination, six days before her death. The reason this case is notable is because the treatments began when she was about seventy years old, a stage of life when people are physically less resilient.

Another way to look at this question is with animal studies. Since ECT successfully treats mood disorders when other treatments have not been effective, animal models have been used to try to understand how ECT works. The brains of animals are not as sophisticated as the human brain, but the properties of the cells and the basic structure are the same. Unlike the human brains that have been studied after the person died, in research studies the animals were sacrificed under conditions that preserve the brain tissue. These studies then examined the brain with high-resolution microscopes and other chemical techniques. These modern highly sensitive approaches have not found any signs that the treatment causes damage to the animal brains.[34] These results were further supported by a review published in 2020 by Drs. An and Shi. They reviewed forty-five articles that studied the effects of ECS (animal ECT). They concluded that there were "no damaging effects of ECS on the brain."[35]

This question has also been studied by high-resolution structural brain imaging scans in patients receiving ECT. Instead of finding damage, the scans have shown that certain brain regions get bigger, especially the hippocampus, an area of the brain that is important in the memory circuit. Ironically, the growth seen in the hippocampus may cause the majority of the memory difficulties that can occur during a course of ECT.

This unexpected finding has been reported in several studies. The largest is from a group of ECT researchers known as the Global ECT-Magnetic Resonance Imaging Research Collaboration. They studied the effects of ECT on the volume of the hippocampus using structural magnetic resonance imaging in 281 patients.[36] Their results showed an increase in hippocampal volume in subjects receiving unilateral or bilateral ECT, while the 95 control subjects who did not receive ECT did not show changes between the two scans. This result is consistent with that of a review of the published imaging studies of ECT's effects on the brain's structure by Drs. Gbyl and Videbech.[37] They reviewed thirty-two studies with 467 patients and 285 controls. They drew the following conclusions: **None of the studies they reviewed reported evidence of brain damage. Instead, they found that hippocampal volume as well as other cortical and subcortical regions showed increases in volume.** These same authors also reviewed five MRI studies that used a technique known as diffusion tensor magnetic resonance imaging. This technique looks at the integrity of the fiber tracts that connect different brain regions. These studies had a total of ninety-two ECT patients and sixty-two controls. The changes they found indicated increased, not decreased, organization of the fibers that connect the frontal and temporal lobes after ECT. The authors noted that the increases in brain volume tended to occur in regions of the brain thought to malfunction during an episode of depression.[38]

Lastly, from a functional perspective, our group recently published a study on one hundred patients who had received at least fifty ECT treatments, thirty-six of whom received one hundred ECT treatments as part of an acute course of ECT that transformed into maintenance treatment. Cognitive function as measured by the Montreal Cognitive Assessment essentially did not change in either group.[39]

This chapter was designed to give you a balanced introduction to ECT. It was also designed to answer questions that you might have about the treatment based on the questions my patients have asked me over the years. Two things bear repeating: ECT is a safe and modern treatment that has little in common with how it is portrayed in the movies, and ECT does not cause brain damage. The memory circuits do change during treatment, but they change through the same processes that make it hard for you to remember what you had for a snack on this date ten years ago. You knew it at one point, but the memory faded.

ECT has helped a number of very ill people over the years. If in reading this chapter you are seeing yourself as a potential candidate for this treatment, I hope you will talk to your clinician about it.

Key Takeaways

- ▶ Convulsive therapy, which originally involved inducing seizures using medication, has evolved into the modern practice of ECT.
- ▶ As practiced today, ECT is primarily used for treatment-resistant depression and other severe psychiatric disorders.
- ▶ Modern ECT uses personalized dosing regimens and brief anesthesia to maximize effectiveness while minimizing side effects and patient discomfort.
- ▶ While the memory side effects of ECT remain the most difficult for some people to handle, rigorous scientific investigation suggests that it is likely they reflect the **remodeling of the memory circuit during treatment, not damage**.

Chapter 9

How Do I Get ECT?

If you are asking how to get ECT treatment, it means that you are struggling with a difficult illness. As you know better than anyone else, depression also causes you to see everything in a negative light, and you may believe that nothing will work to make it go away. But asking this question means that you want to address it, which is hard to do when you are in the throes of a severe illness. As you have seen, there *are* powerful treatments that work when the front-line treatments have failed. I hope I have dispelled the myths around the treatments discussed in this book, specifically ECT, as these get in the way of people experiencing not just relief but a real elimination of the suffering.

Most people who come in for an ECT consultation have been suffering for quite a while and have tried many different medications, psychotherapy, and other treatments. Some have been completely immobilized by their depression, while others are exhausted from the struggle to keep their lives together in the face of an unrelenting depression. Despite the severity and often long-standing nature of their illness, very few people who come in to see me have asked their mental health provider to refer them for ECT. In fact, some people flat-out refuse the recommendation and continue to struggle with their depression. When asked, the primary reason they give is their fear of ECT. They have heard it "fries your brain." They have genuine concerns about losing their memory and not being able to recognize themselves or their family. If you will permit me a little humor, in all the years I've been treating people with ECT, no one has ever forgotten their relatives, even the ones they wanted to forget! Understandably, people often refer to movies, such as *One Flew Over the Cuckoo's Nest*, where the misuse of ECT was portrayed as having devastating effects on the people receiving it.

Like so many others, Angela feared ECT because of false impressions about it. She was a forty-eight-year-old married mother of three children who also held down a high-powered position in the financial services industry when the wheels came off her life. Her husband of fourteen years abruptly announced he was leaving her to move back to his native Italy. She was quite upset but determined to not let this turn of events disrupt her children's lives. She got through the summer and thought she had things figured out. That fall her usually mild seasonal depression seemed a little darker. By Thanksgiving, she was really struggling and wasn't keeping up on all she had to do. Things were bad enough that she went to her primary care doctor for a checkup. The doctor ordered labs, which showed she was perimenopausal but had no other medical issues that would explain what she was experiencing. Her doctor started her on escitalopram (Lexapro) and gave her a referral to a psychiatrist.

Angela went to the psychiatrist but noted that instead of feeling better, the escitalopram had made her "edgy." She was snapping at people at work and finding it hard to focus enough to do her work. Her sleep was terrible. Her boss called her into his office to tell her how concerned he was and suggested she take some time off to "regroup." Over the next six months Angela and her psychiatrist made several medication changes. They tried adding aripiprazole (Abilify) to the escitalopram, which only seemed to make things worse. Then she came off the escitalopram and aripiprazole and added quetiapine (Seroquel). Even at 300 mg/day, she was still depressed, and to make matters worse, now she was groggy all day and started to eat everything in sight. When she gained ten pounds in two weeks, she demanded to be switched to another medication. She refused lithium because she didn't want any more weight gain. The psychiatrist prescribed lamotrigine (Lamictal), and Angela's dose was steadily increased up to 200 mg/day. She was a little less agitated but still felt quite depressed. In frustration, she asked her psychiatrist if there was anything else she could try. She rejected his medication suggestions because of the weight issue. TMS was not suitable because he thought she likely had type II bipolar disorder, and besides, her insurance wouldn't cover it. Finally, he recommended a trial of ECT.

When Angela came into my office for the initial ECT consultation, she was quiet and obviously depressed. As we went through her history, she was surprised at the number of mood episodes, both hypomanic and depressed, she had gone through during her adult life. After we discussed how she was likely to respond to ECT and how the treatment would be tailored to her, she asked one final question: Am I really sick enough that I need ECT?

Is My Depression Bad Enough to Make Me a Good Candidate for ECT?

People often ask this question when their psychiatrist or other members of their treatment team raise the question of ECT. There are a couple of important concepts that I want to make sure you are aware of as you consider your health, both physical and mental. First, depression is not good for your brain or your overall health. Depression and anxiety have been shown to speed up the aging process. Secondly, **if you have not responded to two antidepressants, your chances of responding to a third are about 20 percent.**[1] Lastly, depression is associated with a loss of friends and social supports. In middle-aged and older adults, this loss of connectedness can be devastating.[2] This realization, that untreated and treatment-resistant depression can have profound and lasting negative effects on the person and the people around them, is why physicians and mental health professionals recommend ECT, as well as some of the other treatments discussed in this book, sooner rather than later in a course of depression.

Therefore, I usually answer the question of whether someone is "sick enough" for ECT with a question: **If your depression does not get better for another year, can you afford the impact it is having on your health and well-being for that long?** For most people with significant depressive symptoms, the answer is no. ECT has helped many people who have also answered no to that question.

How Do I Begin?

Once you have decided you are open to learning more about ECT as a potential treatment, the next step is to schedule an initial consultation. As with ketamine and TMS, your mental health provider or primary care physician will likely have a clinic or hospital that they usually refer to. If not, the local chapter of the Depression and Bipolar Support Alliance or the National Alliance on Mental Illness may be able to provide you with a list of local treatment centers.

The primary goal of the initial consultation is for you to learn more about the clinicians and the treatment offered by that service and for them to get to know you. From the ECT consultant's perspective, there are at least four goals for the initial consultation: (1) gather current and past history to decide if ECT is likely to be helpful; (2) address your concerns about the potential risks and benefits of the treatment;

(3) determine the need for pretreatment testing to minimize risks; and (4) convey the information needed to obtain informed consent and proceed with treatment. Please keep in mind that the interview may not proceed in this order but may go back and forth as needed to collect the information and address your concerns.

If you find these types of consultations stressful, and most people do, I recommend bringing someone you trust with you to take notes and make sure you get your questions answered. Also, writing down your treatment history before the appointment may ensure that you don't forget to convey important details about what you have tried in the past (see Appendix B for some prompts).

Will My Insurance Cover ECT?

Your insurance company will likely need to agree to pay for the treatment before it starts. This is known as prior authorization. Depending on your insurance, that may leave you with a copayment that you are responsible for. Insurance companies usually agree to pay for ECT. Studies have consistently shown that ECT is a cost-effective treatment option for treatment-resistant depression.[3] A recent study found that starting ECT at the beginning of a hospital stay led to both a shorter stay in the hospital for the patient and a lower overall cost.

Is ECT Likely to Help Me?

The answer depends on a couple of factors. Do you have a single disorder that usually responds to ECT, or are there other illnesses that make treatment complicated? For example, when treating a person who has been referred for ECT because of a first episode of depression in which they experience suicidality, a good response to ECT is very likely. In comparison, a person who has chronic depression complicated by a history of childhood trauma and chronic excessive alcohol use and who has failed extensive medication trials is still likely to respond to ECT, but in these types of cases, the average response rate is going to be lower.[4] When I start a consult, the first question I ask myself is, Does this person have an illness likely to respond to ECT?

In the United States, **ECT is most commonly used to treat mood disorders, usually depression**.[5] The term *mood disorder* includes both unipolar and bipolar disorders.

ECT can also be used to treat the opposite of depression, **bipolar mania**. Again, before proceeding with ECT, it is important to determine whether the person's primary condition is a different psychiatric illness, medical illness, or substance-use disorder that is causing the symptoms.

As mentioned in the previous chapter, **catatonia** is another set of illnesses that respond well to ECT. Catatonia is a severe condition that can be caused by bipolar disorder, schizophrenia, or autoimmune and other medical illnesses. The first line of therapy is usually medications and targeted medical treatments, but in the cases where those do not help or the person's general health starts to deteriorate, ECT is often quite effective.

As we discussed previously, although ECT is generally not used to treat schizophrenia and other psychotic illnesses, there are certain situations where it is indicated. **Psychosis** that is not responding to medications, especially when there are hallucinations telling the person to harm themselves or others, usually can be effectively treated with ECT. Depression with concurrent psychotic symptoms usually responds poorly to medications but exquisitely to ECT. It has been argued that ECT should be the first-line treatment of choice for this illness.

There are other more specialized uses of ECT, but they are outside of the scope of this discussion and will not be included here. Your health care provider will work with you to assess the source of your depression to rule out other causes and to see if ECT is right for you.

As part of the initial consultation, health care professionals must make sure the person is not suffering from a medical illness that can masquerade as depression. One example is anemia. Anemia is a group of illnesses that are characterized by low red blood cell counts, which can cause severe fatigue and inertia similar to depression. Another common example is thyroid disease. Hypothyroidism, or an underactive thyroid gland, can also cause fatigue, excessive sleeping, and difficulty with motivation similar to that seen in depression. In contrast, hyperthyroidism, or an overactive thyroid gland, can cause restlessness, insomnia, increased energy, and activation that mimics the symptoms of mania. Different ECT centers approach medical workups differently. Some order labs themselves to rule out other causes of depression symptoms, while others have the person "medically cleared" by their primary care provider.

Psychiatric illnesses can also mimic mood disorders at times. Personality disorders (such as narcissistic personality disorder and borderline personality disorder), for example, are characterized by an inflexible approach to dealing with the world regardless of the situation. As you can imagine, these individuals often have a lot of difficulty with interpersonal relationships, housing, and employment. This leads to real-life losses, and the grieving can often be confused with an episode of major depression.[6]

Excessive use of alcohol and other substances can also cause symptoms of depression directly or through the toll they take on relationships and careers. The challenge is to sort out who is self-medicating a mood or anxiety disorder from those whose primary problem is the substance use or abuse. Both types of people are suffering and need help; the question is what type of help.

What About More Meds and Therapy?
Or Should I Do ECT Now?

Once it is clear that you have a condition that is likely to respond to ECT, the next question is whether ECT is indicated at this time.

Generally, people who proceed to ECT fall into one or more of five categories: they are treatment resistant to medications and psychotherapy, they are unable to tolerate those treatments, they need to get better urgently, they have responded to ECT in the past, or they prefer ECT over medication.

Treatment-Resistant Depression

This is a frequently given indication for ECT. As we discussed in the previous chapter, treatment-resistant depression is hard to define. This is due to the ever-increasing number of antidepressant medications and psychotherapies available and the definition of an adequate trial of a treatment. However, there are some concepts to keep in mind.

Augmenting Medications. First, when a medication is ineffective, the next medication you and your team try should work through a different mechanism or at least target an additional receptor that has not been targeted before. A trial of citalopram followed by a trial of escitalopram, thought to be the active ingredient in citalopram, is not likely to provide much information about the person's illness if it doesn't work. In contrast, a trial of citalopram, a serotonergic drug, followed by trial of duloxetine, a serotonergic and noradrenergic drug, tells you the person's illness requires treatments that work through other neurotransmitter systems. This is where augmentation strategies, such as adding lithium or thyroid hormone and neuro-modulation treatments such as ECT or rTMS, come into the treatment plan. Ketamine, which modulates the glutamate system, is another option when trying to find a treatment with a different mechanism of action.[7]

Dose Matters. Another important concept is that dose matters. For a medication to work, it has to get to the brain in a sufficient amount to cause enough change for you to feel better. This is where the genetic differences in drug metabolism can be quite important. People who break down a drug very quickly, known as extensive metabolizers, may require larger than usual doses of a medication for it to work. Genomic testing is a significant advancement because it sheds light on whether an individual metabolizes medications faster or more slowly than average.[8] The tests are not yet capable of identifying the medication that should be chosen on the basis of the mechanism of action. Also, remember that with the possible exception of ketamine and stimulants, antidepressant medications don't work immediately; they require at least two and sometimes up to sixteen weeks to see an antidepressant response. It is important that an adequate amount of the medication gets to the mood circuitry for a long enough time to change the person's mood.[9]

Inability to Tolerate Medications

A less common, but not insignificant, reason why some people get ECT is because they find it **difficult to tolerate antidepressant medications**. Some people have very strong psychological, cognitive, or physical side effects of the medications at very low doses. This is where genomic testing can be helpful. Just as some individuals rapidly metabolize medications and the amount reaching the brain can be insufficient, there are some individuals who break down medications much more slowly than average. The amount of the medication in their blood and brain reaches much higher levels than normal, and they will have significant side effects. Alternatively, these individuals may have brain circuits that react strongly to even small amounts of medication. When these individuals are identified, the dose can be reduced, and they may be able to tolerate a therapeutic trial.

Another reason why some people cannot "tolerate" a medication is that they do not want to assume the potential risks associated with taking it. A good example of this are the newer antipsychotics whose FDA-approved indications have been expanded to include augmenting antidepressants. Older women who have been through menopause are at higher risk for developing a movement disorder called tardive dyskinesia when taking these drugs. They may refuse the drug altogether or try it very briefly and then stop it out of concern that they will develop the side effect. If you are having side effects from the medications you are taking, you should discuss them with your clinician, especially if you are considering stopping them. You may also want to discuss any anxieties you have about the medications. It not uncommon for people to worry about the long-term effects and the stigma associated with psychiatric illnesses and treatment. If these side effects and concerns cannot be addressed effectively, then proceeding to ECT to get out of your depression is reasonable.

Partial Treatment Resistance

Once someone has responded to an antidepressant, they may still seek or even need ECT to boost their antidepressant response. This is often because they have only a partial response, or **partial treatment resistance**, to a medication where they feel better but not completely well. This usually reflects a combination of the elimination of some symptoms and a reduction in the intensity of other symptoms of the depressive episode. Someone who has responded but is not in remission may still have a significant burden of illness, and **people with residual symptoms are more likely to relapse back into depression.**[10] A short course of ECT followed by maintenance treatment is often quite effective in treating these residual symptoms.

Urgency

Some people start ECT after just one or two medication trials because they or their treatment team feel they **need to get better quickly**. This can be because psychiatrically they are at too high of a risk of killing themselves or hurting others, even though they are in the hospital. It can also reflect a need to keep their life together, such as keeping their job or taking care of other family members. Others start ECT quickly because they are so medically depleted from their illness that they are in danger of dying from malnutrition. ECT can quickly deescalate those types of situations.[11]

Aggressive forms of catatonia are another class of psychiatric illness that can make treatment with ECT an emergent necessity. In certain types of catatonia, especially malignant catatonia or "lethal catatonia," the rigidity causes the person's muscles to start to break down. This causes their kidneys and other crucial bodily systems to begin shutting down. Fortunately, catatonia is highly responsive to ECT, and the effects of the illness can usually be halted before they become fatal.

Prior Experience with ECT

It probably won't surprise you to learn that a significant number of people starting a new course of ECT have had **a positive response to ECT in the past**. Mood disorders tend to be recurrent, lifelong illnesses and most antidepressants act through similar mechanisms, so it is not unusual that they would eventually have a break-through episode. It makes sense to come back to a treatment you have had a positive response to in the past. One patient I treated years ago spent the month of August on an inpatient psychiatric unit trying different antidepressants and mood stabilizers. Finally, in frustration, her treatment team asked for an ECT consult. She clearly met the criteria for treatment and underwent a course of ten unilateral treatments. She was discharged home on mood stabilizing and antidepressant medications. She did reasonably well until the beginning of the following summer, when she relapsed into depression. This time when the treatment team proposed more medication trials, she refused and demanded ECT. She again went into remission.

A slightly different variant of this is when people have a family member who has had a positive response to ECT, as mentioned earlier. There is a clear-cut genetic component to mood disorders, and people sometimes realize that their symptoms are very similar to those of their aunt or uncle who did not get better with medications but did well with ECT. They will flat-out say, "I don't want to go through all those medications and side effects only to find out that medications don't work, like my uncle experienced" and "I'm pretty sure the ECT will work."

Am I Healthy Enough for ECT?

Let us return to Angela's journey with ECT. After we had gone over her history in detail, it was clear that she had a primary mood disorder that was likely to respond to ECT. She had well-controlled high blood pressure but was otherwise healthy and at low risk for serious complications from the treatment. We ordered routine prescreening testing—namely, an electrocardiogram—and a basic metabolic panel to assess her general health. Angela did not have these health issues, but there are medical conditions that can increase the risks associated with ECT. Fortunately, active management of any condition can reduce the risk greatly, and many frail eighty- and ninety-year-old patients have been treated without their extensive list of medical illnesses causing a problem.

To help you answer the question of being healthy enough for ECT for yourself, let us briefly discuss the physiologic changes that occur during an individual ECT treatment and different medical illnesses that can be affected by them.

During ECT the electricity induces a seizure, which is an episode of continuous firing of the brain's neurons. The result is that the brain has a significant increase in its need for oxygen and other nutrients. Since the person has received general anesthesia and a muscle relaxant, there is usually little movement in the rest of the body. There is a significant increase in blood pressure and heart rate, which increases blood flow to the brain. On average the volume of blood in the brain increases two- to fourfold during the seizure. This means that patients with significant underlying conditions of their brain and heart may need the treatment modified to reduce the risk of a stroke or heart attack. Only rarely does a person have a condition that makes treatment with ECT too risky.

For people with an underlying **seizure disorder**, or a history of concussion or other brain injury, the seizure induced by the treatment may be prolonged or may require more intensive treatment to stop it. Fortunately, this risk can be managed through careful assessment, consultation with a neurologist, and the preemptive use of antiseizure medications when indicated. In the rare instance when a seizure lasts too long, it is usually stopped by giving the patient additional anesthesia and/or an anticonvulsant.

People with diseases of the blood vessels, or vascular system, in the brain should be evaluated by a neurologist to assess the risks associated with treatment. **The increase in blood pressure and heart rate that occurs during ECT puts stress on the blood vessels, also known as the vascular system, throughout the body.** Narrowing of the arteries to the brain or a history of a prior stroke increases the risks associated with ECT. **Vascular conditions usually require careful evaluation and monitoring.**[12] If a region of brain tissue gets damaged, it can become irritated and prolong the seizure, or, if not well healed, bleed. Aneurysms, which are an outpouching in the wall of a blood vessel, have an increased risk of rupture and severe bleeding. The same is true for arteriovenous malformations, which are a tangle of blood vessels with very weak walls that are vulnerable to bursting during increases in blood pressure.

Another brain condition that increases the risk of doing ECT is when the person has a **mass in their brain**. These can result from tumors or pockets of blood known as hematomas. Tumors can cause problems by taking up space and increasing pressure in the brain or by bleeding. When blood pressure increases due to the increase in blood volume, the only place the brain tissue can go is down and back. If the brain is pushed too far down, it damages the centers that cause the person to breathe, causing death. While there have been reports of using medication to reduce the pressure on the brain followed by successful ECT, most ECT clinicians would not proceed with treatment until the tumor had been treated.[13] Hematomas can accumulate in the brain when an older person hits their head or sustains some other head injury. They slowly increase over time and also cause problems by taking up some of the limited space inside the bony skull.

During the treatment, when the stimulus is applied, the person's heart will initially slow down and then, once the seizure starts, speed up significantly. The heart rate will remain high until the seizure stops, when it may again slow down significantly. In patients with healthy hearts, these changes are temporary and do not negatively affect them. In patients with heart disease, this can cause a number of problems. The **cardiac problems** that occur during ECT fall into two categories: the person has a conduction problem, which leads to an abnormal rhythm, or has partial blockages in the arteries so that blood flow through the heart cannot meet the increased demand during the treatment.

Atrial fibrillation, which is an abnormal rhythm of the heart, increases the risk that clots will form in the upper chambers of the heart, called the atria. **Any clots that are present in the upper chamber of the left side of the heart can head to the brain and cause a stroke.** If you have a history of atrial fibrillation, your provider will need to make sure you are on anticoagulation medication, otherwise known as a blood thinner, for at least six weeks prior to starting treatment.

Abnormal rhythms in the lower chamber of the heart, known as **ventricular arrhythmias**, can also increase the risks from ECT. The increase in heart rate associated with ECT can worsen abnormal ventricular rhythms and lead to cardiac arrest. If you suffer from this condition, it can be managed with the help of your cardiologist.

If the heart's conduction pathways are working well, the other way that ECT can trigger cardiac problems is if you have partial blockages of the arteries in your heart, known as **coronary artery disease**. ECT greatly increases the amount of work the heart has to do for a very brief period of time. If the arteries of the heart are significantly blocked, they cannot supply the muscles with enough blood to meet the increased need for oxygen and nutrients to do the work, and some of the heart muscle may be injured. Again, active monitoring and medications can be used to limit the increase in the amount of work the heart does and protect it. If you are dealing with coronary artery disease, the team will likely ask you to see your cardiologist to make sure your protective medications have been optimized.[14]

People with **a history of problems with their spine** also have increased risk from ECT. The risks include compression and erosion of the discs that sit between the individual vertebrae to cushion the contact between them that occurs with everyday activity, as well as fractures of the vertebrae that make up the bony spinal column. The muscle relaxant medication used during anesthesia greatly reduces the risk by reducing movement during the seizure, but individual differences in blood flow and drug breakdown can cause less than optimal protection for some patients, especially during the early treatments. The most common way these problems present is with pain and/or numbness. ECT usually does not worsen these conditions, but a careful neurological assessment prior to treatment and extra caution with the degree of muscle relaxation during the treatment is a good idea.

Thyroid disease can also increase the risk of ECT. Thyroid hormone regulates metabolism. Too little (hypothyroidism) causes the person to have no energy, gain weight, and feel depressed. Too much (hyperthyroidism) causes the person to be hyper, have difficulty sleeping, have a rapid heart rate, and experience weight loss. If a person receives an ECT treatment while their thyroid is overactive, the additional increase in heart rate and metabolic activity may push the person into an abnormal heart rhythm or a dangerously high blood pressure.[15] If you do have thyroid issues, it is much safer to treat your overactive thyroid gland first before proceeding with ECT.

One important note of caution is not starting ECT while you are being treated with lithium. Lithium is usually stopped during a course of ECT because it increases the risk for severe confusion. Lithium also reduces the thyroid gland's ability to release thyroid hormone, which can lead to an increase in TSH (thyroid stimulating hormone). If you are being treated with thyroid hormone and stop lithium for ECT, you may have a rebound increase in the release of thyroid hormone. The increase in blood pressure and heart rate associated with elevated thyroid hormone is something we try to avoid with ECT.[16]

While the preceding section covers most of the major medical concerns about ECT, it is not exhaustive. It is generally a good idea to see your primary care provider for medical clearance before beginning a course of ECT.

Will I Be Getting Unilateral or Bilateral Treatment?

Going back to Angela's experience, once we had finished our review of her health, we moved to a discussion of the details of the treatment plan. We started with the difference between unilateral and bilateral electrode placement for the treatment. When ECT was initially developed, the electrodes were placed on both sides of the patient's head (bilateral). It wasn't until twenty years after the first ECT that the electrodes were unilaterally placed.[17] The study staff reported that patients treated with unilateral or bilateral ECT showed comparable improvement, but importantly, the amount of time to become reoriented was reduced and short-term memory side effects were less pronounced in the group treated with unilateral ECT.

In addition to reporting the numbers, the researchers also added their clinical impression that bilateral electrode placement was more effective than unilateral. This was further corroborated by an analysis of several studies that also found that bilateral ECT is slightly more effective. This clinical impression has been used by some groups to justify only using bilateral electrode placement in ECT. While these groups help people get better and the cognitive side effects fade with time, these side effects can be distressing for people. I explained to Angela that because unilateral ECT has fewer cognitive (memory) side effects, and bilateral ECT is more effective, for most people, only in very severe cases, I recommended she undergo optimized right unilateral ECT.

Another part of the strategy for optimizing unilateral ECT for Angela would be to start with ultra-brief pulse width for the stimulus. Electricity travels in waves. The pulse width refers to the slice of the wave that is delivered to the patient. Over time, the pulse widths used in ECT have become shorter, and a pulse width of 0.3 milliseconds is now considered ultra-brief whereas a pulse width of 0.5 milliseconds or greater is considered brief. One of the main ways that unilateral ECT has been optimized to limit cognitive side effects while retaining antidepressant effect is to use an ultra-brief pulse width. However, this is where clinical expertise and the "art" of medicine come in. The cognitive side effects of ECT are decreased with ultra-brief pulse treatment when compared with longer pulse widths. However, the cost seems to be one to two additional treatments to achieve treatment response, and the response may be less than those achieved with the longer pulse widths.[18]

I also discussed with Angela the strategy our service uses for "dosing" the amount of charge given during the treatment. Specifically, we start out by measuring the seizure threshold and then in subsequent treatments using a dose that significantly exceeds that threshold but is not excessive as determined by earlier research. Work by Dr. Harold Sackeim and his team at Columbia University has shown that this approach is as effective as using higher doses of charge.[19] Since anti-seizure medications, which are frequently used to treat mood disorders, can affect the seizure threshold, they are often adjusted prior to starting a course of ECT. The same is true for sedative hypnotics such as loraze-pam (Ativan). You will learn more about adjusting medications during ECT later. For now, know that balancing the interplay among stimulus parameters, the person's daily medications, and the dose and timing of the anesthetic can be the difference between being able to treat with ultra-brief pulses and needing to switch to brief-pulse ECT.

I'm Starting ECT Treatment.
What Should I Expect?

In this section I'm going to walk you through a course of ECT treatment.

The night prior to each treatment, be sure you have been drinking enough fluids and are not dehydrated. A thirty-two-ounce bottle of one of the various sports drinks that are currently on the market the evening prior to treatment will do the trick (as long as it does not contain caffeine). Depending on the anesthesia department's usual practice, you may be asked to take nothing by mouth after midnight or you may be allowed clear liquids up until a few hours before the treatment.

Once you arrive for treatment you will be checked in at the front desk and then escorted back to the treatment area when the team is ready for you. Your informed consent documentation, medical status, and medications will be verified. An intravenous, or IV, line will be placed. The treatment team will ask you how your mood is and assess your safety. Depending on the service, you may be asked to fill out rating scales prior to your treatment.

Will I Be Awake for the Procedure?

As has been previously described, you will be given an intravenous injection of a medicine that induces general anesthesia. The goal of the anesthetic is to make you sleep through the treatment and relax your muscles to minimize the risk of injury for the one to two minutes the treatment lasts. At the start of your treatment course, the team will choose which anesthetic medications they want to use and what the dosage will be. Depending on your reaction to the first treatment, they may fine-tune the regimen at the second treatment.

Since the total duration of the general anesthesia is about fifteen minutes, short-acting anesthetics are preferred. In the United States, the drug most often used is methohexital, which has a long track record of being used safely for ECT. Alternatively, some hospitals use etomidate, an anesthetic medication that acts quickly and does not raise seizure threshold as much. This is a desirable trait since the seizure is thought to be how ECT works and raising the threshold with the anesthetic may reduce its efficacy. However, etomidate must be used with care as it can suppress the production of a hormone that supports healthy blood pressure. Usually it is well tolerated, but if etomidate is used for your treatment, you should let your team know if you experience any episodes of dizziness or lightheadedness in between treatments.[20]

Another anesthetic drug that has been used frequently in ECT is propofol. This medication does raise seizure threshold and shortens seizure duration, but it also dampens the increase in blood pressure and heart rate during the ECT treatment. Therefore, it is quite useful in special populations, such as patients with cardiovascular disease. However, using propofol as the medication to induce anesthesia can increase the number of treatments needed to get better.[21]

Once you are asleep, you will be given a muscle relaxant medication intravenously. Most commonly, succinylcholine is used because it is very short-acting and well tolerated. You will probably have some muscle aches after the first one or two treatments. I usually describe them as similar to that soreness you get after your first workout when you haven't been to the gym in a while. People usually attribute it to moving a lot during the seizure, but it is a side effect of the muscle relaxant that occurs even in people who are completely relaxed and show no visible movement during the treatment.

If you find that you are waking up from the treatment feeling short of breath or having difficulty breathing, you should let the team know. This sensation usually can be easily treated by increasing the anesthetic or decreasing the muscle relaxant. Rarely, it can be a sign of something called pseudocholinesterase deficiency. Pseudocholinesterase is an enzyme in the bloodstream that inactivates succinylcholine and thereby reverses muscle relaxation. This deficiency, which occurs in about one in three thousand people, is a genetic condition that otherwise causes few, if any, symptoms.[22]

There are some special situations that require the use of other muscle relaxants: when the patient has a history of extensive burns, is immobilized by catatonia, or has significant paralysis. In these individuals, succinylcholine puts them at increased risk for an abnormal heart rhythm. The team can use other muscle relaxants to remove this risk. If you have one of these conditions, the anesthetist will be able to describe your options to you. Fortunately, the other muscle relaxant medications typically recommended are also usually well tolerated.

Whatever muscle relaxant is used, you will be asleep and unable to move for about three to five minutes. During this time the anesthesia team will support your breathing. Once the muscle relaxant has had time enough to work, the electrodes will be placed on your head and a small amount of electricity will be used to induce a grand mal seizure. Initially you will tense up and then, depending on the degree of muscle relaxation, you may begin to have rhythmic movements of your extremities and other muscles. The heart rate initially slows and then as the seizure takes hold it increases significantly along with the blood pressure. These changes are mediated by a part of the brain responsible for maintaining the body's physiology known as the brainstem. The seizure itself lasts anywhere from twenty seconds to about two minutes.

After the seizure stops, your heart rate will slow, and your blood pressure will likely be increased. Over the next five to fifteen minutes your heart rate and blood pressure and muscle relaxation return to normal as you gradually wake up. You should be awake and oriented by thirty minutes after the treatment ends. When you are fully oriented, you will be discharged home with an escort. An escort is very important since some of the anesthetic will still be in your system and you may not realize how much it is affecting your judgment and reflexes. Some patients need to go home and rest, but some leave ready to carry on with their day. Because the treatments are usually administered very early in the morning, the day is young when you leave the hospital or clinic. Some people go out for breakfast before heading home or to work. Since you have had a brief but general anesthetic, it is best to take it easy for the rest of the day. You must not drive or operate machinery on the day of treatment.

How Many Treatments Will I Need?
What Is a Standard Course?

The average acute course of ECT, or the number of treatments needed to treat your depression, is usually six to ten treatments. Once you are better, the next question is whether to do maintenance ECT or treat you with medications or both. Your prescribing clinician may have decided that along with the acute course of ECT you should change your antidepressant medications. If you are on a medication that works differently from anything you have taken before, stopping ECT and closely observing yourself for signs of depression is reasonable. However, if you stop ECT and continue with medications similar to what you were taking prior to starting ECT, your risk of relapse is high. Your chances of staying well are better with maintenance ECT, and they are best with a combination of medications and maintenance ECT.

What About Side Effects?

The most common side effect of ECT is the memory difficulties that people experience during a course of treatment. Opponents of ECT have used the memory side effects to argue that ECT causes brain damage. As I explained earlier, it does not. In fact, ECT causes an increase in the volume of certain brain regions, including the hippocampus, an important component of the memory circuitry of the brain. Functionally, the memory side effects of the treatment reflect the remodeling of the memory circuit as at least one of its key components increases in size over the course of the treatment.

During a course of ECT, most people usually find that their ability to learn new things is reduced; in other words, they have immediate and short-term memory problems. Some people also report that during the course of ECT they have forgotten periods of time from their past. I know that this can be quite distressing. I generally find reassurance to be helpful and remind them that we expect their memory to rebound once the treatment stops. For most people, once the treatments are finished, their memory stabilizes for a week or two and then begins to rebound. Some people find that their immediate and short-term memory is better after ECT than it was before the treatment.[23]

The immediate side effects that commonly occur with ECT are usually relatively mild and resolve within hours after the treatment. After ECT, because of the general anesthesia, it is common to feel a little groggy and disoriented. You can also expect disorientation and mild confusion posttreatment (these side effects are very common). The good news is that for about 90 percent of people, the grogginess and confusion will go away within thirty minutes of the seizure.[24] Because of the combined effects of the anesthesia and ECT, a small number of patients do not remember having their treatment and, after the disorientation wears off, will ask when their turn is coming. Once they are reminded that they had the treatment already, they usually remember falling asleep with the anesthetic.

Headache is also not unusual following an ECT treatment. When a headache occurs, it often reflects a preexisting vulnerability, such as a history of migraine or temporomandibular joint (TMJ) disease. Depending on the type of headache, it can usually be prevented. Acetaminophen taken orally with just enough water to swallow the pills is often quite effective in preventing a headache. Your provider may also use intravenous fluids and prochlorperazine to prevent a migraine (or treat it after ECT). Unfortunately, TMJ-associated headaches are more difficult to prevent. This is because when the stimulus is delivered to initiate the seizure, the muscle that controls the chewing muscle of the jaw, the masseter muscle, is directly stimulated by the electricity. This causes the muscle to tense up and the underlying misalignment of the jaw then triggers the headache. An ice pack applied to the area after treatment along with acetaminophen or ibuprofen usually reduces the intensity or eliminates the headache.

Nausea is another transient side effect common after anesthesia. Usually this can be prevented with intravenous fluids and/or medications as pretreatment. **Muscle aches** are also common after the first one or two ECT treatments. This is a side effect of the muscle relaxant and usually goes away with continued ECT treatment.

Several studies have shown that the seizure is the active component of the treatment. The anesthesia is given to prevent injury. Before effective anesthesia was developed, patients often suffered fractures and dislocations in their limbs during the seizure. Now that anesthesia and muscle relaxants are used, the incidence of such injuries is estimated at less than 0.4 percent,[25] and it has been estimated that the risk of dying from ECT is consistent with the risk of general anesthesia for a minor surgical procedure—and much lower than your lifetime risk of dying from crossing the street.[26]

Will I Continue or Start Medications While Receiving ECT?

This is an area where there is some disagreement. A recent study that looked at the impact of the major classes of psychiatric medications, including anticonvulsants, taken while undergoing ECT found that they didn't make a difference in the seizure threshold.[27] I do not believe this study, however. Earlier work by Drs. Jha and Stein in London found that benzodiazepine sedatives, such as lorazepam, decreased the effectiveness of unilateral ECT, even when the treatment seemed to be adequate.[28] This makes sense since the therapeutic agent is the seizure and sedatives like lorazepam are anticonvulsant. Based on this work, the approach I have taken is to reduce antiseizure medications as much as can safely be done prior to starting the ECT and continue to slowly taper during the treatment course. The popularity of antiepileptic drugs, such as lamotrigine (Lamictal), for treating mood disorders has made the task more complicated. On the flip side of the coin, one thing I have learned is not to cut the dosage too much too quickly, as that seems to make the brain irritable. Usually, the patient wakes up gradually and quietly, but patients who have had their medications tapered off a little too quickly or had an underlying vulnerability to seizures can be quite disoriented and agitated. This can be dealt with by an extra dose of a sedative, but it is a situation I try to avoid in the first place.

The validity of this approach was recently brought home to me by another patient. This gentleman, who is in his forties, has bipolar disorder. When his medications are augmented by ECT, he is a well-respected professional who is well liked by his coworkers and friends. Recently, he was doing so well that he stopped his maintenance ECT.

Unfortunately, he relapsed into a manic and psychotic state. He was hospitalized and started on an antiepileptic medication, divalproex (Depakote), to treat his mania, and he continued taking his other medications. He resumed his ECT treatments while still taking divalproex. After eight treatments with no benefit, even though the intensity of the treatment had been increased significantly, the divalproex was discontinued. By the end of the next four treatments, he was visibly better, and by the end of the sixth treatment, he felt well. His coworkers were glad to see him when he went back to work a couple of weeks later.

Another medication that requires attention when combined with ECT is lithium. Not often, but too often if it happens to you, people taking lithium and receiving ECT can become very confused and disoriented. Typically, our team stops lithium the night before starting an acute course of treatment and restarts it at the end. Stopping the lithium sooner exposes the patient to the risk of losing the antisuicide effects of lithium while still depressed.[29] ECT is also thought to have antisuicide properties and should protect the patient during treatment. During maintenance ECT, most people on lithium do not have a problem with confusion if they skip their dose the night before the treatment and resume it afterward.[30]

Will I Need to Take Time Off Work to Undergo ECT?

If you are working a job that requires you to remember details, it is best to plan to take four to six weeks off from work to allow your memory time to recover after the acute course of treatments is completed. If you and your treatment team feel that ongoing, less frequent treatment, otherwise known as continuation or maintenance treatment, is indicated for your care, then you may need a couple of additional weeks before heading back to work. These timelines are offered as general guidelines. You should discuss your particular situation with your treatment team.

Does It Really Work?

That ECT is still used in modern medicine more than eighty years after it was first developed is a testament to its ability to treat severe psychiatric illnesses. During those eighty years, the treatment has been refined both in terms of the anesthetics used for patient comfort and safety and how the treatment stimulus is tailored to the needs of the patient. It is important to realize that the severe mood disorders and other psychiatric illnesses described in these chapters can have serious long-term consequences. ECT has a high degree of success in treating these illnesses, and early treatment is the best way to minimize their impact on your life and your family.

To summarize, as you know well, treatment-resistant depression causes a great deal of suffering and has long-term effects on the person's family, health, and career. ECT has demonstrated efficacy in treating depression as well as severe mood disorders, psychosis, and catatonia. As it is practiced today, ECT is a safe and highly effective treatment that has literally been lifesaving for some people and positively life altering for many others. Refinements in our understanding of which illnesses to treat and when to use it have significantly improved the practice of ECT. Significant advances have been made in the anesthesia used, the machines that deliver ECT, and the management of medications during ECT.

Key Takeaways

► ECT as it is practiced today has been modernized and is much improved when compared to old-fashioned shock therapy.

► The anesthetic medications used today have made the treatment much safer and much more comfortable for the patient.

► ECT remains the most effective treatment available for severe or treatment-resistant depression, mania, and catatonia. It is also used in treatment-resistant psychotic illnesses, especially when the person is having suicidal thoughts.

► In addition to diagnosis, other considerations that factor into the use of ECT include severity of illness, safety concerns (suicidality/risk of violence), treatment resistance, inability to tolerate other treatments, and patient preference.

► Memory side effects are common and temporary. Some people do have longer-lasting memory side effects. This has been studied many different ways, and the findings indicate that this is the result of remodeling in the memory circuits, not damage.

► Discuss the medications you are taking with your psychiatric provider and try to minimize or eliminate medications that interfere with seizures, such as antiepileptic medications and sedative-hypnotics—for example, lorazepam (Ativan).

Part III

Adjunct Therapies and the Future of Treatment

Chapter 10

Exercise, Nutrition, and Sleep

The treatments presented in this book are quite potent and have changed the lives of many people suffering from chronic and severe mood disorders. But they are acute treatments, while these illnesses tend to recur over the life span. Fortunately, we have begun to understand that mental illness, and severe depression in particular, affects the health of the entire body and, conversely, that the health of the entire body can influence the course of the person's mood disorder. The good news is that medical science has found that lifestyle changes that improve overall health and reduce inflammation in the body can improve and, in some cases, completely treat a person's mood disorder. You will probably not be surprised by the list: exercise, a more plant-based diet, and improved sleep patterns. This chapter will explain why they are effective and describe the available data supporting each of these treatments. We will end with a discussion of inflammation, specifically which blood markers to monitor and how to strategize with your doctor should the markers not respond to exercise, diet, and improved sleep.

Doesn't Everyone Need More Exercise?

Most people know that they need more exercise, but people suffering from depression usually don't believe it can help and find it difficult to get started. The frustration people with depression feel when hearing a recommendation to exercise more was brought home to me in a recent meeting. We were discussing health care provider burnout when one of the providers in the room became visibly upset. When asked what was bothering him, he said, "If another person tells me to exercise, do yoga, or meditate, I'm going to scream!" This was coming from a person who knows the data from all the studies on exercise, diet, meditation, and regular sleep, but he was tired and frustrated. He needed relief quickly and not more items added to his to-do list. The suggestion to do more made him feel like he was failing again. Although, to my knowledge, he was not suffering from depression, he had a similar response to the recommendation that most people with depression have. **The fatigue and mental fog of depression make recommending that you start exercising and making other changes sound ridiculously out of touch and insensitive.** Yet to not inform you of the antidepressant effects of these interventions might miss an opportunity to point you to self-directed changes that can help your depression now and have lifelong benefits for your health.

How Do I Get Started Exercising?

It is important to start by reminding you that **if you do have any health issues, please discuss any new exercise program with your primary care provider**.

Starting or increasing the amount of exercise you are doing requires making changes in your daily routine. This is doable, but not as easy as saying, "I'm going to start exercising." So how do you get started? The number of gym memberships that go unused a month after the start of each New Year should give you some idea of how common it is for people to want to make changes in their life and how hard they find it to sustain these changes. Fortunately, we have scientists who study personal change and growth quite intensely. They have found that the process of making life changes can be broken down into five stages: pre-contemplation, contemplation, preparation, action, and maintenance.[1]

Briefly, *precontemplation* is the mindset you are in before you realize there is a change you want to make. In this case, it is the stage before learning that exercise can have antidepressant benefits or even that the "rut" you are in is depression. The contemplation phase is when you are trying to decide if you should make a change and are thinking about how you might want to do it. Questions you might be asking at this stage include:

- Should I have a checkup with my primary care provider? (YES)
- Should I see a therapist? (YES)
- Should I start exercising? (YES)

The preparation phase is when you plan what you are going to do, and the action phase is when you start to carry out the plan. This would be when you decide the type of exercise you want to do, when you are going to do it, and where. The maintenance phase is when you have to keep the changes you've made going. Some authors also include a relapse phase, which acknowledges that change can be difficult and people may fall back into old patterns of behavior.[2] Since you are reading this section of the book, you are at least in the contemplation phase, so let us get more specific about how to add exercise into your treatment using this framework.

This Seems Like a Lot of Work!

This is one of the (probably many) reactions my health care colleague was having when people started telling him about yoga and meditation.

The same is true for people struggling with depression. As I mentioned, when you are feeling that bad, being told to exercise can feel like a cruel joke. But it's not! Well-designed studies show that movement really does reduce people's depression.[3] The trick is to find a way to get the support and equipment you need so you can do only what feels impossible. For starters, we can streamline the process significantly. We only need to answer four questions:

1. What type of exercise should you do?
2. What schedule will you follow?
3. How long will each session of exercise last?
4. What do you need for equipment and space?

I will suggest some answers here and then we will discuss the science behind these suggestions in greater detail later on in the chapter. The **type of exercise** can be almost anything that helps you break a sweat, **especially if you enjoy doing it**, because that makes it more likely that you will keep it up. Most people try to exercise three to five times weekly. The length of the sessions will vary from person to person, but a **general target is 150 to 160 minutes per week**.[4] The newer wearable devices that measure heart rate and other health variables tend to be very helpful in making these measurements. These targets combined with the number of sessions you can fit in each week will help you determine your target duration for each workout.

Will All This Work Really Make a Difference?

To give you a more concrete example of what I am talking about, consider Sam's struggle with depression and their "accidental treatment" with exercise. Sam was a nineteen-year-old college sophomore when they came under my care for bipolar depression. Sam has an extensive family history of bipolar disorder with their maternal grandmother,

mother, two maternal uncles, and a sibling all having struggled with bipolar disorder. Over the next year and a half, we tried multiple medications, including lithium, lamotrigine (Lamictal), quetiapine (Seroquel), lurasidone (Latuda), and cariprazine (Vraylar). The medications caused side effects but did not improve Sam's mood. We also tried escitalopram (Lexapro) and bupropion (Wellbutrin XL), but both had to be stopped when they triggered an increase in Sam's suicidal thoughts. Finally, we settled on lamotrigine and fish oils, which combined with weekly psychotherapy provided some modest relief from the depressive symptoms. Feeling "better enough," Sam signed up for the fall semester of their senior year. The depression had been pretty intense in the summer, and they were late arranging housing for the school year. In addition, funds were tight, so the apartment was about five miles from school. To save money, they rode their bicycle to and from school most days, a good ten miles round trip. After a couple of weeks, Sam noticed that their mood had started to improve, and they felt significantly better. Initially, we attributed it to the change in seasons, but I also noted that Sam's mood usually cycled down in the fall. During the Thanksgiving break, Sam went home to their parents' house, where their need to commute ceased. By the end of the weeklong break, Sam noticed that their mood had dropped. They also noticed that their mood started to pick up a few days after they had resumed cycling to and from school. Sam continued to cycle almost every day for the rest of the school year, and their mood stayed pretty close to how they felt before the depression started.

If I had told Sam that they needed to start exercising as a way to treat their depression, they would have found it hard, more likely impossible, to get started. In fact, during the pandemic when Sam experienced another episode of depression, they found it difficult to exercise regularly, even though they knew the potential benefit and the gym in their apartment building was only three floors down. It was the economic necessities of needing to finish their degree and keep their commuting costs to a minimum that unintentionally led Sam to a regular and intense exercise program.

I Don't Know If I Can Do It . . .

I hope you find that exercise helps your mood and becomes an enjoyable part of your weekly routine. As you probably already know, regular exercise benefits almost every aspect of your health, so the question becomes, How can you make it a regular habit? As I mentioned, this is an area that has also been well studied. For something to become a habit, you have to start doing it. In golf, it has been estimated that it takes ten thousand quality swings to become a professional. Fortunately, we are not trying to become professional exercisers, just someone who is trying to feel better using exercise as a tool. For a behavior to become a habit, most people need to do something for at least two months or sixty-six times.[5] This is clearly more attainable than ten thousand times.

When trying to form a new habit it is useful to define a reasonable, clear-cut goal. Simply saying, "I'm going to exercise regularly" is too vague. Compare that to saying, "I'm going to ride an exercise bike at moderate resistance for thirty minutes three days a week by one month after I start." This goal is clearly measurable, and the target of one month after starting acknowledges that you will likely need to build up to the goal.

Another useful concept is linking the habit you want to develop to a habit you already have. In his book *Atomic Habits*, James Clear describes the process of "stacking habits."[6] One example he uses for exercise is to link it to changing your clothes after work. "When you change out of your work clothes, you change into your exercise clothing." If your depression is preventing you from working on a regular schedule, link getting dressed in exercise clothing to getting out of bed for the first time in the day. Then start your workout. Alternatively, you could plan your workout before your first meal of the day, as long as your physical health permits this type of schedule. People with diabetes, for example, may need to delay a workout until after they have eaten.

Social support and sharing your goals can also be helpful. One of the major negative downstream effects of depression is that during an episode of depression, people drift away from their friends. As you get older this becomes harder to reverse. It is even hard for people who are not depressed, so much so that the *Wall Street Journal* recently published an article on making and keeping friends in middle age.[7] If you can get a reliable friend who doesn't take no for an answer to be your workout partner, that is usually very helpful. Otherwise, regularly exercising in a group or in a class may have the added benefit of sustaining and even improving your social network.

Will Exercise Work for My Depression?

In short, there is no way to predict who will have a robust antidepressant response to exercise versus who will have a limited response. What does seem clear is that movement helps most people to some degree. Even if it does not boost your mood, it is likely that the rest of your body will benefit.

Reports documenting the potential antidepressant effects of exercise first began to appear in the scientific literature in the 1970s.[8] Over the ensuing fifty years, this literature has expanded to where the antidepressant effects of exercise seem pretty clear. Also, when these studies are looked at in combination, they cover the full age spectrum from adolescence to the elderly.[9]

As we go through some of these studies, an important consideration is whether the studies were placebo controlled. The early studies were exploratory and did not always include a placebo. As pointed out by Dr. James Blumenthal and colleagues, depression is an illness that sometimes has a good response to sugar pills.[10] Therefore, it is important that studies have a good placebo control group, for example, giving people participating in the study's control group information about their illness or some other exercise equivalent of a sugar pill. Having a placebo treatment group as part of the study helps control for the benefits of having other people more interested than usual in how you are doing because you are participating in research. Without a control group, the researchers might incorrectly conclude that their intervention is helping when the real benefit is coming from increased social interaction or another aspect of the study.

Another important question to be answered is whether exercise helps depression in all age groups. We know that depression that starts in adolescence is different from depression that starts later in life. For one, depression that starts later in life usually is associated with vascular disease and other signs of chronic inflammation that contribute to the illness. We also know that the body's ability to recover and benefit from exercise is different at different ages. The initial data demonstrating the benefits of exercise for depression came from young adults.

Since older adults have less resilient physiologies and in general a greater burden of physical illness, it was not clear that exercise would have the same benefits for them as it does for younger people. However, in 1999, Dr. James Blumenthal and his colleagues from Duke University reported the results of a study that compared sixteen weeks of treatment with aerobic exercise alone, antidepressant medication alone, or a combination of both treatments.[11] All of the treatments produced an antidepressant response, but none of them was significantly better than the other. Unfortunately, they did not include a placebo control group. This makes the results difficult to interpret because just taking the positive steps to get out and enroll in a study may benefit people's mood. It's unlikely, but possible.

Subsequently, two approaches to using exercise as an antidepressant in the elderly have emerged. The first is to try to avoid medication and use exercise to treat the depression. Currently, Dr. Lopez-Torres Hidalgo and the DEP-EXERCISE group recently reported on a study in patients over the age of sixty-five where the participants were randomly selected to be in either a group that exercised twice weekly or one that took medications, over six months. At one month the two treatments did not differ in effectiveness, but at three and six months the antidepressant medication was more effective than twice-weekly exercise, although the medication group reported more side effects.[12]

The current clinical approach is to combine exercise with antidepressant medications. One such study looked at 121 subjects with late-life depression who were randomly selected to (1) take an antidepressant but not do exercise, (2) do lower-intensity exercise and take an antidepressant, or (3) do higher-intensity exercise that got progressively harder and take an antidepressant medication. After twenty-four weeks of treatment, the antidepressant-alone group had a 45 percent remission rate, the lower-intensity exercise group had a 73 percent remission rate, and the higher-intensity group had an 81 percent remission rate. **In sum, regular exercise boosted the traditional antidepressant medications. More convincingly, it did so in a dose-dependent fashion, meaning the more intense the exercise, the greater the response.**[13]

Which Types of Movement Have the Most Antidepressant Benefit?

First and foremost, I cannot stress enough how important it is to choose an exercise regimen that you enjoy. This gives you the best chance of sticking with it, and just getting moving seems to be the most important part. Nonetheless, given the number of different types of exercise available to us, it is important to consider whether one type of exercise has a greater physical impact on the body and whether that matters for depression. For example, is aerobic exercise that focuses on raising heart rate for an extended period of time better than walking, strength training, or stretching? Is high-intensity interval training better than constant-intensity training? How often and how much exercise should you do to treat your depression? Fortunately, I think the answers to these questions can be distilled down to a couple of general principles.

When I discuss the different types of exercise that have been shown to be effective with patients, I like to break things down into aerobic exercise versus strength training. Aerobic exercise is intended to get the heart rate elevated for an extended period of time. How you do that, whether through running, swimming, biking, Nordic walking, or other activity, is up to you.[14] Another important consideration is whether the aerobic exercise is done at a fairly consistent pace or whether the pace is varied with some of the workout done at a high-intensity pace. The latter approach is an emerging trend that is known as high-intensity interval training (HIIT), and it may produce greater gains in strength and stamina than the traditional approach of maintaining a fairly consistent pace.

Strength training, on the other hand, usually refers to lifting weights or some other form of resistance training. Depending on the intensity and pace of the workout, it can elevate the heart rate, but mostly it is intended to build muscle mass and strength. This helps depression and supports long-term health in a couple of ways. During an episode of depression, people tend to be less active. It only takes a couple of weeks to start to lose muscle mass and stamina.[15] As a result, you burn fewer calories. Unless you dramatically reduce your food intake, you will also gain weight. An increase in fat, especially abdominal fat, also results in an increase in inflammation and damages healthy tissues, especially blood vessels. (I'll talk more about inflammation on page 184.) In the elderly, decreased strength and increased body mass also increases the risk of falls and broken bones. Strength training works to reverse these trends, and increased muscle mass burns more calories, even at rest.

Which Type of Exercise Is Better for Me?

At the present time the answer to that question is not clear. There have only been a limited number of studies that directly compared aerobic exercise to resistance (strength) training for their antidepressant effects. The available data suggests that the two are equally effective. Interestingly, resistance training may have a greater antianxiety effect while aerobic exercise may be more beneficial in individuals with an increased risk for cognitive problems or who are in the early stages of cognitive impairment.[16] In light of these findings, it would be reasonable to combine the two types of exercise, if possible. However, the most important thing is to get started, and trying to begin two types of exercise may feel too overwhelming when you're depressed. One encouraging statistic reported across a number of these studies was that roughly **80 percent of the people with depression who started an exercise study were able to complete the study.[17] Like you, these people had symptoms severe enough to warrant a diagnosis of major depression.**

It is worth mentioning other exercise regimens that have not been as well studied in depression but appear to hold promise. These include high-intensity interval training and Nordic walking.

In HIIT workouts the individual does an initial warm-up and then has brief intervals where they exercise near their peak output. The intervals of peak output are followed by low-intensity intervals, and the process is then repeated multiple times. One pattern that is used in HIIT is to exercise near maximal capacity for sixty seconds followed by one to two minutes of low-intensity exercise. After that, the cycle is repeated. The total workout can be as brief as fifteen minutes in duration and has been shown to offer greater improvement in exercise capacity than moderate-intensity continuous exercise performed over thirty to forty minutes.[18] Given that this is a relatively new approach to designing workout regimens, there are few studies on its usefulness in depression. However, the available studies suggest that HIIT has more antidepressant effect than moderate-intensity continuous training.[19]

In Nordic walking, the individual adds special poles to their walking regimen. Unlike walking poles that are used for balance, Nordic walking poles increase the amount of exercise by increasing the amount of work the arms are doing. It has been estimated that walking uses approximately 50 percent of the muscles in your body, while Nordic walking uses about 80 to 90 percent.[20] While this has been shown to increase aerobic capacity, the antidepressant effects were more modest, so additional research is needed.[21]

How Much Exercise Should I Do?

In people with either depression or cognitive decline, 150 minutes per week of aerobic exercise has documented brain benefits. Since there is some variability between people, a target of 150 to 160 minutes per week is likely to be helpful. Dr. Andrea Dunn and her colleagues at the Cooper Institute and the University of Texas Southwestern Medical Center compared groups of people with depression who exercised three times weekly using stretching sessions, low-intensity aerobic exercise, or high-intensity aerobic exercise.[22] Both the low- and high-intensity subjects were further separated into groups that exercised either three or five times per week. The high-intensity five-times-per-week group showed a 64 percent response rate versus a 31 percent response rate for both the high-intensity and low-intensity three-times-weekly groups. The study subjects who were in the five-times-per-week group did 150 to 200 minutes per week of exercise, which is part of why I say that 150 to 160 minutes per week is a good goal. Note that the World Health Organization recommends that individuals over the age of sixty-five have 150 minutes of moderate-intensity aerobic exercise or 75 minutes of high-intensity aerobic exercise every week to reduce their risk of dementia.[23]

Sleep and Depression

Disrupted sleep afflicts almost 90 percent of people suffering from depression.[24] In fact, sleep disturbance is one of the nine criteria that psychiatry's diagnostic bible, the *DSM-5*, uses to make a diagnosis of major depression.[25] This connection between sleep and depression is further illustrated by the finding that people whose primary problem is a sleep disorder also have an increased risk of depression.[26] The sleep disturbances associated with depression can be broken down into difficulty falling asleep, also known as early insomnia; difficulty staying asleep, or middle insomnia; and waking up too early, or late insomnia. It is not uncommon to have more than one type of insomnia during an episode of depression. Some people experience the opposite, hypersomnia, where they sleep too much. Whether people have insomnia or hypersomnia, they are constantly dragging. The associated fatigue is one of the most frustrating and disabling symptoms of depression.

Changes in a person's sleep pattern often precede a relapse into depression or an upward mood swing into mania. When I first start working with someone new to my practice, one of the topics I make sure to discuss very early on is their sleep. We talk about why they should be vigilant for changes in their sleep pattern and to reach out to me sooner than later if changes start to occur. We also discuss what is known as sleep hygiene. Briefly, this means setting yourself up for a restful night's sleep when you go to bed.

Part of this discussion focuses on foods and other substances that can affect sleep. As you probably already know, caffeinated drinks can make it difficult to fall asleep. Alcohol, although it tends to make people sleepy, causes sleep to be disrupted and of poor quality, leaving the person tired or, worse, hung over, in the morning.[27] I also generally recommend against cannabis use. Cannabis has been shown to help sleep in the short term, but some people experience rebound sleep difficulties when they stop using it. Said another way, discontinuation of cannabis has been associated with sleep disturbances for up to forty-five days, and sleep disturbance increases the risk of relapse into continued cannabis use.[28] There is also data to suggest that people with mood disorders who use cannabis tend to have more episodes of their illness.[29] Many people also try cannabidiol, or CBD, for pain and anxiety with and without depression. There is minimal data about whether CBD is helpful or not.

Another part of my initial discussion with new patients covers setting up the environment for sleep. One of the most important things to do is to turn off computer, tablet, and cell phone screens at least an hour before trying to sleep. This is because they emit light at the blue end of the visible spectrum. Blue light reduces the amount of melatonin in the brain, and melatonin is the main chemical produced by the brain to induce sleep. Another important consideration is to make sure the room is sufficiently dark and quiet, and the temperature is comfortable for you. Lastly, since you don't want your brain to associate the bed with hanging out or other activities, you want to train your brain to equate the bed with sleeping. Sleep specialists recommend that people try to use the bed only for sleep and sex.

Here are some further tips for better sleep:

- Avoid alcohol, smoking or nicotine (e.g., vaping), and caffeinated drinks at least four hours before bedtime.[30]
- Remove all blue light devices (phone, tablet, computer) from your sleeping area.
- Use your bed only for sleep and sex.
- Be aware of your sleep patterns, and talk to your health care provider if changes start to occur.

What Can I Do About My Insomnia?

If you find that your anxiety gets much worse before you try to go to sleep, you are not alone. A significant number of people with depression and insomnia avoid going to bed because they anticipate another night of tossing and turning in total frustration. Over the years, the treatment of insomnia has gone from sedative medications such as diazepam (Valium), to sleep hygiene, to cognitive behavioral treatment of insomnia, or CBT-I. Currently, CBT-I is considered the first-line treatment for insomnia, and it has been shown to be highly effective in people with depression and insomnia.[31] Your providers may know a local CBT-I therapist; if not, a quick online search may be helpful. There is also a CBT-I app that has been developed by the US Department of Veterans Affairs and is available online.[32]

CBT-I consists of several components:

- **Stimulus control** aims to reestablish bed as a place where you sleep. To accomplish this goal, the person sets a morning wake time and then is in bed only when sleepy or asleep. Naps greater than thirty minutes are avoided as they can disrupt nighttime sleep.
- **Sleep restriction** aims to align the amount of time a person spends in bed with the amount of time they are asleep. The idea is to figure out the amount of time you sleep at night and then limit the number of hours you spend in bed to that amount of time.
- **Reducing activating stimuli** focuses on establishing a calm and quiet sanctuary for sleep. It focuses on relaxation as preparation for sleep and setting up a safe place for sleep.
- Part of creating a sanctuary for sleep is to **avoid foods and substances** such as alcohol, caffeine, and other stimulants that can increase alertness during the time you are trying to sleep.
- CBT-I tries to **align the time of your circadian clock** with the hours you are in bed.

If the CBT-I approach does not alleviate your sleep problems, there are several medications that can be used in conjunction with CBT-I. They must be used with care, as some of them can lead to misuse and dependence. A significant number of them can also cause side effects like next-day sleepiness, sleepwalking, and increased risk of automobile accidents. It should be noted that the American Association of Sleep Medicine 2017 practice guidelines for the use of medicines to treat chronic insomnia found that the data supporting the efficacy of medications was limited.[33] The classes of medications that it did find data on included the benzodiazepines (e.g., temazepam), the nonbenzodiazepine sedative-hypnotics (e.g., zolpidem), antihistamines (e.g., diphenhydramine), antidepressants (e.g., trazodone, doxepin), melatonin and melatonin-like drugs (e.g., ramelteon), and the more recently developed orexin blocker medications (e.g., suvorexant). The length of this list, which is not exhaustive, highlights two facts. First, insomnia is a problem for many people, and second, the currently available medications are not very effective.

If Sleep Disruption Causes Mood Problems, Why Did My Depression Get Better After I Pulled an All-Nighter in College?

In individuals with bipolar disorder, switches into manic episodes usually begin between 2:00 a.m. and 4:00 a.m. Observing this, several researchers have used sleep deprivation as an antidepressant treatment. Studies have shown that if a group of depressed people stay up all or most of the night, approximately two-thirds of them will not be depressed by morning.[34] Unfortunately, once they go back to sleep, their depressive symptoms will reemerge. It seems paradoxical, but sleep difficulties often herald depression relapses and are frequent during an acute episode of depression, while deliberate sleep deprivation for one or several nights in a row has antidepressant effects.

One of the more common ways that people find out they have an antidepressant or promanic response to sleep deprivation is through airplane travel across multiple time zones. One middle-aged woman I treated had been depressed for a number of years before her trip to New Zealand. She was very much looking forward to the trip and was not able to sleep during her flight. When she arrived, she noticed that her mood was much brighter, and it stayed that way for the duration of her trip. She never exhibited any signs of mania. About six months after her return home, her mood dropped again. Armed with the knowledge that her depression had been lifted by temporary sleep deprivation, and that she had an extensive list of medications she had tried and failed in the past, we tried a night of sleep deprivation. Again, her mood improved, and she stayed well for several months.

I must stress that this case is unusual. In our psychiatric emergency room, it is common for people without prior illness to be brought in from the airport in a manic, decompensated state after an overnight international flight.

Does Diet Really Matter That Much?

It probably will not surprise you to learn that the typical Western diet of high fat, high salt, and high sugar is associated with an increased risk of depression.[35] This diet often leads to obesity, which is thought to increase the risk of depression.[36] It has been proposed that one mechanism by which the Western diet and obesity can contribute to causing depression is through increased inflammation.

Whereas the Western diet may increase the risk of depression in vulnerable individuals, studies have found that traditional diets, such as the Mediterranean diet, with their emphasis on nonprocessed foods, especially fish, vegetables, fruit, and fiber, were associated with a 30 percent reduction in the risk of developing depression in university students.[37] More encouraging is the finding that dietary counseling in mildly depressed elderly adults was associated with a significant reduction in depression scores two years later.[38]

One question that is under active investigation is what about these diets causes their effects on mood. For the Western diet, the available data shows that repeatedly eating foods that cause a sudden rise in blood sugar leads to obesity, and this is related to inflammation.

The Western diet also changes the types of bacteria that live in the intestines, otherwise known as the microbiome. The changes induced in the microbiome increase the "leakiness" (permeability) of the intestines, allowing food particles to escape from the intestines into the bloodstream and trigger a local inflammatory response to what the body perceives as a foreign invader. The altered microbiome also produces a number of chemicals that can cross the blood-brain barrier and enter the brain, stressing it and decreasing the resilience of the circuitry that regulates mood.[39]

Another important pathway by which the intestines influence the brain is through the vagus nerve. The word *vagus* means "wandering" in Latin, and it reflects the vast area of the digestive system to which the vagus nerve sends and receives information. More specifically, it provides input into centers in the brainstem, which in turn provide input into the prefrontal areas of the brain that are an important component of the mood circuit. The vagus nerve provides a direct route for the intestines to tell the brain, "We are not doing well!" When this occurs chronically, it can trigger a depression, especially in those individuals who have an underlying vulnerability to a mood disorder.[40] The vagal nerve's direct connection to the brain is the basis for using vagal nerve stimulation to treat depression. I will discuss this treatment in greater detail in Chapter 11.

What About Supplements?

Remember Sam, whom I introduced earlier in this chapter? You may remember that we augmented their lamotrigine with fish oils. Fish oils and other nutritional supplements have been labeled nutraceuticals. As you might imagine, there are a number of supplements that have been tried in the treatment of depression. In addition to fish oils, they include probiotics, magnesium, zinc, and vitamin D, to name the most common. One limitation of the data about the nutraceuticals is that they have never been reviewed by the FDA for the treatment of mood disorders and there is debate about their benefits. Another thing to keep in mind as you think about supplements is whether they work in people who are not suffering from a dietary deficiency of the nutrient. For example, the antidepressant effects of zinc seem to be greatest in those who are deficient in zinc.[41]

The supplement I most frequently prescribe when trying to elevate mood by augmenting medications is omega-3 fatty acids. Most of the time this means fish oils. Some people who do not want to consume animal products will try alpha-linolenic acid, or ALA, but there is little data to support this, and my experience is that the omega-3 fatty acids eicosapentaenoic acid (EPA) and docosahexaenoic acid (DHA) have a stronger antidepressant effect.[42] I generally try to target a dose of 1000 mg of DHA and EPA combined. Some researchers have advocated for using one or the other, but there is data that the combination is effective, possibly additive.[43] Generally, the fish oils are well tolerated, but some preparations can leave a fishy taste or the "burps." When this occurs, I find that putting the capsules in the freezer and swallowing them while frozen eliminates the problem. If that does not work for you, there are brands of omega-3 fatty acids that claim not to have a fishy aftertaste. They can be expensive. But if you simply cannot tolerate the others, then they are an option you should be aware of.

In terms of the other supplements, probiotics have been reported to have an antidepressant effect working through the gut. As you probably know, the human gut is host to millions of bacteria that aid digestion and contribute to our general health. When those beneficial bacteria are replaced with bacteria that negatively impact digestion, they can cause inflammation and send out chemical signals that increase depression in the brain. If you are having gastrointestinal symptoms, such as bloating or flatulence, then a trial of probiotics may be helpful.[44] One thing to be careful about is making sure that the probiotic you choose has active cultures. Sitting on the shelf in a grocery store and crossing the stomach to get into the digestive tract can greatly reduce the number of active cultures available to improve your mood.[45]

Vitamin D supplementation has also been reported to have antidepressant effects. It appears that people with depression and vitamin D deficiency get the most benefit. Similarly, magnesium and zinc have shown antidepressant effects, but again those effects are most pronounced in people who start out with a deficiency.[46]

If you want to try any of these supplements, it is best to discuss them with your prescriber beforehand (especially to make sure there are no contraindications with any medications you are taking) and have baseline and monitoring blood levels drawn when they are available. For example, with magnesium, have a baseline level drawn and recheck it a week or two after starting the supplement to ensure you are not taking too much.

I Hear a Lot About Inflammation and Depression. Does Inflammation Cause Depression?

While chronic inflammation increases the risk and severity of depression, it is unlikely that inflammation alone causes mood disorders.[47] There are many people who do not have signs of increased inflammation in their bloodstream, yet they struggle with depression and other mood disorders. Also, these disorders tend to start when the person is young, when their brain is most resilient and can best tolerate the effects of short-term inflammation. What is more likely is that mood disorders cause a long-term increase in inflammation. Over time, this increases the wear and tear on the brain and decreases the resilience of the mood circuit as well as the rest of the body.

What Is Inflammation?

As you probably know, we live in a world that is full of disease-causing bacteria and viruses. Most of the time the immune system, which includes our white blood cells and a host of other circulating chemicals, prevents these potential invaders from causing serious illness. The immune system gets triggered when an infection occurs. An inflammatory response follows.

Since a picture is worth a thousand words, to get a better idea of what inflammation does, think about a sinus infection. Your nose is red, and your nasal passages are swollen. Everything is clogged up; you produce a lot of mucous that isn't clear, and you likely have a fever. What happened was that the virus or bacteria that caused the infection attacked some of the cells in the lining of your sinuses. Local immune cells recognized a foreign invader, and they began to attack. In the process they released chemicals that caused the blood vessels to become leaky and caused other white cells in the circulating blood to be called to the site of the infection. These cells also attacked and amplified the process until the bacteria causing the infection were eliminated. As part of the process a number of enzymes were activated and released to destroy the bacteria's membranes and other structures.

Among the chemicals produced were compounds known as free radicals. Under normal conditions, the production of free radicals is tightly controlled, and they are used for a number of important cellular functions, including energy production. When they are released during the inflammatory process, they damage cell membranes and proteins through a chemical process known as oxidation. This process is usually buffered by a class of chemicals called antioxidants. When the amount of oxidative activity exceeds the antioxidants, the body is considered to be under oxidative stress.[48] The proteins and other molecules damaged by oxidation then become recognized by the immune system as foreign and the cycle of inflammation continues. In the brain, this process can directly damage neurons and other cells that are important for the functioning of the mood circuit. It can also damage the lining of blood vessels and can cause blockages that reduce blood flow to important organs such as the heart and brain.[49] In short, the inflammatory response is protective and important for our survival in the microscopic jungle of germs in which we live. Inflammation becomes problematic when it becomes chronic and damages healthy tissue.

How Can I Tell If I Have Chronic Inflammation?

People have realized that inflammation plays an important role in many diseases and premature aging. As a result, there is a dizzying array of lab tests that you can do to measure inflammation. Unfortunately, our understanding of what the results mean and how to treat elevated values is still preliminary.

As a first step to figuring out whether you have increased inflammation, you can simply start by measuring your waist. To measure your waist, take a tape measure and start at the top of your hip and loop it around yourself so that it fits snugly. It should not pull any of your belly in, and the tape should be sitting at the level of the belly button. A waist circumference of greater than forty inches for men and thirty inches for women is associated with an increased risk of type 2 diabetes and cardiovascular disease. Inflammation contributes significantly to both diseases and likely reflects the increase in white fat that occurs in the abdomen with obesity. Over time people have found that the waist-to-height ratio somewhat increases the sensitivity of the measure in people of short stature.[50] However, the difference is small, and if you are close to having too large a waist, you should discuss it further with your doctor.

Some of the more commonly measured blood markers of inflammation to know about are C-reactive protein (CRP), tumor necrosis factor-alpha (TNF-α), and the interleukins.

CRP is a protein synthesized by the liver. During an infection, it binds to bacteria and damaged cells to aid the immune system in clearing them. CRP, which is measured in the blood, can be elevated in a number of conditions, including gum disease. Chronically elevated levels of CRP increase your risk of heart disease and type 2 diabetes and are associated with lower muscle mass.[51]

TNF-α is a protein with multiple functions. It is elevated in several autoimmune illnesses, such as psoriasis. It is one of a complex family of proteins that play a key role in the immune response. If too much TNF-α is released, it can cause damage to healthy cells. The elevated levels of TNF-α seen in chronic low-grade inflammation are thought to be produced by fatty tissue. Increased levels have been associated with prediabetes and type 2 diabetes, increased vascular disease, and dementia. Conversely, exercise is associated with decreases in TNF-α levels as well as reduced premature mortality.[52]

Interleukins are another major class of molecules that regulate the immune response on several levels. It is an area of active research, and the available data is sometimes contradictory and difficult to interpret. For example, interleukin-6 is considered proinflammatory, yet it is released in significant amounts by the muscles during exercise and exercise is anti-inflammatory.[53] There are some studies that show increased interleukin-6 in depressed individuals, while others do not.[54] At the time of this writing, researchers are still helping us learn how to interpret interleukin levels. What we have learned so far is not anything we can apply in treating patients in a clinic.

What Can I Do to Prevent Chronic Inflammation?

This is where the advice to exercise, improve diet, lose weight, and get more rest comes in. All four reduce chronic inflammation. We will discuss how each one is thought to do so, helping you treat your depression and, downstream, decrease recurrences of mood disorders.

How Does Exercise Reduce Inflammation?

I don't know about you, but the stiffness I feel every time I climb the stairs a few hours after a vigorous workout makes it very hard to believe that exercise can reduce inflammation. However, over time, each workout becomes easier: that is the difference between a single workout and regular exercise. The same is true for the inflammatory response to exercise. When you are starting out on an exercise program, you actually experience muscle injury that triggers an inflammatory response, hence the stiffness and pain. Over time blood flow and muscle mass increase, reducing the amount of injury that occurs with exercise. In addition, regular exercise increases the amount of anti-inflammatory proteins that are released during a workout. These proteins act to reduce the intensity of the inflammatory response to injury. So not only is there more muscle to manage the workload and therefore less damage, but there is also a muted response to any muscle injury. Even so, exercise creates a minor level of inflammation.

Regular exercise reduces inflammation overall, in part by increasing the efficiency of energy production and reducing oxidative stress. As we briefly touched on above, one of the main mechanisms by which chronic inflammation causes damage is oxidative stress. The cells use the oxidation process to convert sugars into a chemical known as adenosine triphosphate, or ATP. ATP powers most of the energy-requiring functions of cells. Under normal conditions, this process is well contained in a cellular structure, or organelle, known as mitochondria. As mitochondria age, they become "leaky," allowing free radicals to cause damage to the cell. Regular exercise causes cells to produce more mitochondria, thereby increasing the energy production capacity of the cells.[55] Also, the new mitochondria are better able to contain the electrons produced during ATP production.

Another mechanism by which exercise reduces inflammation is by changing the types of immune cells that populate the abdominal fat so that more of them are ones that reduce the magnitude of the inflammatory response when it is triggered.[56]

Lastly, it is worth noting that exercise also has direct effects on the brain, such as increasing plasticity—that is, the ability of certain parts of the brain to increase in volume and connectedness between neurons. The hippocampus, which is an important component of the mood circuit, is one of the brain regions whose volume increases with consistent exercise. Since increased volume is thought to reflect increased activity, this suggests that exercise reduces depression by increasing positive input from the hippocampus. Exercise also leads to an increased release of endorphins, neurotransmitters that act on the opiate system in the brain. Certain types of opiates have been shown to have direct antidepressant effects, and there is data that shows that endorphins are important in social functioning, which is reduced in depression.[57] Exercise also leads to a decrease in glutamate production and release. Based on the antidepressant effects of ketamine, excess glutamate release and neurotransmission is thought to play a central role in depression.

How Can Dietary Changes Lower Inflammation?

As we discussed, the Western diet emphasizes high-carbohydrate, calorie-dense meals and snacks. Believe it or not, this not only increases your waist circumference but also changes the type of fat in your belly. There are at least two types of fat: white and brown. White fat is pro-inflammatory while brown fat is anti-inflammatory. Diets that emphasize nutrient-dense whole foods, with minimal refined sugar, tend to not cause obesity and allow the anti-inflammatory brown fat of the body to be dominant.[58] These diets also promote the growth of healthier

bacteria in the intestines and reduce the inflammatory proteins produced in the intestines over the long term.

Can I Sleep My Way to Lower Inflammation?

If you are having trouble getting a restful night's sleep, then improving
your sleep routine will most likely help lower inflammation. Some people are very resilient and don't show the negative effects of inflammation even though they are not exercising, are overweight, and are having
sleep difficulties. The data indicates that there is a high likelihood they
will eventually suffer the results of excess and chronic inflammation.
Sleep problems have been associated with an increased risk of obesity
and early death.[59] They have also been associated with increased levels
of inflammatory proteins in the bloodstream of people both with and
without depression.[60]

In addition to poor sleep's effect on inflammation, research is exploring other explanations for the adverse health effects of sleep problems
and may offer a better explanation for why sleeplessness is so detrimen-
tal. Regardless of whether inflammation is mainly responsible for the
mood effects and sleep difficulties or not, treating insomnia has been
associated with a decrease in depressive symptoms and, most notably,
suicidal ideation.[61]

Key Takeaways

► Exercising, improving your diet, and dealing with sleep problems can significantly reduce your depression and improve your overall health.

► If it seems hard to change your habits, **know that using principles from the science of change, such as forming specific goals, "stacking habits," and rallying social supports can make the seemingly impossible achievable**.

► The type of exercise you do is less important than doing something enjoyable so that you are more likely to do it; 150 to 160 minutes of exercise per week is a reasonable target.

► Diets that minimize sugar content and emphasize lean proteins and vegetables—that is, nutrient-dense foods— can decrease obesity and improve your mood.

► Sleep disturbances are common, especially in depression and other mood disorders. Treating them can also help antidepressant treatments be more effective and improve overall health.

► Inflammation contributes to depression. People can get stuck in a vicious cycle where the inactivity caused by depression leads to elevated inflammation and the inflammation makes the depression worse.

► Exercise, a healthy diet, and regular sleep reduce inflammation.

Chapter 11

Up-and-Coming Treatments:
Hallucinogens, Psychedelics, VNS, and DBS

When you mention LSD, psylocibin, or mushrooms as a potential treatment for intractable depression, you get a range of reactions. People who have heard about their use in Silicon Valley and the stories of improved creativity and decreased anxiety will tune in and enthusiastically ask questions. People who have grown up thinking that drug use is harmful to your health or have experienced addiction in their family will express their misgivings fairly quickly. Most people will fall somewhere in between. The available data suggests that both sides are correct. Psychedelics and other hallucinogens (some of which you will learn about shortly) are very potent medications that seem to have powerful antidepressant and antianxiety effects.[1] However, in vulnerable people, such as those with a personal or family history of severe psychiatric illness (such as schizophrenia) or addiction, they can be quite dangerous. Even for people without those vulnerabilities, hallucinogens can be dangerous when used in the wrong setting and without appropriate support.[2]

You may ask, If these drugs are potentially dangerous, why continue trying to develop them as treatments for depression and anxiety? After all, they were effectively banned in 1967 when they were reclassified as schedule I drugs, the most restrictive classification possible, by the UN convention on drugs and the FDA. The reclassification ended their clinical use but was not based on side effects seen in clinical use or in research studies.[3] It was based on the realization that these compounds had "escaped" the clinic and the lab and were being used by people without the guidance of a medical health professional.

Why Are Psychedelics Illegal?

In his book *How to Change Your Mind: What the New Science of Psychedelics Teaches Us About Consciousness, Dying, Addiction, Depression, and Transcendence*, Michael Pollan argues that psychedelics were banned because they were fueling a counterculture that was increasingly unwilling to fight an unpopular war in Vietnam. The full story is more complicated and colorful than that.[4]

In the 1950s, the Central Intelligence Agency (CIA) started giving unsuspecting people LSD; it stopped the experiment in 1964 after deciding LSD was too dangerous. In the 1960s, Timothy Leary and Richard Alpert, of Harvard University, "discovered" psychedelics and began experimenting with LSD. Soon after, they and others began "preaching" about these drugs, and their recreational use increased significantly, especially among those in the anti–Vietnam War movement. People were using them without appropriate safeguards over extended periods of time.[5]

With increased use came reports of LSD-induced mental illnesses and psychosis-induced violence as well as accidental deaths from LSD-induced delusions. It was not uncommon to hear of people who had jumped off buildings while under the influence of LSD or some other psychedelic. This, combined with an increasing epidemic of abuse of other drugs, such as opiates and stimulants, led to a change in society's and the medical establishment's view of the psychedelics. Even some people who had viewed psychedelics as medications capable of providing a profound calming and life-changing mystical experience now saw them as dangerous drugs. This led to the 1967 reclassification, and possession of psychedelics was outlawed in the United States in 1968.

Why Are Psychedelics and Hallucinogens Being Studied Now?

Despite their negative image, interest in the therapeutic potential of psychedelics and hallucinogens persists because of their positive effects, especially the profound sense of peace and mystical experiences reported by patients with terminal cancer. The more recent success of ketamine in treating depression has also contributed to renewed interest in the potential for using hallucinogens to treat other types of depression and mental illness. Depression, anxiety, and trauma are leading causes of disability throughout the world. The amount of suffering caused by these illnesses justifies an aggressive search for better treatments.[6]

In addition to patient need, there are three other broad trends that have fueled the interest in developing psychedelics for the clinic. First was the realization that not much progress had been made in developing new antidepressants since the introduction of the SSRIs. This reached its peak in 2010 when a major pharmaceutical company announced it was stopping its research into antidepressant medications altogether.[7] Second was the popularity of festivals such as Burning Man, with their emphasis on expanded consciousness, and separate reports of microdosing of LSD in Silicon Valley to enhance cognition and creativity. These experiences brought together psychedelics and people who could afford to sponsor research into their potential. Lastly, the discovery of the antidepressant properties of ketamine contributed greatly to the acceptance of this line of research.

Despite an exceptional physical safety profile, ketamine's clinical use was waning until recently. On the street, it was known to cause a dissociative high (feelings of being detached from yourself and your senses) and was often abused. The finding that it had significant benefit in severe depression and that its risk of abuse could be managed supported the idea that the same could be true for other psychedelics. This was further supported by a long history of safety in religious and medicinal uses of some of these compounds. Naturally occurring psychedelics, such as psilocybin, which is found in certain types of nonpoisonous mushrooms, had been used by the native peoples of Mexico and Central America in religious ceremonies for centuries before the Spanish "discovered" the Americas.[8] Peyote, which is made from cactus and contains mescaline, is still used in Native American tribal religious ceremonies.

Prior to its reclassification in 1967, LSD was extensively studied. Early research reported positive clinical effects not only in depression but also in treating the distress and reactive depression seen in people with terminal illnesses, post-traumatic stress disorder, obsessive-compulsive disorder, alcohol dependence, and nicotine dependence. However, these research studies were mostly done with less statistically rigorous designs than are required today, so the conclusions that can be drawn based on their results are limited. Nonetheless, they did include a total of almost forty thousand subjects and attest to the safety of these medications when used by skilled clinicians.[9]

As of this writing, there are over two hundred clinical trials listed for psychedelics and hallucinogens on the ClinicalTrials.gov website of the US National Library of Medicine. We still don't have FDA approval for the use of psychedelics, but I'd like to walk you through what these drugs are, dispel some myths, and provide information on how they may be instrumental in the future treatment of depression.

Are There Different Types of Hallucinogens?

Hallucinogens fall into three classes: dissociative anesthetics, psychedelics, and entactogens[10] (Table 11.1 lists some of the common members of each of these classes). The dissociative anesthetics, such as ketamine and esketamine, as we discussed earlier, are now well-established antidepressants. They are thought to act by blocking the activity of the NMDA subtype of the glutamate receptor, and although they can produce hallucinations, they primarily cause a mind-body disconnection or dissociation. Psychedelics, such as psilocybin and LSD, primarily act by enhancing the action of the serotonin type 2A receptor and produce classical visual, auditory, and tactile hallucinations.[11] But it is the mystical experiences that usually occur while a person is under the influence of psychedelics that have potential for treating anxiety and depression. People often describe these experiences as "transformative" and as giving them a sense of connectedness that has deep personal meaning. The entactogens, such as MDMA, or ecstasy, induce a state of increased empathy and social connection. Mechanistically, they act on several brain systems. They block the serotonin, norepinephrine, and dopamine reuptake transporters to increase levels of these chemicals. They can also cause an increase in the release of the hormones oxytocin, vasopressin, and cortisol.[12] As you know, serotonin, norepinephrine, and dopamine are neurotransmitters that boost mood. Oxytocin is a hormone that is released during physically intimate moments, such as when hugging, cuddling, or having an orgasm (in short, experiences that increase the person's sense of psychological closeness). While most people think of cortisol as a stress hormone, it can also produce a sense of well-being or even euphoria. As you might expect from the increased sense of connection they generate in people, entactogens also seem to have positive effects when added to psychotherapy, especially for PTSD.

Table 11.1: Common Hallucinogens (and their street names)

Psychedelics	Dissociative Anesthetics	Entactogens
Psilocybin (magic mushrooms)	Phencyclidine (PCP)	Methylenedioxyethylamphetamine (MDMA, ecstasy, or molly)
D-lysergic acid dieth-ylamide (LSD)	Ketamine (special K) Esketamine	+ 3,4 -methylenedioxyamphetamine (MDA, sass)
Peyote	Dextromethorphan (DXM)	Mephedrone (meow meow)
Mescaline		
N, N-dimethyltrypt-amine (DMT)		Methylone
Ayahuasca		

What Are the Risks?

When people hear about using psychedelic medications to treat psychiatric illness, they often get a puzzled look on their faces. They usually think of these medications as ruining lives through addiction. While there is some data that these drugs can be habit forming and that people can develop tolerance to them, they do not appear to have the same addictive potential as drugs like alcohol, opiates, or cocaine. Anecdotally, LSD is thought to have contributed to the sobriety of Bill Wilson, the cofounder of Alcoholics Anonymous.[13] In addition, prior to psychedelics being banned, there were six clinical trials using LSD to treat alcoholism. A recent reanalysis of that data affirmed that LSD was effective for treating alcohol addiction.[14] More recent studies using psilocybin have also shown efficacy in treating alcohol use disorder and smoking.[15]

People sometimes fear psychedelic medications because these drugs have been known to cause chronic psychotic illnesses. Ingesting the drug can result in hallucinations and other perceptual disturbances that resemble acute psychosis. Usually, these symptoms end when the drug is cleared from the body. Unfortunately, some people who have used hallucinogens recreationally have gone on to develop chronic psychotic disorders. But remember these diseases also occur in people who have never used hallucinogens. Also, the people using them recreationally are usually in their late teens and early twenties. This is the prime window of vulnerability for developing chronic psychotic illnesses such as schizophrenia and schizoaffective disorder. The people who develop a chronic psychotic disorder were likely to develop it whether or not they used the drug. The problem is that there is no way to know who is vulnerable beforehand, except for those who have had prior episodes or have a family history of illness. This underscores the need to not use these medications on your own. If you want to find out whether these medications can help your depression or your PTSD, work with a practitioner who has experience assessing people for these medications and administering them. At present, this usually means signing up for a clinical research study.

What Is a "Bad Trip"?

With any medication that induces hallucinations, it is possible to have an intense unpleasant experience, or a "bad trip." Emergency rooms have surely seen their share of patients going through one. One of the first recorded bad trips with LSD was described by Dr. Albert Hoffman, the chemist who first synthesized the drug. He described it as follows: "Familiar objects and pieces of furniture assumed grotesque, threatening forms. They were in continuous motion, animated as if driven by an inner restlessness. . . . A demon had invaded me, taken possession of my body, mind, and soul. I jumped up and screamed, trying to free myself from him, but then sank down and lay helpless on the sofa. . . . My ego was suspended somewhere in space and I saw my body lying dead on the sofa."[16]

Today's clinical trials have a number of safeguards in place to manage any unpleasant effects of hallucinogens. Specifically, people have realized that the setting is important. Instead of a sterile clinic room, researchers now use comfortable rooms with sofas and a male and female guide to sit with the patient. They also pay attention to the person's mindset. They now prep patients, use calming medications when needed, and help people process the experience afterward. Clearly, this is a very different experience than the average recreational user has and highlights the need to use these powerful medications under medical supervision.[17]

What Does Research Tell Us About These Medications' Effectiveness?

The results of the studies I mention here suggest these medications can be quite effective for treating depression, anxiety, psychological distress that results from life transitions (bolstering psychotherapy), and alcohol dependence, among others. What is unique about these medications is that they not only reduce symptoms of illness but also often cause a mystical experience that has positive benefits in healthy individuals without psychiatric symptoms. The modern studies that have reported results to date are mostly small ones designed to lay the foundation for the larger trials needed for FDA approval. While the following list is not exhaustive, it will give you an idea of the type of studies that are going on and what researchers are learning.

Psychedelics

It has long been recognized that a diagnosis of a terminal illness can create tremendous distress and impair quality of life in a significant number of people. One of the most consistent findings from the early work with LSD and psilocybin was that users often described a profoundly positive and mystical experience with an enduring sense of peace. When researchers got the approval to begin to explore the therapeutic potential of the psychedelics, they started with terminally ill cancer patients.

Dr. Roland Griffiths and colleagues at Johns Hopkins Bayview Medical Center studied the effects of very low-dose versus high-dose psilocybin in fifty-one cancer patients with life-threatening diagnoses and anxiety and/or depression. The study used a crossover design so that each person got both doses, but they were randomized as to which they received first. Greater than 80 percent of the study subjects reported improved well-being and life satisfaction with the greatest effects occurring after the high-dose treatment. Also, a mystical-type response to psilocybin correlated with long-term improvement.[18]

Another major mental health issue people struggle with is depression, which has been made even worse by the COVID pandemic. The antidepressant effects of LSD and the other psychedelics were well described before they were banned. One of the problems with the prior studies was their design: everybody knew which subjects received the LSD. The most rigorous study design for evaluating a new drug is to use a double-blind placebo-controlled study. In this design neither the subject nor the researcher evaluating the effects of the drug know which treatment the person received. A challenging problem in designing this type of study for psychedelics is what to use for the inactive comparator so that the subject does not know which treatment they received.[19] As soon as the subject has a hallucination, both the subject and the rater know which treatment it is.

Despite these methodological challenges, Dr. Robin Carhart-Harris and colleagues at Imperial College in London just reported on their study of fifty-nine subjects with major depression.[20] They compared a regular dose (25 mg) of psilocybin combined with a placebo to a microdose (1 mg) of psilocybin with the antidepressant (SSRI) escitalopram (10–20 mg). In both arms of the study, the psilocybin was dosed only twice with a three-week interval between doses. The placebo and escitalopram were given daily for six weeks. At the end of the trial, the antidepressant response and remission rate were greater in the group that received the two regular doses of psilocybin than in the group that received six weeks of daily escitalopram, but the difference did not reach statistical significance.[21]

One key takeaway from the studies has to do with the simple facts of administering the treatment. As described, when administering psychedelics therapeutically, it is important to learn from the early experiences with these medications and prepare and support the patient emotionally and provide a safe environment. That means professionals are on hand with medications and training to make the patient comfortable should they begin to have an unpleasant experience. In all three of these studies, subjects were provided supportive psychological guidance during the administration of the psilocybin.

An important point that bears repeating about these studies is that they are small initial proof-of-concept studies. By definition, their findings need to be verified by research studies involving larger groups of people. However, their results are consistent with the earlier human studies done in the 1960s as well as studies done in animal models that are used to screen for antidepressants and antianxiety medications. These findings are also supported by brain imaging studies that show changes in functional connectivity in the mood circuit similar to those we see with other antidepressant treatments.[22]

Dissociative Anesthetics

I described the antidepressant effects of the dissociative anesthetics, mostly ketamine and esketamine, in previous chapters. To briefly recap, ketamine has demonstrated antidepressant effects in pilot studies that looked for a glutamate-based antidepressant mechanism, as well as several follow-up studies. However, the studies needed for FDA approval are cost-prohibitive because the patent on ketamine has run out. Fortunately, esketamine, a constituent of ketamine, has shown antidepressant effects in large multicenter, controlled studies. It has received FDA approval as an add-on medication to boost antidepressant treatment. The challenges are side effects and being able to access treatment and have it paid for.

Entactogens

The most commonly used entactogen is MDMA. **While it falls under the hallucinogen label, MDMA generally does not cause hallucinations.** It has been shown to primarily increase the person's sense of connection and feelings of trust and empathy. These changes in the person's emotional state can be explained by MDMA's effects on neurotransmitters in the brain in combination with its effects on hormones such as oxytocin, which facilitates interpersonal connectedness (for example, maternal-child bonding). As such, MDMA has been explored as an adjunct to psychotherapy, particularly when the patient has post-traumatic stress disorder (PTSD) and is flooded by negative memories of their trauma. With PTSD, patients often cannot tolerate their feelings long enough to stay in treatment.

The effectiveness of MDMA-augmented psychotherapy in PTSD has been reported in six clinical trials. A recent analysis of the long-term (twelve months or greater) follow-up data from those six trials was recently published by Dr. Lisa Jerome and colleagues.[23] One to two months after the final MDMA-assisted psychotherapy session, 56 percent of subjects no longer exhibited enough symptoms to meet criteria for a diagnosis of PTSD. By the twelve-month posttreatment assessment, that number had climbed to 67 percent. This contrasts with the limited relief provided by traditional antidepressants, sedatives, and antiseizure medications that are the medications currently used to treat this illness. PTSD symptoms have caused a great deal of suffering and even suicide in a great number of people afflicted with the illness. Because of the positive results of these studies and data showing MDMA's safety, a large-scale multicenter trial is underway at the time of this writing.

What About Side Effects?

As I noted previously, it is true that in vulnerable people, hallucinogens can trigger episodes of major mental illnesses. Currently there is no way to know who is vulnerable beforehand. We do know that those who have had prior episodes or who have a strong family history of psychotic illnesses and addiction are at increased risk. In addition to potentially triggering these illnesses, these compounds have side effects that reflect their chemical activities in the body.[24]

Let us consider some of these compounds in greater detail, skipping over ketamine and esketamine, which you learned about in Part II. The information here is not intended to be exhaustive, but it will give you a good foundation for understanding what we know about hallucinogens used for depression treatment.

Psilocybin

Recreational use of psilocybin has been associated with visual hallucinations, an altered perception of time, anxiety, panic, and paranoia. Similar to the other hallucinogens, excessive use has been associated with persistent hallucinations and other visual disturbances such as halos and trails attached to moving objects. In contrast, in clinical trials, where subjects are given a limited number of doses that are usually spread out over time, the incidence of persistent side effects has been minimal. The typical psychological adverse effects seen with psilocybin include an altered sense of self and time, anxiety, confusion, and paranoia. Physical side effects include headache, nausea, trembling, palpitations, and increased blood pressure and heart rate. The good news is that these effects have usually been limited to the duration of the drug in the body. In clinical trials, there have been *no* long-term side effects.[25]

LSD

LSD has many of the same properties as psilocybin, and both drugs' side effect profiles are similar. The psychological side effects experienced shortly after ingestion of LSD include anxiety, panic attacks, paranoia, visual hallucinations, a sense of being disconnected from your body and reality, and a mixing of auditory and visual phenomena, or synesthesia. The physical side effects are also similar to psilocybin: increased heart rate, blood pressure, body temperature, and pupil size while under the influence of the drug.

The best-known delayed side effect of LSD is the "flashback," or delayed reexperiencing of a trip days, weeks, months, or even perhaps years afterward. When flashbacks cause significant distress or anxiety and impair function, they are classified as hallucinogen-persisting perception disorder. Of note, subjects who participated in current research studies and/or have past clinical experience have rarely reported such significant flashbacks. These findings suggest that the amount of LSD ingested and the frequency with which it is taken contribute to the development of hallucinogen-persisting perception disorder. Likewise, there are some reports of LSD triggering aggression. The data on this is very limited, but what is available indicates that it is a rare side effect and that individuals with underlying psychiatric illnesses were most at risk.

MDMA

When used in a therapeutic setting with pharmaceutical-grade medication, MDMA is generally well tolerated with fewer than 8.4 percent of research participants reporting an adverse effect during the treatment phase and only 3.1 percent reporting persistence of those symptoms at twelve months.[26] Most of the adverse effects that have been described with MDMA use are those seen with recreational use and misuse. Adverse effects experienced in the short term when under the influence of MDMA can include teeth clenching or grinding, chills, sweating, blurred vision, nausea, and muscle cramping. Delayed effects commonly seen after moderate use of the drug include irritability, aggressiveness, depression, anxiety, sleep difficulties, and memory and attentional problems. This cluster of symptoms, sometimes seen after a weekend of recreational use, has the nickname of "hangover Tuesday."

It is very important that MDMA not be taken with a selective serotonin reuptake inhibitor (SSRI) or serotonin norepinephrine reuptake inhibitor (SNRI) antidepressant, such as fluoxetine (Prozac), escitalopram (Lexapro), or venlafaxine (Effexor). The combination can lead to serotonin syndrome, which involves a very high buildup of serotonin in the system and is characterized by muscle rigidity, increased reflexes, and fever. Importantly, **serotonin syndrome is potentially lethal**.

What Is Microdosing?

Microdosing of psychedelics has recently gained some attention in the mainstream press. In the case of psychedelics, it refers to the practice of taking doses of LSD or psilocybin that are much smaller than the doses needed to produce hallucinations. The practice has been used by engineers, creative artists, and others as a way of increasing creativity and cognitive performance. Other reported uses of microdosing include treating depression, migraines, chronic fatigue syndrome, and anxiety. Dr. Daniel Rosenbaum and colleagues surveyed 729 subjects via social media, 414 of whom reported microdosing of LSD, psilocybin, or both.[27] One of their more interesting findings was that 20 percent of the people who microdosed reported suffering from ADHD. They note that there is very little safety data on this practice of repeated dosing and strongly advocate for well-designed clinical trials to better understand its potential benefits as well as the risks.[28]

The discovery of ketamine and the rebirth of the psychedelics, dissociative anesthetics, and entactogens (MDMA) has provided new ways of thinking about depression and anxiety disorders. Although these medications have shown a potential for abuse when used outside of the medical clinic, in the hands of skilled professionals who know how to prepare the patient and guide the experience, they have been shown to be safe and have a relatively low risk of misuse.

The majority of the safety data is from the earlier trials that did not use modern clinical trial methodologies. More data on safety and efficacy is needed before these approaches can be adopted in mainstream clinical practice, and more data is needed on dosages that are safe and effective, but hallucinogens offer significant hope for those suffering from depression and anxiety that has been resistant to current treatments.

Finally, I want to touch on two other treatments that have been showing promising outcomes.

Vagal Nerve Stimulation

You may remember that we briefly discussed how the vagus nerve connects the brain with the gut and that the gut can affect a person's mood. It turns out that stimulating the vagus nerve directly with electricity and indirectly with magnets can have antidepressant effects.[29] Vagal nerve stimulation (VNS) was first developed as an add-on treatment for the management of seizures in the early 1990s by the Cyberonics corporation. During the epilepsy clinical trials, it was noticed that people with depressive symptoms felt better, irrespective of whether their seizure control improved.[30] This led to some initial pilot studies and a large multicenter clinical trial.[31] The data from these studies was sufficiently positive that the FDA cleared the device for use in treatment-resistant depression. However, insurance companies, who were used to the standard of the FDA requiring effectiveness in two large multicenter trials as the basis of approval, argued that it was still an experimental treatment. If this is confusing, it was for me as well at the time. The issue reflected the difference between the devices division of the FDA clearing a device and the pharmaceuticals division of the FDA approving a new medication. The net effect is that it was difficult to get for patients.

One patient whom I was able to get approval for was Britney. Britney was a thirty-four-year-old divorced mother of two whose depression started after the birth of her second child. Over the course of the next three years, she tried multiple antidepressant medications, mood stabilizers, augmenting antipsychotics, and ECT along with intensive psychotherapy. She was hospitalized six times, and the hospitalizations were intense and stormy. After she had her vagal nerve stimulator placed, her course began to slowly change. Over the next three years, she was hospitalized only three times. The hospitalizations were less intense and shorter. Her mood also began to improve slowly, and she was gradually able to begin participating in her children's lives again. Her medications were simplified, the frequency of her ECT was reduced, and she feels well.

When it was initially developed, VNS involved surgically implanting a wire around the left vagus nerve in the neck and running that wire down to a pacemaker that was implanted outside the rib cage in the upper left chest. After recovering from the surgery, patients tolerated it pretty well. The pacemaker was set to stimulate the nerve every few minutes, and this caused the person's voice to quaver. Patients were given a magnet by which they could pause the pacer if they had to do any public speaking or other activity where they did not want their voice to change. Today, there are two noninvasive approaches to VNS that are being explored, one that applies magnetic stimulation to the neck and one that applies magnetic stimulation to the ear.[32] It turns out the vagus, or "wandering nerve,"[33] really lives up to its name and has a branch that innervates the ear.

At this point it is not clear which type of VNS will prove most beneficial nor is it clear which patients will benefit most from it. However, it does have antidepressant effects, and you should discuss with your treaters if it makes sense in your case.

Deep Brain Stimulation

Throughout this book we have presented depression as a disease of the mood circuit. With VNS we have just discussed implanting pacemakers and wires on a permanent basis to indirectly stimulate the brain. There are still patients who do not get better despite heroic medication trials, psychotherapy, and the other interventions discussed in this book. The next logical step is to implant electrodes into the components of the mood circuit in the brain. That is just what a couple of research groups did. It is called deep brain stimulation, or DBS. Helen Mayberg's group at Emory University in Atlanta and others reported promising results in small open-label clinical trials that did not replicate in a larger-scale multicenter trial.[34] For the moment, interest in using DBS to treat depression seems to have waned, but it has been shown to be effective in treating Parkinson's disease. This has led to the development of adaptive deep brain stimulation, which adjusts the intensity of the stimulation to the brain's underlying activity.[35] Whether this approach will prove useful in depression remains to be seen.

The combination of dextromethorphan and buproprion as the compounded medication Auvelty utilizes two approaches to treating depression described earlier in this book: targeting the NMDA receptor and blocking the cytochrome P450 enzymes in the liver that break down medications to increase the time they can act in the brain. Dextromethorphan blocks the NMDA receptor and the sigma opioid receptor in a manner similar to ketamine. But when taken alone it is inactivated by the cytochrome P450 2D6 enzyme in the liver too quickly to produce an antidepressant response. The addition of a low dose of the antidepressant bupropion partially blocks the enzyme and triples the amount of time the dextromethorphan circulates in the body. In two large-scale clinical trials, the combination showed an antidepressant response in one to two weeks. In the first trial the combination was compared to a placebo. The second trial compared the combination to low-dose bupropion alone, confirming that dextromethorphan is the active antidepressant.[36]

If you are considering a trial of ketamine or esketamine, you should ask your prescriber about this option, which does not require the extensive in-person monitoring needed with ketamine and esketamine.

Key Takeaways

► Psilocybin given along with psychological support has the potential to alleviate the severe anxiety and depression frequently seen in terminal cancer patients.

► Preliminary data also suggests that it has potential as an antidepressant in treatment-resistant depression.

► MDMA combined with psychotherapy has shown significantly positive results in the treatment of PTSD.

► MDMA must not be combined with SSRI or SNRI antidepressants so as to avoid serotonin syndrome, which can be lethal.

► When used in a controlled setting for a limited number of doses, the potential for addiction to these medications so far appears to be low.

► The results of research into hallucinogens' effectiveness in treating depression are just one of the reasons to be hopeful about relieving depression even when your depression has been treatment resistant.

► Deep brain stimulation (DBS) has shown efficacy in certain brain disorders, such as Parkinson's disease, but for depression it has struggled to reproduce the antidepressant effects seen in small trials.

► Vagal nerve stimulation (VNS) has been cleared by the FDA for the treatment of depression. Clinical trials are underway to better define how to tailor the treatment to the patient and optimize treatment response.

Afterword:
Hope for the Future

Thank you for taking the time to read this book. I titled the introduction of this book "Don't Give Up Hope," and *hope* is a word I would also like to leave you with. The partner of one of my patients said it much better than I ever could. Her partner underwent one of the treatments in this book. She described their experience like this: "Before working with you, we were told that we had tried pretty much everything, and I did not see a path ahead. I thank you not only for working so closely with us to find an effective treatment but also for showing us that there is—and always will be—hope. At our lowest lows, both of these things, the effective treatments and this hope, made all the difference in the world." The treatments discussed in this book have been life changing for many people, and my hope is that you will find one that works for you.

Resources

Suicide Prevention

US National Suicide Prevention Lifeline: 800-273-8255, text TALK to 741741 or go to https://www.SpeakingOfSuicide.com/resources

Samaritans Suicide Prevention Hotline: https://samaritanshope.org

General

Depression and Bipolar Support Alliance: https://www.dbsalliance.org

National Alliance on Mental Illness: https://www.nami.org

Substance Abuse and Mental Health Services Administration: https://www.samhsa.gov/find-help/national-helpline

Centers for Disease Control, Tools and Resources: https://www.cdc.gov/mentalhealth

Therapy

Psychology Today: https://www.psychologytoday.com

Healthline: https://www.healthline.com/mental-health

Sleep Foundation: https://www.sleepfoundation.org/insomnia/treatment/cognitive-behavioral-therapy-insomnia

Sleep, CBT-I: https://mobile.va.gov/app/cbt-i-coach

Transcranial Magnetic Stimulation

Transcranial Magnetic Stimulation: https://www.neurostar.com

Deep Transcranial Magnetic Stimulation: https://www.brainsway.com/patients-faqs/find-deep-tms-therapy-near-me

Esketamine

Esketamine: https://www.spravato.com (click on the Find a Center tab)

ECT

International Society for ECT and Neurostimulation: https://www.isen-ect.org/find-a-provider

Appendix A: Questions to Ask at an Initial Consultation

ECT/TMS/Esketamine Consultation

1. **Do You Think My Condition Is Likely to Respond to the Treatment?**
   While there have been some reports of predictors of response, they are not robust enough to guide an individual's treatment.

   Esketamine is approved by the FDA for use in treatment-resistant depression and major depression with suicidal behavior. TMS has been cleared by the FDA for the treatment of major depression, obsessive-compulsive disorder, and smoking cessation. ECT has been cleared by the FDA to treat major depression and catatonia. It is also used to treat refractory cases of mania.

   Your access to these different treatment options can vary depending on where you live. You may find that your treatment team strongly favors one over the others or that one of these treatments is better suited to the supports available to you (rides, for example). In which case, these considerations are likely to guide your treatment.

2. **How Many Treatments Are Typically Given for My Condition?**
   An acute course of TMS is usually about thirty treatments spread out over six weeks. Additional treatment is usually only given if there is improvement but persistence or reemergence of symptoms. An acute course of esketamine is twice weekly for four weeks followed by maintenance treatment. An acute course of ECT is usually six to ten

treatments administered on a three-times-a-week schedule, and maintenance treatments are sometimes needed. As with all of these, your treatment team should have a clear-cut plan for handling any reemergence of symptoms.

3. **How Long Have You Been Administering the Treatment?**

   In medicine, practice matters. With experience, your treaters get used to anticipating and preventing side effects and other problems. Therefore, it is reasonable to ask how much experience the practice has administering the treatment.

4. **Is My Insurance Accepted by the Practice?**

   The reality is that these treatments are costly and if not covered by insurance out of reach for many patients.

5. **How Do You Handle Emergencies?**

   Most side effects from these treatments are short-lived and handled by the staff on site. Sometimes treatments can trigger heart conditions and other health issues that require more intensive treatment. Most facilities that are not in hospitals send these patients to a hospital. If the hospital they send you to is not covered by your insurance, things can get expensive quickly. After going through all that, getting a large medical bill is the last thing you need.

Psychotherapy Consultation

1. **Is My Insurance Accepted by the Practice?**

   Therapists handle finances in many different ways. Certain therapists (including psychiatrists) only accept cash payments; others, only certain insurances. It might be very disruptive to you if you start a therapy you cannot afford to finish or one that puts you into significant debt unless you have no other options.

2. **How Long Do You Usually Work with a Person?**

   Some types of therapy have a very time-limited, focused approach. This usually works better when the problem has recently started or is very limited in nature. Other types of therapy take a less focused approach and may go deeper into the root of the problem.

3. **How Much Guidance Do You Usually Give?**

   Some therapists use a skills-based approach and are very directive by design. They may even give homework. Other therapists try to say very little on purpose. The goal is to guide the patient to their own solutions. This approach works to ensure that it is the patient who solves the problem. The most important point is that you know there are different approaches, and if your current therapy is not working, then you should discuss it with your therapist.

4. **What Do You Think My Main Issue Is?**

   After the practitioner has taken your history, they should be able to give you their understanding of why you are starting therapy. This should be fairly consistent with your view of why you are starting therapy. Some people describe it as an ah-ha moment where they feel that somebody finally understands what they are going through.

5. **Does Your Usual Approach Generally Work for This Problem?**

   This is intended to politely ask if the therapist has had much success with patients whose symptoms are similar to yours.

Appendix B: Information to Bring with You to a Consultation

The Current Episode

Mood Symptoms

1. When did you start to not feel well or feel different?
2. What changed first when it started?
3. Why are you coming in for this consultation at this time?
4. Were there any changes in your sleep, your appetite, or your ability to focus?
5. How is your energy level?
6. Do you feel very optimistic or that you can do things others can't?
7. Are you more irritable than usual?

Anxiety Symptoms

1. Did you start to feel more anxious? Did you have panic attacks?
2. Has this episode brought back memories of past trauma?
3. Has it caused any of them to worsen or be more intense?

Psychotic Symptoms

1. Do you hear voices when you are alone? Can you stop the voices if you want?
2. Have you had any unusual experiences, such as seeing people or things that weren't there?

Recreational Substance Use

1. How often and how much alcohol do you drink?
2. How much cannabis/THC/edibles are you using? How often?
3. Are you using any other substances regularly?

Your Safety

1. Have things ever been so bad that you have thought of killing yourself?
2. Have you ever done anything to prepare for ending your life?
3. Have you ever attempted to kill yourself?
4. Have you ever thought of hurting yourself?
5. Have you ever taken steps to prepare for hurting yourself?
6. Have you ever done anything to hurt yourself?

Current Treatment

1. Do you have a therapist or counselor? If yes, how often do you meet with them?
2. Do you feel they are helpful and focused on what's important to you?
3. Do you have a treater who prescribes you medication?
4. If yes, what medications are you taking?
5. When did you start them?
6. Do you take medicines for other medical conditions? Which ones and at what doses?

Past Episodes

1. Have you ever felt like this before?
2. Have you ever been hospitalized psychiatrically before?
3. Have you been treated with psychiatric medications in the past?
4. Which ones? Please give doses and how long you took them for if possible (see suggested worksheet at the end of these questions).
5. Did any of them help? Do you remember why you stopped them?
6. Have you ever had therapy for a similar problem in the past?
7. Was it helpful?

Developmental History

1. Did your mother have any health problems when she was carrying you?
2. Did she catch the flu during her pregnancy with you?
3. Any issues with your birth?
4. Did you require any special care or intensive care (NICU) as a newborn?
5. Did you walk, talk, read (hit developmental milestones) on time?
6. Did you have problems sitting still or focusing in the early grades?
7. If yes, do you still have them today?

Social History

1. Who do you live with today?
2. Are there any issues at home?
3. Is anyone making you feel unsafe at home or elsewhere?
4. Do you have a best friend?
5. Do you have supportive friendships?
6. How do you support yourself?
7. Are there any issues at work?
8. How are your finances?

Suggested Medication Worksheet

Current Medications

Medication	Maximum Dose	When Started	Response: Yes/No/ Partial	Side Effects

Past Medication Trials

Medication	Maximum Dose	How Long Taken	Response: Yes/No/ Partial	Reason for Stopping

Acknowledgments

There are many people who contributed to this book in so many ways, and I owe each of them a debt of gratitude. I would like to start by thanking my wife, Dot, and our grown children, Paul, Nikki, and Mike, for their sustained support and tolerance of the time and mental energy taken over the years to pursue my career and, especially, to write this book. I also owe a deep debt of gratitude to the talented individuals who were my teachers and not only taught me information but also inspired me to pursue psychiatry and ways to improve the treatment of severe mood disorders. I also want to thank my current and past colleagues, especially the ones who took time to read and comment on parts of this manuscript. Your collective drive for excellence in patient care and research motivates me to reach inside for my best effort every day.

Most importantly, I want to thank my patients. You have given me the privilege of working with you on your journey to restoring your health. Along the way I have gotten to know you as people and appreciate how hard you work to get better every day. I hope you see this book as a snapshot of what you have taught me and hope that you find it useful in your journey.

As with any endeavor, there are also the people who make things work and who I would like to thank for their efforts and support. Irene Goodman, my agent, who identified the need for this book and then found a way to get it published. Renee Sedliar, my patient editor, who kept the book focused and on track and provided very helpful feedback. Jennifer Crane, my book editor, who provided very helpful and timely editing that kept the project moving forward. And the rest of the team at Hachette Go: Alison Dalafave, Julianne Lewis, Zach Polendo, Mike Giarratano, Michael Barrs, Michelle Aielli, and Mary Ann Naples, who believed in the book from the beginning and worked to get it out into the world.

Notes

1 Introduction

1. Klaus Martiny, "Novel Augmentation Strategies in Major Depression," *Danish Medical Journal* 64, no. 4 (2017): 277–89; Agnès Le Port, Alice Gueguen, Emmanuelle Kesse-Guyot, Maria Melchior, Cédric Lemogne, Hermann Nabi, Marcel Goldberg, Marie Zins, and Sébastien Czernichow, "Association between Dietary Patterns and Depressive Symptoms Over Time: A 10-Year Follow-Up Study of the GAZEL Cohort," *PLoS ONE* 7, no. 12 (2012): e51593, doi:10.1371/journal.pone.0051593.

2. Waguih William IsHak, Khanh Ha, Nina Kapitanski, Kara Bagot, Hassan Fathy, Brian Swanson, Jennice Vilhauer, Konstantin Balayan, Nestor Ian Bolotaulo, and Mark Hyman Rapaport, "The Impact of Psychotherapy, Pharmacotherapy, and Their Combination on Quality of Life in Depression," *Harvard Review of Psychiatry* 19, no. 6 (2011): 277–89, doi:10.310 9/10673229.2011.630828.

3. Maryia Zhdanava, Dominic Pilon, Isabelle Ghelerter, Wing Chow, Kruti Joshi, Patrick Lefebvre, and John J. Sheehan, "The Prevalence and National Burden of Treatment-Resistant Depression and Major Depressive Disorder in the United States," *Journal of Clinical Psychiatry* 82, no. 2 (2021), doi:10.4088/jcp.20m13699.

4. Manuella P. Kaster, Morgana Moretti, Mauricio P. Cunha, and Ana Lúcia S. Rodrigues, "Novel Approaches for the Management of Depressive Disorders," *European Journal of Pharmacology* 771 (2016): 236–40, doi:10.1016/j.ejphar.2015.12.029.

5. Ravi K. Sharma, Gajanan Kulkarni, Channaveerachari Naveen Kumar, Shyam Sundar Arumugham, Venkataramaiah Sudhir, Urvakhsh M. Mehta, Sayantanava Mitra, Milind Vijay Thanki, and Jagadisha Thirthalli, "Antidepressant Effects of Ketamine and ECT: A Pilot Comparison," *Journal of Affective Disorders* 276 (2020): 260–66, doi:10.1016/j.jad.2020.07.066; Jian-jun Chen, Li-bo Zhao, Yi-yun Liu, Song-hua Fan, and Peng Xie, "Comparative Efficacy and Acceptability of Electroconvulsive Therapy versus Repetitive Transcranial Magnetic Stimulation for Major Depression: A Systematic Review and Multiple-Treatments Meta-Analysis," *Behavioural Brain Research* 320 (2017): 30–36, doi:10.1016/j.bbr.2016.11.028.

Chapter 1

1. Alan M. Gruenberg and Reed D. Goldstein, "Depressive Disorders," in *Psychiatry*, ed. A. Tasman, J. Kay, and J. A. Lieberman, 990–1019 (Philadelphia: W. B. Saunders, 1987).

2. Brittany Mason, E. Brown, and Paul Croarkin, "Historical Underpinnings of Bipolar Disorder Diagnostic Criteria," *Behavioral Sciences* 6, no. 3 (2016): 14, doi:10.3390/bs6030014; American Psychiatry Association, "DSM History," accessed July 13, 2022, https://www.psychiatry.org/psychiatrists/practice/dsm/history-of-the-dsm.

3. American Psychiatric Association, *Diagnostic and Statistical Manual of Mental Disorders*, 5th ed. (Arlington, VA: American Psychiatric Association, 2013).

4. Lakshmi N. Yatham, Sidney H. Kennedy, Sagar V. Parikh, Ayal Schaffer, David J. Bond, Benicio N. Frey, Verinder Sharma, et al., "Canadian Network for Mood and Anxiety Treatments (CANMAT) and International Society for Bipolar Disorders (ISBD) 2018 Guidelines for the Management of Patients with Bipolar Disorder," *Bipolar Disorders* 20, no. 2 (2018): 97–170, doi:10.1111/bdi.12609.

5. Alessandro Cuomo, Andrea Aguglia, Eugenio Aguglia, Simone Bolognesi, Arianna Goracci, Giuseppe Maina, Ludovico Mineo, Paola Rucci, Silvia Sillari, and Andrea Fagiolini, "Mood Spectrum Symptoms during a Major Depressive Episode: Differences between 145 Patients with Bipolar Disorder and 155 Patients with Major Depressive Disorder; Arguments for a Dimensional Approach," *Bipolar Disorders* (2019), doi:10.1111/bdi.12855; Eduard Vieta, Estela Salagre, Iria Grande, Andre F. Carvalho, Brisa S. Fernandes, Michael Berk, Boris Birmaher, Mauricio Tohen, and Trisha Suppes, "Early Intervention in Bipolar Disorder," *American Journal of Psychiatry* 175, no. 5 (2018), https://doi.org/10.1176/appi.ajp.2017.17090972.

6. Mason, Brown, and Croarkin, "Historical Underpinnings of Bipolar Disorder Diagnostic Criteria."

7. American Psychiatric Association, *Diagnostic and Statistical Manual of Mental Disorders*, 5th ed.

8. Ciro Marangoni, Lavinia De Chiara, and Gianni L. Faedda, "Bipolar Disorder and ADHD: Comorbidity and Diagnostic Distinctions," *Current Psychiatry Reports* 17, no. 8 (2015): 67, doi:10.1007/s11920-015-0604-y.

9. Alexander H. Fan and Joseph Hassell, "Bipolar Disorder and Comorbid Personality Psychopathology: A Review of the Literature," *Journal of Clinical Psychiatry* 69, no. 11 (2008): 1794–803, doi:10.4088/jcp.v69n1115; Joel Paris and Donald W. Black, "Borderline Personality Disorder and Bipolar Disorder," *Journal of Nervous and Mental Disease* 203, no. 1 (2015): 3–7, doi:10.1097/nmd.0000000000000225.

10. American Psychiatric Association, *Diagnostic and Statistical Manual of Mental Disorders*, 5th ed.

11. Paris and Black, "Borderline Personality Disorder and Bipolar Disorder."

12. Eve Caligor, Kenneth N. Levy, and Frank E. Yeomans, "Narcissistic Personality Disorder: Diagnostic and Clinical Challenges," *American Journal of Psychiatry* 172, no. 5 (2015): 415–22, doi:10.1176/appi.ajp.2014.14060723.

13. Vieta et al., "Early Intervention in Bipolar Disorder."

14. Patrick Luyten and Sidney J. Blatt, "Psychodynamic Treatment of Depression," *Psychiatric Clinics of North America* 35, no. 1 (2012): 111–29, doi:10.1016/j.psc.2012.01.001.

15. "Reserpine," MedlinePlus, accessed July 22, 2022, https://medlineplus.gov/druginfo/meds/a601107.html; Gonzalo A. Aillon, "Biochemistry of Affective Disorders," *Psychosomatics* 12, no. 4 (1971): 260–72, doi:10.1016/s0033-3182(71)71517-5; Jennifer J. G. Steffensmeier, Michael E. Ernst, Michael Kelly, and Arthur J. Hartz, "Do Randomized Controlled Trials Always Trump Case Reports? A Second Look at Propranolol and Depression," *Pharmacotherapy: The Journal of Human Pharmacology and Drug Therapy* 26, no. 2 (2006): 162–67, doi:10.1592/phco.26.2.162.

16. M. B. Keller and R. J. Boland, *Antidepressants in Psychiatry*, ed. A. Tasman, J. Kay, and J. A. Lieberman (Philadelphia: W. B. Saunders, 1997).

17. Keller and Boland, *Antidepressants in Psychiatry*.

18. Kathleen Merikangas and Nancy C. P. Low, "The Epidemiology of Mood Disorders," *Current Psychiatry Reports* 6, no. 6 (2004): 411–21, doi:10.1007/s11920-004-0004-1.

19. Robert G. Robinson, Kenneth L. Kubos, Lyn Book Starr, Krishna Rao, and Thomas R. Price, "Mood Disorders in Stroke Patients: Importance of Location of Lesion," *Brain* 107, no. 1 (1984): 81–93, doi:10.1093/brain/107.1.81.

20. Helen S. Mayberg, "Positron Emission Tomography Imaging in Depression: A Neural Systems Perspective," *Neuroimaging Clinics of North America* 13, no. 4 (2003): 805–15, doi:10.1016/s1052-5149(03)00104-7.

Chapter 2

1. A. M. Guenberg and R. D. Goldstein, *Depressive Disorders in Psychiatry*, ed. A. Tasman, J. Kay, and J. A. Lieberman (Philadelphia: W. B. Saunders, 1997); American Psychiatric Association, *Diagnostic and Statistical Manual of Mental Disorders*, 4th ed., text revision (Washington, DC: American Psychiatric Association, 2000).

2. Guenberg and Goldstein, *Depressive Disorders in Psychiatry*.

3. E. S. Paykel, "Partial Remission, Residual Symptoms, and Relapse in Depression," *Dialogues in Clinical Neuroscience* 10, no. 4 (2008): 431–37, doi:10.31887/dcns.2008.10.4/espaykel.

4. Alice Caldiroli, Enrico Capuzzi, Ilaria Tagliabue, Martina Capellazzi, Matteo Marcatili, Francesco Mucci, Fabrizia Colmegna, Massimo Clerici, Massimiliano Buoli, and Antonios Dakanalis, "Augmentative Pharmacological Strategies in Treatment-Resistant Major Depression: A Comprehensive Review," *International Journal of Molecular Sciences* 22, no. 23 (2021): 13070, doi:10.3390/ijms222313070.

5. Spyros Kolovos, Annet Kleiboer, and Pim Cuijpers, "Effect of Psychotherapy for Depression on Quality of Life: Meta-Analysis," *British Journal of Psychiatry* 209, no. 6 (2016): 460–68, doi:10.1192/bjp.bp.115.175059.

6. Waguih IsHak, Konstantin Balayan, Catherine Bresee, Jared Greenberg, Hala Fakhry, Scott Christensen, and Mark Rapaport, "A Descriptive Analysis of Quality of Life Using

Patient-Reported Measures in Major Depressive Disorder in a Naturalistic Outpatient Setting," *Quality of Life Research* 22, no. 3 (2013): 585–96, doi:10.1007/s11136-012-0187-6.

7. Keming Gao, Meilei Su, Jennifer Sweet, and Joseph R. Calabrese, "Correlation between Depression/Anxiety Symptom Severity and Quality of Life in Patients with Major Depressive Disorder or Bipolar Disorder," *Journal of Affective Disorders* 244 (2018): 9–15, doi:10.1016/j. jad.2018.09.063.

8. Ziggi Ivan Santini, Ai Koyanagi, Stefanos Tyrovolas, Catherine Mason, and Josep Maria Haro, "The Association between Social Relationships and Depression: A Systematic Review," *Journal of Affective Disorders* 175 (2015): 53–65, doi:10.1016/j.jad.2014.12.049; John T. Cacioppo, Mary Elizabeth Hughes, Linda J. Waite, Louise C. Hawkley, and Ronald A. Thisted, "Loneliness as a Specific Risk Factor for Depressive Symptoms: Cross-Sectional and Longitudinal Analyses," *Psychology and Aging* 21, no. 1 (2006): 140–51, doi:10.1037/0882-7974.21.1.140; I. M. J. Saris, M. Aghajani, S. J. A. Werff, N. J. A. Wee, and B. W. J. H. Penninx, "Social Functioning in Patients with Depressive and Anxiety Disorders," *Acta Psychiatrica Scandinavica* 136, no. 4 (2017): 352–61, doi:10.1111/acps.12774.

9. Saris et al., "Social Functioning in Patients with Depressive and Anxiety Disorders," 352–61.

10. Julianne Holt-Lunstad, Timothy B. Smith, and J. Bradley Layton, "Social Relationships and Mortality Risk: A Meta-Analytic Review," *PLoS Medicine* 7, no. 7 (2010): e1000316, doi:10.1371/journal.pmed.1000316.

11. Barbara Biasi, Michael S. Dahl, and Petra Moser, "Career Effects of Mental Health," BarbaraBiasi.com, December 30, 2020, www.barbarabiasi.com/uploads/1/0/1/2/101280322 /biasidahlmoser_mentalhealth.pdf.

12. M. Weck, S. Fischer, M. Hanefeld, W. Leonhardt, U. Julius, W. Gräser, B. Schneider, and H. Haller, "Loss of Fat, Water, and Protein during Very Low Calorie Diets and Complete Starvation," *Klinische Wochenschrift* 65, no. 23 (1987): 1142–50, doi:10.1007/bf01734837.

13. Dean Ornish, *The Spectrum* (New York: Ballantine Books, 2007).

14. Alessandro Serretti and Laura Mandelli, "Antidepressants and Body Weight: A Comprehensive Review and Meta-Analysis," *Journal of Clinical Psychiatry* 71, no. 10 (2010): 1259–72, doi:10.4088/jcp.09r05346blu.

15. Serretti and Mandelli, "Antidepressants and Body Weight," 1259–72.

16. Julieta Schachter, Jan Martel, Chuan-Sheng Lin, Chih-Jung Chang, Tsung-Ru Wu, Chia-Chen Lu, Yun-Fei Ko, Hsin-Chih Lai, David M. Ojcius, and John D. Young, "Effects of Obesity on Depression: A Role for Inflammation and the Gut Microbiota," *Brain, Behavior, and Immunity* 69 (2018): 1–8, doi:10.1016/j.bbi.2017.08.026.

17. M. Kondo, Y. Nakamura, Y. Ishida, and S. Shimada, "The 5-HT3 Receptor Is Essential for Exercise-Induced Hippocampal Neurogenesis and Antidepressant Effects," *Molecular Psychiatry* 20, no. 11 (2014): 1428–37, doi:10.1038/mp.2014.153; Suk Yau, Ang Li, Ruby L. C. Hoo, Yick Ching, Brian R. Christie, Tatia M. C. Lee, Aimin Xu, and Kwok-Fai So, "Physical Exercise-Induced Hippocampal Neurogenesis and Antidepressant Effects Are Mediated by the

Adipocyte Hormone Adiponectin," *Proceedings of the National Academy of Sciences* 111, no. 44 (2014): 15810–15, doi:10.1073/pnas.1415219111.

18. J. B. Savitz and W. C. Drevets, "Imaging Phenotypes of Major Depressive Disorder: Genetic Correlates," *Neuroscience* 164, no. 1 (2009): 300–30, doi:10.1016/j.neuroscience.2009.03.082.

19. Jennifer Townsend and Lori L. Altshuler, "Emotion Processing and Regulation in Bipolar Disorder: A Review," *Bipolar Disorders* 14, no. 4 (2012): 326–39, doi:10.1111/j.1399-5618.2012.01021.x.

20. Savitz and Drevets, "Imaging Phenotypes of Major Depressive Disorder," 300–30.

21. Savitz and Drevets, "Imaging Phenotypes of Major Depressive Disorder," 300–30.

22. Savitz and Drevets, "Imaging Phenotypes of Major Depressive Disorder," 300–30.

23. Kevin S. LaBar and Roberto Cabeza, "Cognitive Neuroscience of Emotional Memory," *Nature Reviews Neuroscience* 7, no. 1 (2006): 54–64, doi:10.1038/nrn1825.

24. P. Zanos and T. D. Gould, "Mechanisms of Ketamine Action as an Antidepressant," *Molecular Psychiatry* 23, no. 4 (2018): 801–11, doi:10.1038/mp.2017.255; Xiangxiang Zhao, Yanpeng Li, Qing Tian, Bingqian Zhu, and Zhongxin Zhao, "Repetitive Transcranial Magnetic Stimulation Increases Serum Brain-Derived Neurotrophic Factor and Decreases Interleukin-1β and Tumor Necrosis Factor-α in Elderly Patients with Refractory Depression," *Journal of International Medical Research* 47, no. 5 (2018): 1848–55, doi:10.1177/0300060518817417; Iris Dalhuisen, Eveline Ackermans, Lieke Martens, Peter Mulders, Joey Bartholomeus, Alex de Bruijn, Jan Spijker, Philip van Eijndhoven, and Indira Tendolkar, "Longitudinal Effects of rTMS on Neuroplasticity in Chronic Treatment-Resistant Depression," *European Archives of Psychiatry and Clinical Neuroscience* 271, no. 1 (2021): 39–47, doi:10.1007/s00406-020-01135-w; K. Gbyl and P. Videbech, "Electroconvulsive Therapy Increases Brain Volume in Major Depression: A Systematic Review and Meta-Analysis," *Acta Psychiatrica Scandinavica* 138, no. 3 (2018): 180–95, doi:10.1111/acps.12884; Chadi Abdallah, Lynette A. Averill, Katherine A. Collins, Paul Geha, Jaclyn Schwartz, Christopher Averill, Kaitlin E. DeWilde, et al., "Ketamine Treatment and Global Brain Connectivity in Major Depression," *Neuropsychopharmacology* 42 (2017): 1210–19, https://www.ncbi.nlm.nih.gov/pmc/articles/PMC5437875/pdf/npp2016186a.pdf.

Chapter 3

1. Joseph M. Cerimele, Lydia A. Chwastiak, Sherry Dodson, and Wayne J. Katon, "The Prevalence of Bipolar Disorder in Primary Care Patients with Depression or Other Psychiatric Complaints: A Systematic Review," *Psychosomatics* 54, no. 6 (2013): 515–24, doi:10.1016/j.psym.2013.05.009.

2. Michael E. Thase, "STEP-BD and Bipolar Depression: What Have We Learned?," *Current Psychiatry Reports* 9, no. 6 (2007): 497–503, doi:10.1007/s11920-007-0068-9.

3. T. A. Wehr and F. K. Goodwin, "Can Antidepressants Cause Mania and Worsen the Course of Affective Illness?," *American Journal of Psychiatry* 144, no. 11 (1987): 1403–11, doi:10.1176/ajp.144.11.1403.

4. American Psychiatric Association, *Diagnostic and Statistical Manual of Mental Disorders*, 5th ed.

5. Pim Cuijpers, Matthias Berking, Gerhard Andersson, Leanne Quigley, Annet Kleiboer, and Keith S. Dobson, "A Meta-Analysis of Cognitive-Behavioural Therapy for Adult Depression, Alone and in Comparison with Other Treatments," *Canadian Journal of Psychiatry* 58, no. 7 (2012): 376–85, doi:10.1177/070674371305800702.

6. Kai-Jo Chiang, Jui-Chen Tsai, Doresses Liu, Chueh-Ho Lin, Huei-Ling Chiu, and Kuei-Ru Chou, "Efficacy of Cognitive-Behavioral Therapy in Patients with Bipolar Disorder: A Meta-Analysis of Randomized Controlled Trials," *PLoS ONE* 12, no. 5 (2017): e0176849, doi:10.1371/journal.pone.0176849.

7. Jennifer L. Hames, Christopher R. Hagan, and Thomas E. Joiner, "Interpersonal Processes in Depression," *Annual Review of Clinical Psychology* 9, no. 1 (2013): 355–77, doi:10.1146/annurev-clinpsy-050212-185553.

8. Alan E. Kazdin, "Understanding How and Why Psychotherapy Leads to Change," *Psychotherapy Research* 19, no. 4–5 (2009): 418–28, doi:10.1080/10503300802448899.

9. Aaron Kandola, Garcia Ashdown-Franks, Joshua Hendrikse, Catherine M. Sabiston, and Brendon Stubbs, "Physical Activity and Depression: Towards Understanding the Antidepressant Mechanisms of Physical Activity," *Neuroscience & Biobehavioral Reviews* 107 (2019): 525–39, doi:10.1016/j.neubiorev.2019.09.040.

10. James A. Blumenthal, Michael A. Babyak, P. Murali Doraiswamy, Lana Watkins, Benson M. Hoffman, Krista A. Barbour, Steve Herman, et al., "Exercise and Pharmacotherapy in the Treatment of Major Depressive Disorder," *Psychosomatic Medicine* 69, no. 7 (2007): 587–96, doi:10.1097/psy.0b013e318148c19a.

11. André F. Carvalho, Manu S. Sharma, André R. Brunoni, Eduard Vieta, and Giovanni A. Fava, "The Safety, Tolerability and Risks Associated with the Use of Newer Generation Antidepressant Drugs: A Critical Review of the Literature," *Psychotherapy and Psychosomatics* 85, no. 5 (2016): 270–88, doi:10.1159/000447034.

12. Carvalho et al., "Safety, Tolerability and Risks Associated with the Use of Newer Generation Antidepressant Drugs," 270–88.

13. K. Demyttenaere and P. Haddad, "Compliance with Antidepressant Therapy and Antidepressant Discontinuation Symptoms," *Acta Psychiatrica Scandinavica* 101, no. s403 (2000): 50–56, doi:10.1111/j.1600-0447.2000.tb10948.x.

14. A. A. Nierenberg, N. E. McLean, J. E. Alpert, J. J. Worthington, J. F. Rosenbaum, and M. Fava, "Early Nonresponse to Fluoxetine as a Predictor of Poor 8-Week Outcome," *American Journal of Psychiatry* 152, no. 10 (1995): 1500–03, doi:10.1176/ajp.152.10.1500.

15. Maurizio Fava, Jonathan Alpert, Andrew Nierenberg, Isabel Lagomasino, Shamsah Sonawalla, Joyce Tedlow, John Worthington, Lee Baer, and Jerrold F. Rosenbaum, "Double-Blind Study of High-Dose Fluoxetine versus Lithium or Desipramine Augmentation of Fluoxetine in Partial Responders and Nonresponders to Fluoxetine," *Journal of Clinical Psychopharmacology* 22, no. 4 (2002): 379–87, doi:10.1097/00004714-200208000-00008.

16. Alice Caldiroli, Enrico Capuzzi, Ilaria Tagliabue, Martina Capellazzi, Matteo Marcatili, Francesco Mucci, Fabrizia Colmegna, Massimo Clerici, Massimiliano Buoli, and Antonios Dakanalis, "Augmentative Pharmacological Strategies in Treatment-Resistant Major Depression: A Comprehensive Review," *International Journal of Molecular Sciences* 22, no. 23 (2021): 13070, doi:10.3390/ijms222313070.

17. Wilmar M. Wiersinga, "Thyroid Hormone Replacement Therapy," *Hormone Research in Paediatrics* 56, suppl 1 (2002): 74–81, doi:10.1159/000048140.

18. Richard C. Shelton, Olawale Osuntokun, Alexandra N. Heinloth, and Sara A. Corya, "Therapeutic Options for Treatment-Resistant Depression," *CNS Drugs* 24, no. 2 (2010): 131–61, doi:10.2165/11530280-000000000-00000.

19. Mauricio Tohen, Eduard Vieta, Joseph Calabrese, Terence A. Ketter, Gary Sachs, Charles Bowden, Philip B. Mitchell, et al., "Efficacy of Olanzapine and Olanzapine-Fluoxetine Combination in the Treatment of Bipolar I Depression," *Archives of General Psychiatry* 60, no. 11 (2003): 1079–88, doi:10.1001/archpsyc.60.11.1079.

20. Yatham et al., "Canadian Network for Mood and Anxiety Treatments (CANMAT) and International Society for Bipolar Disorders (ISBD)," 97–170.

21. Giulio Perugi, Pierpaolo Medda, Cristina Toni, Michela Mariani, Chiara Socci, and Mauro Mauri, "The Role of Electroconvulsive Therapy (ECT) in Bipolar Disorder: Effectiveness in 522 Patients with Bipolar Depression, Mixed-State, Mania and Catatonic Features," *Current Neuropharmacology* 15, no. 3 (2017): 359–71, doi:10.2174/1570159x14666161017233642.

Chapter 4

1. Linda Li and Phillip E. Vlisides, "Ketamine: 50 Years of Modulating the Mind," *Frontiers in Human Neuroscience* 10 (2016): 612, doi:10.3389/fnhum.2016.00612.

2. Li and Vlisides, "Ketamine," 612.

3. Vwaire Orhurhu, Mariam Salisu Orhurhu, Anuj Bhatia, and Steven P. Cohen, "Ketamine Infusions for Chronic Pain: A Systematic Review and Meta-Analysis of Randomized Controlled Trials," *Anesthesia & Analgesia* 129, no. 1 (2019): 241–54, doi:10.1213/ane.0000000000004185.

4. Robert M. Berman, Angela Cappiello, Amit Anand, Dan A. Oren, George R. Heninger, Dennis S. Charney, and John H. Krystal, "Antidepressant Effects of Ketamine in Depressed Patients," *Biological Psychiatry* 47, no. 4 (2000): 351–54, doi:10.1016/s0006-3223(99)00230-9.

5. John H. Krystal, Chadi G. Abdallah, Gerard Sanacora, Dennis S. Charney, and Ronald S. Duman, "Ketamine: A Paradigm Shift for Depression Research and Treatment," *Neuron* 101, no. 5 (2019): 774–78, doi:10.1016/j.neuron.2019.02.005.

6. Carlos A. Zarate, Jaskaran B. Singh, Paul J. Carlson, Nancy E. Brutsche, Rezvan Ameli, David A. Luckenbaugh, Dennis S. Charney, and Husseini K. Manji, "A Randomized Trial of an N-methyl-D-aspartate Antagonist in Treatment-Resistant Major Depression," *Archives of General Psychiatry* 63, no. 8 (2006): 856–64, doi:10.1001/archpsyc.63.8.856.

7. Jennifer Swainson, Rejish K. Thomas, Shaina Archer, Carson Chrenek, Mary-Anne MacKay, Glen Baker, Serdar Dursun, Larry J. Klassen, Pratap Chokka, and Michael L. Demas,

"Esketamine for Treatment Resistant Depression," *Expert Review of Neurotherapeutics* 19, no. 10 (2019): 1–13, doi:10.1080/14737175.2019.1640604.

8. Kenji Hashimoto, "Rapid-Acting Antidepressant Ketamine, Its Metabolites and Other Candidates: A Historical Overview and Future Perspective," *Psychiatry and Clinical Neurosciences* 73, no. 10 (2019): 613–27, doi:10.1111/pcn.12902.

9. Jaskaran B. Singh, Maggie Fedgchin, Ella Daly, Liwen Xi, Caroline Melman, Geert De Bruecker, Andre Tadic, et al., "Intravenous Esketamine in Adult Treatment-Resistant Depression: A Double-Blind, Double-Randomization, Placebo-Controlled Study," *Biological Psychiatry* 80, no. 6 (2016): 424–31, doi:10.1016/j.biopsych.2015.10.018.

10. James W. Murrough, Dan V. Iosifescu, Lee C. Chang, Rayan K. Al Jurdi, Charles E. Green, Andrew M. Perez, Syed Iqbal, et al., "Antidepressant Efficacy of Ketamine in Treatment-Resistant Major Depression: A Two-Site Randomized Controlled Trial," *American Journal of Psychiatry* 170, no. 10 (2013): 1134–42, doi:10.1176/appi.ajp.2013.13030392.

11. Anees Bahji, Gustavo H. Vazquez, and Carlos A. Zarate, "Comparative Efficacy of Racemic Ketamine and Esketamine for Depression: A Systematic Review and Meta-Analysis," *Journal of Affective Disorders* 278 (2020): 12473, doi:10.1016/j.jad.2020.09.071.

12. S. E. Strasburger, P. M. Bhimani, J. H. Kaabe, J. T. Krysiak, D. L. Nanchanatt, T. N. Nguyen, K. A. Pough, et al., "What Is the Mechanism of Ketamine's Rapid-Onset Antidepressant Effect? A Concise Overview of the Surprisingly Large Number of Possibilities," *Journal of Clinical Pharmacy and Therapeutics* 42, no. 2 (2017): 147–54, doi:10.1111/jcpt.12497.

13. Ole Kohler, Jesper Krogh, Ole Mors, and Michael Eriksen Benros, "Inflammation in Depression and the Potential for Anti-Inflammatory Treatment," *Current Neuropharmacology* 14, no. 7 (2016): 732–42, doi:10.2174/1570159x14666151208113700.

14. Wenyan Cui, Yuping Ning, Wu Hong, Ju Wang, Zhening Liu, and Ming D. Li, "Cross-Talk between Inflammation and Glutamate System in Depression: Signaling Pathway and Molecular Biomarkers for Ketamine's Antidepressant Effect," *Molecular Neurobiology* (2018): 1–17, doi:10.1007/s12035-018-1306-3.

15. Marieke Niesters, Christian Martini, and Albert Dahan, "Ketamine for Chronic Pain: Risks and Benefits," *British Journal of Clinical Pharmacology* 77, no. 2 (2014): 357–67, doi:10.1111/bcp.12094.

16. Nolan R. Williams, Boris D. Heifets, Brandon S. Bentzley, Christine Blasey, Keith D. Sudheimer, Jessica Hawkins, David M. Lyons and Alan F. Schatzberg, "Attenuation of Antidepressant and Antisuicidal Effects of Ketamine by Opioid Receptor Antagonism," *Molecular Psychiatry* 24, no. 12 (2019): 1779–86, doi:10.1038/s41380-019-0503-4.

Chapter 5

1. Ethan Minkin, "The Ketamine Clinic Craze: Legalities and Possibilities," Harris Bricken, March 4, 2020, https://harrisbricken.com/cannalawblog/the-ketamine-clinic-craze-legalities-and-possibilities.

2. Anees Bahji, Gustavo H. Vazquez, and Carlos A. Zarate, "Comparative Efficacy of Racemic Ketamine and Esketamine for Depression: A Systematic Review and Meta-Analysis," *Journal of Affective Disorders* 278 (2020): 12473, doi:10.1016/j.jad.2020.09.071.

3. Göran Bergström, Margaretha Persson, Martin Adiels, Elias Björnson, Carl Bonander, Håkan Ahlström, Joakim Alfredsson, et al., "Prevalence of Subclinical Coronary Artery Atherosclerosis in the General Population," *Circulation* 144, no. 12 (2021): 916–29, doi:10.1161/circulationaha.121.055340.

4. Bergström et al., "Prevalence of Subclinical Coronary Artery Atherosclerosis in the General Population," 916–29.

5. Yanhui Liao, Yi-lang Tang, and Wei Hao, "Ketamine and International Regulations," *American Journal of Drug and Alcohol Abuse* 43, no. 5 (2017): 1–10, doi:10.1080/00952990.2016.1278449.

6. Linda Li and Phillip E. Vlisides, "Ketamine: 50 Years of Modulating the Mind," *Frontiers in Human Neuroscience* 10 (2016): 612, doi:10.3389/fnhum.2016.00612.

7. Vwaire Orhurhu, Mariam Salisu Orhurhu, Anuj Bhatia, and Steven P. Cohen, "Ketamine Infusions for Chronic Pain: A Systematic Review and Meta-Analysis of Randomized Controlled Trials," *Anesthesia & Analgesia* 129, no. 1 (2019): 241–54, doi:10.1213/ane.0000000000004185.

8. Chittaranjan Andrade, "Ketamine for Depression, 1: Clinical Summary of Issues Related to Efficacy, Adverse Effects, and Mechanism of Action (Clinical and Practical Psychopharmacolgy)," *Journal of Clinical Psychiatry* 78, no. 4 (2017): e415–e419, doi:10.4088/jcp.17f11567.

9. Ewa Wajs, Leah Aluisio, Richard Holder, Ella J. Daly, Rosanne Lane, Pilar Lim, Joyce E. George, et al., "Esketamine Nasal Spray Plus Oral Antidepressant in Patients with Treatment-Resistant Depression: Assessment of Long-Term Safety in a Phase 3, Open-Label Study (SUSTAIN-2)," *Journal of Clinical Psychiatry* 81, no. 3 (2020), doi:10.4088/jcp.19m12891.

10. Esketamine package insert; Andrade, "Ketamine for Depression, 1."

11. Polychronis E. Dilaveris and Harold L. Kennedy, "Silent Atrial Fibrillation: Epidemiology, Diagnosis, and Clinical Impact," *Clinical Cardiology* 40, no. 6 (2017): 413–18, doi:10.1002/clc.22667; Bergström et al., "Prevalence of Subclinical Coronary Artery Atherosclerosis in the General Population."

12. Esketamine package insert; Justin Lin, Yelena Figuerado, Adrienne Montgomery, Jonathan Lee, Mark Cannis, Valerie C. Norton, Richard Calvo, and Harminder Sikand, "Efficacy of Ketamine for Initial Control of Acute Agitation in the Emergency Department: A Randomized Study," *American Journal of Emergency Medicine* 44 (2021): 306–11, doi:10.1016/j.ajem.2020.04.013; Steven M. Green, Mark G. Roback, Robert M. Kennedy, and Baruch Krauss, "Clinical Practice Guideline for Emergency Department Ketamine Dissociative Sedation: 2011 Update," *Annals of Emergency Medicine* 57, no. 5 (2011): 449–61, doi:10.1016/j.annemergmed.2010.11.030.

13. Wenyan Cui, Yuping Ning, Wu Hong, Ju Wang, Zhening Liu, and Ming D. Li, "Cross-Talk between Inflammation and Glutamate System in Depression: Signaling Pathway and Molecular Biomarkers for Ketamine's Antidepressant Effect," *Molecular Neurobiology* (2018): 1–17, doi:10.1007/s12035-018-1306-3.

14. Esketamine package insert.

15. Esketamine package insert.

Chapter 6

1. David Kent, "The History of TMS," From the Desk of Dr. Kent, March 13, 2017, Nume TMS Clinic, https://www.numetms.com/blog/e_34/From-the-Desk-of-Dr.-Kent/2017/3/The -History-of-TMS.

2. Max Fink, *Electroconvulsive Therapy: A Guide for Professionals and Their Patients*, 2nd ed. (New York: Oxford University Press, 2009).

3. John P. O'Reardon, H. Brent Solvason, Philip G. Janicak, Shirlene Sampson, Keith E. Isenberg, Ziad Nahas, William M. McDonald, et al., "Efficacy and Safety of Transcranial Magnetic Stimulation in the Acute Treatment of Major Depression: A Multisite Random-ized Controlled Trial," *Biological Psychiatry* 62, no. 11 (2007): 1208–16, doi:10.1016/j.bio-psych.2007.01.018; M. T. Berlim, F. van den Eynde, S. Tovar-Perdomo, and Z. J. Daskalakis, "Response, Remission and Drop-Out Rates Following High-Frequency Repetitive Transcra-nial Magnetic Stimulation (rTMS) for Treating Major Depression: A Systematic Review and Meta-Analysis of Randomized, Double-Blind and Sham-Controlled Trials," *Psychological Med-icine* 44, no. 2 (2014): 225–39, doi:10.1017/s0033291713000512.

4. Uwe Herwig, Andreas J. Fallgatter, Jacqueline Höppner, Gerhard W. Eschweiler, Mar-tina Kron, Göran Hajak, Frank Padberg, et al., "Antidepressant Effects of Augmentative Transcranial Magnetic Stimulation," *British Journal of Psychiatry* 191, no. 5 (2007): 441–48, doi:10.1192/bjp.bp.106.034371.

5. O'Reardon et al., "Efficacy and Safety of Transcranial Magnetic Stimulation in the Acute Treatment of Major Depression," 1208–16.

6. Mark S. George, Sarah H. Lisanby, David Avery, William M. McDonald, Val-erie Durkalski, Martina Pavlicova, Berry Anderson, et al., "Daily Left Prefrontal Transcra-nial Magnetic Stimulation Therapy for Major Depressive Disorder: A Sham-Controlled Randomized Trial," *Archives of General Psychiatry* 67, no. 5 (2010): 507–16, doi:10.1001/archgenpsychiatry.2010.46.

7. Linda L. Carpenter, Philip G. Janicak, Scott T. Aaronson, Terrence Boyadjis, David G. Brock, Ian A. Cook, David L. Dunner, Karl Lanocha, H. Brent Solvason, and Mark A. Demi-track, "Transcranial Magnetic Stimulation (TMS) for Major Depression: A Multisite, Natural-istic, Observational Study of Acute Treatment Outcomes in Clinical Practice," *Depression and Anxiety* 29, no. 7 (2012): 587–96, doi:10.1002/da.21969.

8. Bradley N. Gaynes, Diane Warden, Madhukar H. Trivedi, Stephen R. Wisniewski, Mau-rizio Fava, and A. John Rush, "What Did STAR*D Teach Us? Results from a Large-Scale, Practical, Clinical Trial for Patients with Depression," *Psychiatric Services* 60, no. 11 (2009): 1439–45, doi:10.1176/ps.2009.60.11.1439.

9. Wanalee Klomjai, Rose Katz, and Alexandra Lackmy-Vallée, "Basic Principles of Transcranial Magnetic Stimulation (TMS) and Repetitive TMS (rTMS)," *Annals of Physical and Rehabilitation Medicine* 58, no. 4 (2015): 208–13, doi:10.1016/j.rehab.2015.05.005.

10. Yiftach Roth, Alon Amir, Yechiel Levkovitz, and Abraham Zangen, "Three-Dimensional Distribution of the Electric Field Induced in the Brain by Transcranial Magnetic Stimulation Using Figure-8 and Deep H-Coils," *Journal of Clinical Neurophysiology* 24, no. 1 (2007): 31–38, doi:10.1097/wnp.0b013e31802fa393.

11. Yechiel Levkovitz, Yiftach Roth, Eiran Vadim Harel, Yoram Braw, Aharon Sheer, and Abraham Zangen, "A Randomized Controlled Feasibility and Safety Study of Deep Transcranial Magnetic Stimulation," *Clinical Neurophysiology* 118, no. 12 (2007): 2730–44, doi:10.1016/j.clinph.2007.09.061.

12. Yechiel Levkovitz, Moshe Isserles, Frank Padberg, Sarah H. Lisanby, Alexander Bystritsky, Guohua Xia, Aron Tendler, et al., "Efficacy and Safety of Deep Transcranial Magnetic Stimulation for Major Depression: A Prospective Multicenter Randomized Controlled Trial," *World Psychiatry* 14, no. 1 (2015): 64–73, doi:10.1002/wps.20199.

13. Mark S. George, "Whither TMS: A One-Trick Pony or the Beginning of a Neuroscientific Revolution?," *American Journal of Psychiatry* 176, no. 11 (2019): 904–10, doi:10.1176/appi.ajp.2019.19090957.

14. Daniel M. Blumberger, Fidel Vila-Rodriguez, Kevin E. Thorpe, Kfir Feffer, Yoshihiro Noda, Peter Giacobbe, Yuliya Knyahnytska, et al., "Effectiveness of Theta Burst versus High-Frequency Repetitive Transcranial Magnetic Stimulation in Patients with Depression (THREE-D): A Randomised Non-Inferiority Trial," *Lancet* 391, no. 10131 (2018): 1683–92, doi:10.1016/s0140-6736(18)30295-2.

15. Nicholas J. Petrosino, Camila Cosmo, Yosef A. Berlow, Amin Zandvakili, Mascha van't Wout-Frank, and Noah S. Philip, "Transcranial Magnetic Stimulation for Post-Traumatic Stress Disorder," *Therapeutic Advances in Psychopharmacology* 11 (2021): 20451253211049920, doi:10.1177/20451253211049921; Noah S. Philip, Jennifer Barredo, Emily Aiken, Victoria Larson, Richard N. Jones, M. Tracie Shea, Benjamin D. Greenberg, and Mascha van't Wout-Frank, "Theta-Burst Transcranial Magnetic Stimulation for Posttraumatic Stress Disorder," *American Journal of Psychiatry* 176, no. 11 (2019): 939–48, doi:10.1176/appi.ajp.2019.18101160.

16. Roth et al., "Three-Dimensional Distribution of the Electric Field," 31–38; George, "Whither TMS?," 904–10.

17. Ruiyang Ge, Jonathan Downar, Daniel M. Blumberger, Zafiris J. Daskalakis, and Fidel Vila-Rodriguez, "Functional Connectivity of the Anterior Cingulate Cortex Predicts Treatment Outcome for rTMS in Treatment-Resistant Depression at 3-Month Follow-Up," *Brain Stimulation* 13, no. 1 (2019): 206–14, doi:10.1016/j.brs.2019.10.012.

Chapter 7

1. Simone Rossi, Mark Hallett, Paolo M. Rossini, Alvaro Pascual-Leone, and the Safety of TMS Consensus Group, "Safety, Ethical Considerations, and Application Guidelines for the Use of Transcranial Magnetic Stimulation in Clinical Practice and Research," *Clinical Neurophysiology* 120, no. 12 (2009): 2008–39, doi:10.1016/j.clinph.2009.08.016.

2. Daniel M. Blumberger, Fidel Vila-Rodriguez, Kevin E. Thorpe, Kfir Feffer, Yoshi-hiro Noda, Peter Giacobbe, Yuliya Knyahnytska, et al., "Effectiveness of Theta Burst versus High-Frequency Repetitive Transcranial Magnetic Stimulation in Patients with Depression (THREE-D): A Randomised Non-Inferiority Trial," *Lancet* 391, no. 10131 (2018): 1683–92, doi:10.1016/s0140-6736(18)30295-2.

3. Adam J. Lerner, Eric M. Wassermann, and Diana I. Tamir, "Seizures from Transcranial Magnetic Stimulation 2012–2016: Results of a Survey of Active Laboratories and Clinics," *Clinical Neurophysiology* 130, no. 8 (2019): 1409–16, doi:10.1016/j.clinph.2019.03.016.

4. Tyler S. Kaster, Jonathan Downar, Fidel Vila-Rodriguez, Zafiris J. Daskalakis, and Daniel M. Blumberger, "Caution When Continuing Benzodiazepines During rTMS: Response to Hunter and Leuchter," *American Journal of Psychiatry* 177, no. 2 (2020): 172–73, doi:10.1176/appi.ajp.2019.19060603r; Tyler S. Kaster, Jonathan Downar, Fidel Vila-Rodriguez, Kevin E. Thorpe, Kfir Feffer, Yoshihiro Noda, Peter Giacobbe, et al., "Trajectories of Response to Dorsolateral Prefrontal rTMS in Major Depression: A THREE-D Study," *American Journal of Psychiatry* 176, no. 5 (2019): 367–75, doi:10.1176/appi.ajp.2018.18091096; Aimee M. Hunter, Michael J. Minzenberg, Ian A. Cook, David E. Krantz, Jennifer G. Levitt, Natalie M. Rotstein, Shweta A. Chawla, and Andrew F. Leuchter, "Concomitant Medication Use and Clinical Outcome of Repetitive Transcranial Magnetic Stimulation (rTMS) Treatment of Major Depressive Disorder," *Brain and Behavior* 9, no. 5 (2019): e01275, doi:10.1002/brb3.1275.

5. Aimee M. Hunter and Andrew F. Leuchter, "Benzodiazepine Use and rTMS Outcome," *American Journal of Psychiatry* 177, no. 2 (2020): 172, doi:10.1176/appi.ajp.2019.19060603.

6. Hunter et al., "Concomitant Medication Use and Clinical Outcome of Repetitive Transcranial Magnetic Stimulation (rTMS) Treatment of Major Depressive Disorder," e01275.

7. Blumberger et al., "Effectiveness of Theta Burst versus High-Frequency Repetitive Transcranial Magnetic Stimulation in Patients with Depression (THREE-D)," 1683–92.

8. Linda L. Carpenter, Philip G. Janicak, Scott T. Aaronson, Terrence Boyadjis, David G. Brock, Ian A. Cook, David L. Dunner, Karl Lanocha, H. Brent Solvason, and Mark A. Demitrack, "Transcranial Magnetic Stimulation (TMS) for Major Depression: A Multisite, Naturalistic, Observational Study of Acute Treatment Outcomes in Clinical Practice," *Depression and Anxiety* 29, no. 7 (2012): 587–96, doi:10.1002/da.21969.

9. Blumberger et al., "Effectiveness of Theta Burst versus High-Frequency Repetitive Transcranial Magnetic Stimulation in Patients with Depression (THREE-D)," 1683–92.

10. Mark S. George, Sarah H. Lisanby, David Avery, William M. McDonald, Valerie Durkalski, Martina Pavlicova, Berry Anderson, et al., "Daily Left Prefrontal Transcranial Magnetic Stimulation Therapy for Major Depressive Disorder: A Sham-Controlled Randomized Trial," *Archives of General Psychiatry* 67, no. 5 (2010): 507–16, doi:10.1001/archgenpsychiatry.2010.46.

11. Sung Wook Chung, Kate E. Hoy, and Paul B. Fitzgerald, "Theta-Burst Stimulation: A New Form of TMS Treatment for Depression?," *Depression and Anxiety* 32, no. 3 (2014): 182–92, doi:10.1002/da.22335.

Chapter 8

1. James Luccarelli, Michael E. Henry, and Thomas H. McCoy, "Demographics of Patients Receiving Electroconvulsive Therapy Based on State-Mandated Reporting Data," *Journal of ECT* 36, no. 4 (2020): 229–33, doi:10.1097/yct.0000000000000692.

2. William Z. Potter and Matthew V. Rudorfer, "Electroconvulsive Therapy—A Modern Medical Procedure," *New England Journal of Medicine* 328, no. 12 (1993): 882–83, doi:10.1056/nejm199303253281213.

3. Mathew V. Rudorfer, Michael E. Henry, and Harold A. Sackeim, *Electroconvulsive Therapy in Psychiatry*, ed. Allen Tasman, Jerald Kay, Jeffrey A. Lieberman (Philadelphia: W. B. Saunders, 1997); Max Fink, *Electroconvulsive Therapy: A Guide for Professionals and Their Patients*, 2nd ed. (New York: Oxford University Press, 2009).

4. Fink, *Electroconvulsive Therapy*.

5. Max Fink, "Meduna and the Origins of Convulsive Therapy," *American Journal of Psychiatry* 141, no. 9 (1984): 1034–41, doi:10.1176/ajp.141.9.1034.

6. Harold A. Sackeim, Joan Prudic, Mitchell S. Nobler, Linda Fitzsimons, Sarah H. Lisanby, Nancy Payne, Robert M. Berman, Eva-Lotta Brakemeier, Tarique Perera, and D. P. Devanand, "Effects of Pulse Width and Electrode Placement on the Efficacy and Cognitive Effects of Electroconvulsive Therapy," *Brain Stimulation* 1, no. 2 (2008): 71–83, doi:10.1016/j.brs.2008.03.001.

7. Rudorfer, Henry, and Sackeim, *Electroconvulsive Therapy in Psychiatry*.

8. Fink, "Meduna and the Origins of Convulsive Therapy," 1034–41.

9. Rudorfer, Henry, and Sackeim, *Electroconvulsive Therapy in Psychiatry*; Andrew Teodorczuk, Brett Emmerson, and Gail Robinson, "Revisiting the Role of Electroconvulsive Therapy in Schizophrenia: Where Are We Now?," *Australasian Psychiatry* 27, no. 5 (2019): 477–79, doi:10.1177/1039856219860033.

10. Rudorfer, Henry, and Sackeim, *Electroconvulsive Therapy in Psychiatry*.

11. Luccarelli, Henry, and McCoy, "Demographics of Patients Receiving Electroconvulsive Therapy Based on State-Mandated Reporting Data," 229–33.

12. Richard D. Weiner, C. Edward Coffey, Laura J. Fochtman, Robert M. Greenberg, Keith E. Eisenberg, Charles H. Kellner, Harold A. Sackeim, and Luois Moench, *The Practice of Electroconvulsive Therapy* (Washington, DC: American Psychiatric Association, 2001).

13. David J. Kupfer, "The Pharmacological Management of Depression," *Dialogues in Clinical Neuroscience* 7, no. 3 (2005): 191–205, doi:10.31887/dcns.2005.7.3/dkupfer.

14. P. Brambilla, A. Cipriani, M. Hotopf, and C. Barbui, "Side-Effect Profile of Fluoxetine in Comparison with Other SSRIs, Tricyclic and Newer Antidepressants: A Meta-Analysis of Clinical Trial Data," *Pharmacopsychiatry* 8, no. 2 (2005): 69–77, doi:10.1055/s-2005-837806.

15. John Simons, "Lilly Goes Off Prozac," *Fortune* 149 (2004), 179–80, 182, 184.

16. Kupfer, "Pharmacological Management of Depression," 191–205.

17. M. E. Thase and A. J. Rush, "When at First You Don't Succeed: Sequential Strategies for Antidepressant Nonresponders," *Journal of Clinical Psychiatry* 58, suppl 13 (1997): 23–29. PMID: 9402916.

18. Roar Fosse, Wenche Ryberg, Merete Kvalsvik Carlsson, and Jan Hammer, "Predictors of Suicide in the Patient Population Admitted to a Locked-Door Psychiatric Acute Ward," *PLoS ONE* 12, no. 3 (2017): e0173958, doi:10.1371/journal.pone.0173958.

19. Sophia Bennett and Alan J. Thomas, "Depression and Dementia: Cause, Consequence or Coincidence?," *Maturitas* 79, no. 2 (2014): 184–90, doi:10.1016/j.maturitas.2014.05.009.

20. W. Vaughn McCall, "Electroconvulsive Therapy in the Era of Modern Psychopharmacology," *International Journal of Neuropsychopharmacology* 4, no. 3 (2001): 315–24, doi:10.1017/s1461145701002437.

21. Peter D. Kramer, *Listening to Prozac: A Psychiatrist Explores Antidepressant Drugs and Remaking of the Self*, rev. ed. (New York: Penguin, 1997).

22. Elżbieta Wyska, "Pharmacokinetic Considerations for Current State-of-the-Art Antidepressants," *Expert Opinion on Drug Metabolism & Toxicology* 15, no. 10 (2019): 1–17, doi:1 0.1080/17425255.2019.1669560.

23. Sherrill Rose, Sarah K. Dotters-Katz, and Jeffrey A. Kuller, "Electroconvulsive Therapy in Pregnancy: Safety, Best Practices, and Barriers to Care," *Obstetrical & Gynecological Survey* 75, no. 3 (2020): 199–203, doi:10.1097/ogx.0000000000000763.

24. Teri Pearlstein, "Depression during Pregnancy," *Best Practice & Research Clinical Obstetrics & Gynaecology* 29, no. 5 (2015): 754–64, doi:10.1016/j.bpobgyn.2015.04.004.

25. Rose, Dotters-Katz, and Kuller, "Electroconvulsive Therapy in Pregnancy," 199–203.

26. L. Maronge and D. Bogod, "Complications in Obstetric Anaesthesia," *Anaesthesia* 73, no. S1 (2018): 61–66, doi:10.1111/anae.14141.

27. Diarmid J. M. Sinclair, Sai Zhao, Fang Qi, Kazare Nyakyoma, Joey S. W. Kwong, and Clive E. Adams, "Electroconvulsive Therapy for Treatment-Resistant Schizophrenia," *Cochrane Database of Systematic Reviews* 3, no. 3 (2019): CD011847, doi:10.1002/14651858. cd011847.pub2.

28. Bjanka Vuksan Cusa, Nataša Klepac, Nenad Jakši, Zoran Bradaš, Marija Boievi, Natalia Palac, and Marina Šagud, "The Effects of Electroconvulsive Therapy Augmentation of Antipsychotic Treatment on Cognitive Functions in Patients with Treatment-Resistant Schizophrenia," *Journal of ECT* 34, no. 1 (2018): 31–34, doi:10.1097/yct.0000000000000463; Max Fink and Harold A. Sackeim, "Convulsive Therapy in Schizophrenia?," *Schizophrenia Bulletin* 22, no. 1 (1996): 27–39, doi:10.1093/schbul/22.1.27.

29. Amber N. Edinoff, Sarah E. Kaufman, Janice W. Hollier, Celina G. Virgen, Christian A. Karam, Garett W. Malone, Elyse M. Cornett, Adam M. Kaye, and Alan D. Kaye, "Catatonia: Clinical Overview of the Diagnosis, Treatment, and Clinical Challenges," *Neurology International* 13, no. 4 (2021): 570–86, doi:10.3390/neurolint13040057.

30. John Read, Sue Cunliffe, Sameer Jauhar, and Declan M. McLoughlin, "Should We Stop Using Electroconvulsive Therapy?," *British Medical Journal* 364 (2019): k5233, doi:10.1136/ bmj.k5233.

31. B. J. Alpers, "The Brain Changes Associated with Electrical Shock Treatment, a Critical Review," *Lancet* 66, no. 11 (1946): 363–69.

32. Danielle Anderson, Robert Wollmann, and Stephen H. Dinwiddie, "Neuropatholog-ical Evaluation of an 84-Year-Old Man after 422 ECT Treatments," *Journal of ECT* 30, no. 3 (2014): 248–50, doi:10.1097/yct.0000000000000062.

33. Jason Scalia, Sarah H. Lisanby, Andrew J. Dwork, James E. Johnson, Elisabeth R. Bernhardt, Victoria Arango, and W. Vaughn McCall, "Neuropathologic Examination after 91 ECT Treatments in a 92-Year-Old Woman with Late-Onset Depression," *Journal of ECT* 23, no. 2 (2007): 96–98, doi:10.1097/yct.0b013e31804bb99d.

34. Erlyn Limoa, Sadayuki Hashioka, Tsuyoshi Miyaoka, Keiko Tsuchie, Ryosuke Arauchi, Ilhamuddin A. Azis, Rei Wake, et al., "Electroconvulsive Shock Attenuated Microgliosis and Astrogliosis in the Hippocampus and Ameliorated Schizophrenia-Like Behavior of Gunn Rat," *Journal of Neuroinflammation* 13, no. 1 (2016): 230, doi:10.1186/s12974-016-0688-2.

35. Xianli An and Xiujian Shi, "Effects of Electroconvulsive Shock on Neuro-Immune Responses: Does Neuro-Damage Occur?," *Psychiatry Research* 292 (2020): 113289, doi:10.1016/j.psychres.2020.113289.

36. Leif Oltedal, Katherine L. Narr, Christopher Abbott, Amit Anand, Miklos Argyelan, Hauke Bartsch, Udo Dannlowski, et al., "Volume of the Human Hippocampus and Clin-ical Response Following Electroconvulsive Therapy," *Biological Psychiatry* 84, no. 8 (2018): 574–81, doi:10.1016/j.biopsych.2018.05.017.

37. K. Gbyl and P. Videbech, "Electroconvulsive Therapy Increases Brain Volume in Major Depression: A Systematic Review and Meta-Analysis," *Acta Psychiatrica Scandinavica* 138, no. 3 (2018): 180–95, doi:10.1111/acps.12884.

38. Gbyl and Videbech, "Electroconvulsive Therapy Increases Brain Volume in Major Depression," 180–95.

39. James Luccarelli, Thomas H. McCoy, Stephen J. Seiner, and Michael E. Henry, "Main-tenance ECT Is Associated with Sustained Improvement in Depression Symptoms without Adverse Cognitive Effects in a Retrospective Cohort of 100 Patients Each Receiving 50 or More ECT Treatments," *Journal of Affective Disorders* 271 (2020): 109–14, doi:10.1016/j.jad.2020.03.152.

Chapter 9

1. B. N. Gaynes, A. J. Rush, M. H. Trivedi, S. R. Wisniewski, D. Spencer, and M. Fava, "The STAR*D Study: Treating Depression in the Real World," *Cleveland Clinic Journal of Medicine* 75, no. 1 (2008): 57–66, doi:10.3949/ccjm.75.1.57.

2. Joan Domènech-Abella, Elvira Lara, Maria Rubio-Valera, Beatriz Olaya, Maria Victoria Moneta, Laura Alejandra Rico-Uribe, Jose Luis Ayuso-Mateos, Jordi Mundó, and Josep Maria Haro, "Loneliness and Depression in the Elderly: The Role of Social Network," *Social Psychia-try and Psychiatric Epidemiology* 52, no. 4 (2017): 381–90, doi:10.1007/s00127-017-1339-3.

3. William M. McDonald, "Is ECT Cost-Effective? A Critique of the National Institute of Health and Clinical Excellence's Report on the Economic Analysis of ECT," *Journal of ECT* 22, no. 1 (2006): 25–29, doi:10.1097/00124509-200603000-00005.

4. Aazaz U. Haq, Adam F. Sitzmann, Mona L. Goldman, Daniel F. Maixner, and Brian J. Mickey, "Response of Depression to Electroconvulsive Therapy," *Journal of Clinical Psychiatry* 76, no. 10 (2015): 1374–84, doi:10.4088/jcp.14r09528.

5. Samuel T. Wilkinson, Edeanya Agbese, Douglas L. Leslie, and Robert A. Rosenheck, "Identifying Recipients of Electroconvulsive Therapy: Data from Privately Insured Americans," *Psychiatric Services* 69, no. 5 (2018): 542–48, doi:10.1176/appi.ps.201700364.

6. American Psychiatric Association, *Diagnostic and Statistical Manual of Mental Disorders*, 5th ed.

7. M. E. Thase and A. J. Rush, "When at First You Don't Succeed: Sequential Strategies for Antidepressant Nonresponders," *Journal of Clinical Psychiatry* 58, suppl 13 (1997): 23–29. PMID: 9402916; Richard C. Shelton, Olawale Osuntokun, Alexandra N. Heinloth, and Sara A. Corya, "Therapeutic Options for Treatment-Resistant Depression," *CNS Drugs* 24, no. 2 (2010): 131–61, doi:10.2165/11530280-000000000-00000.

8. Marta Ramos, Cecilia Berrogain, Julia Concha, Laura Lomba, Cristina García, and Mª Ribate, "Pharmacogenetic Studies: A Tool to Improve Antidepressant Therapy," *Drug Metabolism and Personalized Therapy* 31, no. 4 (2016): 197–204, doi:10.1515/dmpt-2016-0019.

9. Martin Desseilles, Janet Witte, Trina E. Chang, Nadia Iovieno, Christina M. Dording, Heidi Ashih, Maren Nyer, Marlene P. Freeman, Maurizio Fava, and David Mischoulon, "Assessing the Adequacy of Past Antidepressant Trials: A Clinician's Guide to the Antidepressant Treatment Response Questionnaire (ASCP Corner)," *Journal of Clinical Psychiatry* 72, no. 8 (2011): 1152–54, doi:10.4088/jcp.11ac07225.

10. J. E. J. Buckman, A. Underwood, K. Clarke, R. Saunders, S. D. Hollon, P. Fearon, and S. Pilling, "Risk Factors for Relapse and Recurrence of Depression in Adults and How They Operate: A Four-Phase Systematic Review and Meta-Synthesis," *Clinical Psychology Review* 64 (2018): 13–38, doi:10.1016/j.cpr.2018.07.005.

11. Richard D. Weiner, C. Edward Coffey, Laura J. Fochtman, Robert M. Greenberg, Keith E. Eisenberg, Charles H. Kellner, Harold A. Sackeim, and Luois Moench, *The Practice of Electroconvulsive Therapy* (Washington, DC: American Psychiatric Association, 2001).

12. Sheryl Salaris, Martin P. Szuba, and Karen Traber, "ECT and Intracranial Vascular Masses," *Journal of ECT* 16, no. 2 (2000): 198–203, doi:10.1097/00124509-200006000-00012.

13. Ashwin A. Patkar, Kevin P. Hill, Stephen P. Weinstein, and Stephen L. Schwartz, "ECT in the Presence of Brain Tumor and Increased Intracranial Pressure: Evaluation and Reduction of Risk," *Journal of ECT* 16, no. 2 (2000): 189–97, doi:10.1097/00124509-200006000-00011.

14. Weiner et al., *Practice of Electroconvulsive Therapy*; Viji Kurup and Robert Ostroff, "When Cardiac Patients Need ECT—Challenges for the Anesthesiologist," *International Anesthesiology Clinics* 50, no. 2 (2012): 128–40, doi:10.1097/aia.0b013e31824ff57c; Ethan O. Bryson, Dennis Popeo, Mimi Briggs, Rosa M. Pasculli, and Charles H. Kellner, "Electroconvulsive Therapy (ECT) in Patients with Cardiac Disease," *Journal of ECT* 29, no. 1 (2013): 76–77, doi:10.1097/yct.0b013e318271761a.

15. Weiner et al., *Practice of Electroconvulsive Therapy*.

16. John H. Lazarus, "Lithium and Thyroid," *Best Practice & Research Clinical Endocrinology & Metabolism* 23, no. 6 (2009): 723–33, doi:10.1016/j.beem.2009.06.002.

17. Neville Peel Lancaster, Reuben Ralph Steinert, and Isaac Frost, "Unilateral Electro-Convulsive Therapy," *Journal of Mental Science* 104, no. 434 (1958): 221–27, doi:10.1192/bjp.104.434.221.

18. Harm-Pieter Spaans, Esmée Verwijk, Hannie C. Comijs, Rob M. Kok, Pascal Sienaert, Filip Bouckaert, Katrien Fannes, et al., "Efficacy and Cognitive Side Effects after Brief Pulse and Ultrabrief Pulse Right Unilateral Electroconvulsive Therapy for Major Depression," *Journal of Clinical Psychiatry* 74, no. 11 (2013): e1029–e1036, doi:10.4088/jcp.13m08538.

19. Harold A. Sackeim, P. Decina, M. Kanzler, B. Kerr, and S. Malitz, "Effects of Electrode Placement on the Efficacy of Titrated, Low-Dose ECT," *American Journal of Psychiatry* 144, no. 11 (1987): 1449–55, doi:10.1176/ajp.144.11.1449.

20. H. Janouschek, T. Nickl-Jockschat, M. Haeck, B. Gillmann, and M. Grözinger, "Comparison of Methohexital and Etomidate as Anesthetic Agents for Electroconvulsive Therapy in Affective and Psychotic Disorders," *Journal of Psychiatric Research* 47, no. 5 (2013): 686–93, doi:10.1016/j.jpsychires.2012.12.019.

21. Alok Kumar, Devendra Kumar Sharma, and Raghunandan Mani, "A Comparison of Propofol and Thiopentone for Electroconvulsive Therapy," *Journal of Anaesthesiology, Clinical Pharmacology* 28, no. 3 (2012): 353–57, doi:10.4103/0970-9185.98337.

22. "Pseudocholinesterase Deficiency," MedlinePlus, last updated April 1, 2012, https://medlineplus.gov/genetics/condition/pseudocholinesterase-deficiency/.

23. Ravi K. Sharma, Gajanan Kulkarni, Channaveerachari Naveen Kumar, Shyam Sundar Arumugham, Venkataramaiah Sudhir, Urvakhsh M. Mehta, Sayantanava Mitra, Milind Vijay Thanki, and Jagadisha Thirthalli, "Antidepressant Effects of Ketamine and ECT: A Pilot Comparison," *Journal of Affective Disorders* 276 (2020): 260–66, doi:10.1016/j.jad.2020.07.066.

24. Donel M. Martin, Ada Wong, Divya R. Kumar, and Colleen K. Loo, "Validation of the 10-Item Orientation Questionnaire," *Journal of ECT* 34, no. 1 (2018): 21–25, doi:10.1097/yct.000000000000.

25. Mathew V. Rudorfer, Michael E. Henry, and Harold A. Sackeim, *Electroconvulsive Therapy in Psychiatry*, ed. Allen Tasman, Jerald Kay, and Jeffrey A. Lieberman (Philadelphia: W. B. Saunders, 1997).

26. "Odds of Dying," Preventable Deaths, National Safety Council: Injury Facts, https://injuryfacts.nsc.org/all-injuries/preventable-death-overview/odds-of-dying/.

27. Stephanie Chiao, Keith Isenberg, and Carol S. North, "Psychotropic Medication Effects on Seizure Threshold and Seizure Duration during Electroconvulsive Therapy Stimulus Titration," *Journal of ECT* 36, no. 2 (2020): 115–22, doi:10.1097/yct.0000000000000621.

28. A. Jha and G. Stein, "Decreased Efficacy of Combined Benzodiazepines and Unilateral ECT in Treatment of Depression," *Acta Psychiatrica Scandinavica* 94, no. 2 (1996): 101–4, doi:10.1111/j.1600-0447.1996.tb09832.x.

29. L. Tondo and R. J. Baldessarini, "Reduced Suicide Risk during Lithium Maintenance Treatment," *Journal of Clinical Psychiatry* 61, suppl 9 (2000): 97–104. PMID: 10826667.

30. Rikinkumar S. Patel, Anil Bachu, and Nagy A. Youssef, "Combination of Lithium and Electroconvulsive Therapy (ECT) Is Associated with Higher Odds of Delirium and Cognitive Problems in a Large National Sample across the United States," *Brain Stimulation* 13, no. 1 (2020): 15–19, doi:10.1016/j.brs.2019.08.012.

Chapter 10

1. Sarah Fader, "The 5 Stages of Change and What They Mean to You," Betterhelp, March 31, 2022, https://www.betterhelp.com/advice/behavior/the-5-stages-of-change-and-what-they -mean-to-you/.

2. Rachel R. Kleis, Matt C. Hoch, Rachel Hogg-Graham, and Johanna M. Hoch, "The Effectiveness of the Transtheoretical Model to Improve Physical Activity in Healthy Adults: A Systematic Review," *Journal of Physical Activity and Health* 18, no. 1 (2021): 94–108, doi:10.1123/jpah.2020-0334; James O. Prochaska and Wayne F. Velicer, "The Transtheoretical Model of Health Behavior Change," *American Journal of Health Promotion* 12, no. 1 (1997): 38–48, doi:10.4278/0890-1171-12.1.38.

3. Emily M. Paolucci, Dessi Loukov, Dawn M. E. Bowdish, and Jennifer J. Heisz, "Exercise Reduces Depression and Inflammation but Intensity Matters," *Biological Psychology* 133 (2018): 79–84, doi:10.1016/j.biopsycho.2018.01.015; Benjamin Gardner, Phillippa Lally, and Jane Wardle, "Making Health Habitual: The Psychology of 'Habit-Formation' and General Practice," *British Journal of General Practice* 62, no. 605 (2012): 664–66, doi:10.3399/ bjgp12x659466.

4. Kleis et al., "Effectiveness of the Transtheoretical Model to Improve Physical Activity in Healthy Adults," 94–108.

5. Gardner, Lally, and Wardle, "Making Health Habitual," 664–66; Fader, "5 Stages of Change"; Brooklin White, "How to Create a Lasting Behavior Change," Amos Institute, accessed July 16, 2022, https://amosinstitute.com/blog/how-to-create-a-lasting-behavior-change/.

6. James Clear, *Atomic Habits* (New York: Penguin Random House, 2018).

7. Julie Jargon, "How to Find and Keep Friends: A Guide for Middle Age," *Wall Street Journal*, January 29, 2022, https://www.wsj.com/articles/being-a-parent-is-lonelyheres-how-to-find -and-keep-friends-in-2022-11643465968.

8. Charles P. Ransfod, "A Role for Amines in the Antidepressant Effect of Exercise: A Review," *Medicine & Science in Sports & Exercise* 14, no. 1 (1982): 1, doi:10.1249/00005768 -198201000-00001.

9. T. Carter, I. Morres, J. Repper, and P. Callaghan, "Exercise for Adolescents with Depression: Valued Aspects and Perceived Change," *Journal of Psychiatric and Mental Health Nursing* 23, no. 1 (2016): 37–44, doi:10.1111/jpm.12261; Brett R. Gordon, Cillian P. McDowell, Mats Hallgren, Jacob D. Meyer, Mark Lyons, and Matthew P. Herring, "Association of Efficacy of Resistance Exercise Training with Depressive Symptoms: Meta-Analysis and Meta-Regression Analysis of Randomized Clinical Trials," *JAMA Psychiatry* 75, no. 6 (2018): 566, doi:10.1001/jamapsychiatry.2018.0572; Andrea L. Dunn, Madhukar H. Trivedi, James B.

Kampert, Camillia G. Clark, and Heather O. Chambliss, "Exercise Treatment for Depression Efficacy and Dose Response," *American Journal of Preventive Medicine* 28, no. 1 (2005): 1–8, doi:10.1016/j.amepre.2004.09.003; Noora Sjösten and Sirkka-Liisa Kivelä, "The Effects of Physical Exercise on Depressive Symptoms among the Aged: A Systematic Review," *International Journal of Geriatric Psychiatry* 21, no. 5 (2006): 410–18, doi:10.1002/gps.1494.

10. James A. Blumenthal, Michael A. Babyak, P. Murali Doraiswamy, Lana Watkins, Benson M. Hoffman, Krista A. Barbour, Steve Herman, et al., "Exercise and Pharmacotherapy in the Treatment of Major Depressive Disorder," *Psychosomatic Medicine* 69, no. 7 (2007): 587–96, doi:10.1097/psy.0b013e318148c19a.

11. James A. Blumenthal, Michael A. Babyak, Kathleen A. Moore, W. Edward Craighead, Steve Herman, Parinda Khatri, Robert Waugh, et al., "Effects of Exercise Training on Older Patients with Major Depression," *Archives of Internal Medicine* 159, no. 19 (1999): 2349–56, doi:10.1001/archinte.159.19.2349.

12. Jesús López-Torres Hidalgo, Joseba Rabanales Sotos, and DEP-EXERCISE Group, "Effectiveness of Physical Exercise in Older Adults with Mild to Moderate Depression," *Annals of Family Medicine* 19, no. 4 (2021): 302–9, doi:10.1370/afm.2670.

13. Belvederi M. Murri, M. Amore, M. Menchetti, G. Toni, F. Neviani, M. Cerri, L. Rocchi, et al., "Physical Exercise for Late-Life Major Depression," *British Journal of Psychiatry* 207, no. 3 (2015): 235–42, doi:10.1192/bjp.bp.114.150516.

14. Wendy Bumgardner, "Getting Exercise with Nordic Walking," VeryWell, December 28, 2020, https://www.verywellfit.com/nordic-walking-3432907.

15. Brett R. Gordon, Cillian P. McDowell, Mats Hallgren, Jacob D. Meyer, Mark Lyons, and Matthew P. Herring, "Association of Efficacy of Resistance Exercise Training with Depressive Symptoms: Meta-Analysis and Meta-Regression Analysis of Randomized Clinical Trials," *JAMA Psychiatry* 75, no. 6 (2018): 566, doi:10.1001/jamapsychiatry.2018.0572.

16. Matthew P. Herring, Marni L. Jacob, Cynthia Suveg, Rodney K. Dishman, and Patrick J. O'Connor, "Feasibility of Exercise Training for the Short-Term Treatment of Generalized Anxiety Disorder: A Randomized Controlled Trial," *Psychotherapy and Psychosomatics* 81, no. 1 (2011): 21–28, doi:10.1159/000327898; Cindy K. Barha, Liisa A. Galea, Lindsay S. Nagamatsu, Kirk I. Erickson, and Teresa Liu-Ambrose, "Personalising Exercise Recommendations for Brain Health: Considerations and Future Directions," *British Journal of Sports Medicine* 51, no. 8 (2017): 636, doi:10.1136/bjsports-2016-096710.

17. Felipe B. Schuch, Davy Vancampfort, Justin Richards, Simon Rosenbaum, Philip B. Ward, and Brendon Stubbs, "Exercise as a Treatment for Depression: A Meta-Analysis Adjusting for Publication Bias," *Journal of Psychiatric Research* 77 (2016): 42–51, doi:10.1016/j.jpsychires.2016.02.023.

18. Kassia S. Weston, Ulrik Wisløff, and Jeff S. Coombes, "High-Intensity Interval Training in Patients with Lifestyle-Induced Cardiometabolic Disease: A Systematic Review and Meta-Analysis," *British Journal of Sports Medicine* 48, no. 16 (2014): 1227, doi:10.1136/bjsports-2013-092576.

19. Nicole Korman, Michael Armour, Justin Chapman, Simon Rosenbaum, Steve Kisely, Shuichi Suetani, Joseph Firth, and Dan Siskind, "High Intensity Interval Training (HIIT) for People with Severe Mental Illness: A Systematic Review & Meta-Analysis of Intervention Studies—Considering Diverse Approaches for Mental and Physical Recovery," *Psychiatry Research* 284 (2019): 112601, doi:10.1016/j.psychres.2019.112601.

20. Harvard Health Publishing, "Fitness Trend: Nordic Walking," Harvard Medical School, November 1, 2019, https://www.health.harvard.edu/staying-healthy/fitness-trend-nordic-walking.

21. Frank Kruisdijk, Marijke Hopman-Rock, Aartjan T. F. Beekman, and Ingrid Hendriksen, "EFFORT-D: Results of a Randomised Controlled Trial Testing the Effect of Running Therapy on Depression," *BMC Psychiatry* 19, no. 1 (2019): 170, doi:10.1186/s12888-019-2156-x; Bumgardner, "Getting Exercise with Nordic Walking."

22. Dunn et al., "Exercise Treatment for Depression Efficacy and Dose Response," 1–8.

23. World Health Organization, "Physical Activity," November 26, 2020, https://www.who.int/news-room/fact-sheets/detail/physical-activity.

24. Peter L. Franzen and Daniel J. Buysse, "Sleep Disturbances and Depression: Risk Relationships for Subsequent Depression and Therapeutic Implications," *Dialogues in Clinical Neuroscience* 10, no. 4 (2008): 473–81, doi:10.31887/dcns.2008.10.4/plfranzen.

25. American Psychiatric Association, *Diagnostic and Statistical Manual of Mental Disorders*, 5th ed.

26. Dieter Riemann, Lukas B. Krone, Katharina Wulff, and Christoph Nissen, "Sleep, Insomnia, and Depression," *Neuropsychopharmacology* 45, no. 1 (2020): 74–89, doi:10.1038/s41386-019-0411-y.

27. Ian M. Colrain, Christian L. Nicholas, and Fiona C. Baker, "Alcohol and the Sleeping Brain," *Handbook of Clinical Neurology* 125 (2014): 415–31, doi:10.1016/b978-0-444-62619-6.00024-0.

28. Kimberly A. Babson, James Sottile, and Danielle Morabito, "Cannabis, Cannabinoids, and Sleep: A Review of the Literature," *Current Psychiatry Reports* 19, no. 4 (2017): 23, doi:10.1007/s11920-017-0775-9.

29. Daniel Feingold and Aviv Weinstein, "Cannabinoids and Neuropsychiatric Disorders," *Advances in Experimental Medicine and Biology* 1264 (2020): 67–80, doi:10.1007/978-3-030-57369-0_5.

30. Christine E. Spadola, Na Guo, Dayna A. Johnson, Tamar Sofer, Suzanne M. Bertisch, Chandra L. Jackson, Michael Rueschman, Murray A. Mittleman, James G. Wilson, and Susan Redline, "Evening Intake of Alcohol, Caffeine, and Nicotine: Night-to-Night Associations with Sleep Duration and Continuity among African Americans in the Jackson Heart Sleep Study," *Sleep* 42, no. 11 (2019), doi:10.1093/sleep/zsz136.

31. Jasmyn E. A. Cunningham and Colin M. Shapiro, "Cognitive Behavioural Therapy for Insomnia (CBT-I) to Treat Depression: A Systematic Review," *Journal of Psychosomatic Research* 106 (2018): 1–12, doi:10.1016/j.jpsychores.2017.12.012.

32. US Department of Veterans Affairs, "Veterans CBT-iCoach," VAmobile, accessed July 16, 2022, https://mobile.va.gov/app/cbt-i-coach.

33. Michael J. Sateia, Daniel J. Buysse, Andrew D. Krystal, David N. Neubauer, and Jonathan L. Heald, "Clinical Practice Guideline for the Pharmacologic Treatment of Chronic Insomnia in Adults: An American Academy of Sleep Medicine Clinical Practice Guideline," *Journal of Clinical Sleep Medicine* 13, no. 2 (2017): 307–49, doi:10.5664/jcsm.6470.

34. Michael Ioannou, Constanze Wartenberg, Josephine T. V. Greenbrook, Tomas Larson, Kajsa Magnusson, Linnea Schmitz, Petteri Sjögren, Ida Stadig, Zoltán Szabó, and Steinn Steingrimsson, "Sleep Deprivation as Treatment for Depression: Systematic Review and Meta-Analysis," *Acta Psychiatrica Scandinavica* 143, no. 1 (2021): 22–35, doi:10.1111/acps. 13253.

35. Agnès Le Port, Alice Gueguen, Emmanuelle Kesse-Guyot, Maria Melchior, Cédric Lemogne, Hermann Nabi, Marcel Goldberg, Marie Zins, and Sébastien Czernichow, "Association between Dietary Patterns and Depressive Symptoms over Time: A 10-Year Follow-Up Study of the GAZEL Cohort," *PLoS ONE* 7, no. 12 (2012): e51593, doi:10.1371/journal. pone.0051593.

36. Robert E. Roberts, George A. Kaplan, Sarah J. Shema, and William J. Strawbridge, "Are the Obese at Greater Risk for Depression?," *American Journal of Epidemiology* 152, no. 2 (2000): 163–70, doi:10.1093/aje/152.2.163.

37. R. S. Opie, C. Itsiopoulos, N. Parletta, A. Sanchez-Villegas, T. N. Akbaraly, A. Ruusunen, and F. N. Jacka, "Dietary Recommendations for the Prevention of Depression," *Nutritional Neuroscience* 20, no. 3 (2016): 1–11, doi:10.1179/1476830515y.0000000043; Laura R. LaChance and Drew Ramsey, "Antidepressant Foods: An Evidence-Based Nutrient Profiling System for Depression," *World Journal of Psychiatry* 8, no. 3 (2018): 97–104, doi:10.5498/wjp.v8.i3.97.

38. LaChance and Ramsey, "Antidepressant Foods"; Sarah T. Stahl, Steven M. Albert, Mary Amanda Dew, Michael H. Lockovich, and Charles F. Reynolds, "Coaching in Healthy Dietary Practices in At-Risk Older Adults: A Case of Indicated Depression Prevention," *American Journal of Psychiatry* 171, no. 5 (2014): 499–505, doi:10.1176/appi.ajp.2013.13101373.

39. Agata Chudzik, Anna Orzyłowska, Radosław Rola, and Greg J. Stanisz, "Probiotics, Prebiotics and Postbiotics on Mitigation of Depression Symptoms: Modulation of the Brain–Gut–Microbiome Axis," *Biomolecules* 11, no. 7 (2021): 1000, doi:10.3390/biom11071000.

40. Bruno Bonaz, Thomas Bazin, and Sonia Pellissier, "The Vagus Nerve at the Interface of the Microbiota-Gut-Brain Axis," *Frontiers in Neuroscience* 12 (2018): 49, doi:10.3389/fnins.2018. 00049; Jolana Wagner-Skacel, Nina Dalkner, Sabrina Moerkl, Kathrin Kreuzer, Aitak Farzi, Sonja Lackner, Annamaria Painold, Eva Z. Reininghaus, Mary I. Butler, and Susanne Bengesser, "Sleep and Microbiome in Psychiatric Diseases," *Nutrients* 12, no. 8 (2020): 2198, doi:10.3390/ nu12082198.

41. Richard T. Liu, Rachel F. L. Walsh, and Ana E. Sheehan, "Prebiotics and Probiotics for Depression and Anxiety: A Systematic Review and Meta-Analysis of Controlled

Clinical Trials," *Neuroscience & Biobehavioral Reviews* 102 (2019): 13–23, doi:10.1016/j. neubiorev.2019.03.023.

42. Fereidoon Shahidi and Priyatharini Ambigaipalan, "Omega-3 Polyunsaturated Fatty Acids and Their Health Benefits," *Annual Review of Food Science and Technology* 9, no. 1 (2017): 1–37, doi:10.1146/annurev-food-111317-095850; Mansoor D. Burhani and Mark M. Rasenick, "Fish Oil and Depression: The Skinny on Fats," *Journal of Integrative Neuroscience* 16, no. s1 (2017): S115–S124, doi:10.3233/jin-170072.

43. Burhani and Rasenick, "Fish Oil and Depression," S115–S124.

44. Liu, Walsh, and Sheehan, "Prebiotics and Probiotics for Depression and Anxiety," 13–23.

45. Elizaveta A. Trush, Elena A. Poluektova, Allan G. Beniashvilli, Oleg S. Shifrin, Yuri M. Poluektov, and Vladimir T. Ivashkin, "The Evolution of Human Probiotics: Challenges and Prospects," *Probiotics and Antimicrobial Proteins* 12, no. 4 (2020): 1291–99, doi:10.1007/s12602-019-09628-4.

46. Gordon B. Parker, Heather Brotchie, and Rebecca K. Graham, "Vitamin D and Depression," *Journal of Affective Disorders* 208 (2017): 56–61, doi:10.1016/j.jad.2016.08.082.

47. Vyara Valkanova, Klaus P. Ebmeier, and Charlotte L. Allan, "CRP, IL-6 and Depression: A Systematic Review and Meta-Analysis of Longitudinal Studies," *Journal of Affective Disorders* 150, no. 3 (2013): 736–44, doi:10.1016/j.jad.2013.06.004; Piotr Gałecki and Monika Talarowska, "Inflammatory Theory of Depression," *Psychiatria Polska* 52, no. 3 (2018): 437–47, doi:10.12740/pp/76863.

48. Tarique Hussain, Bie Tan, Yulong Yin, Francois Blachier, Myrlene C. B. Tossou, and Najma Rahu, "Oxidative Stress and Inflammation: What Polyphenols Can Do for Us?," *Oxidative Medicine and Cellular Longevity*, 2016: 7432797, doi:10.1155/2016/7432797.

49. Paolo Raggi, Jacques Genest, Jon T. Giles, Katey J. Rayner, Girish Dwivedi, Robert S. Beanlands, and Milan Gupta, "Role of Inflammation in the Pathogenesis of Atherosclerosis and Therapeutic Interventions," *Atherosclerosis* 276 (2018): 98–108, doi:10.1016/j. atherosclerosis.2018.07.014.

50. Robert Ross, Ian J. Neeland, Shizuya Yamashita, Iris Shai, Jaap Seidell, Paolo Magni, Raul D. Santos, et al., "Waist Circumference as a Vital Sign in Clinical Practice: A Consensus Statement from the IAS and ICCR Working Group on Visceral Obesity," *Nature Reviews. Endocrinology* 16, no. 3 (2020): 177–89, doi:10.1038/s41574-019-0310-7.

51. Camilla S. L. Tuttle, Lachlan A. N. Thang, and Andrea B. Maier, "Markers of Inflammation and Their Association with Muscle Strength and Mass: A Systematic Review and Meta-Analysis," *Ageing Research Reviews* 64 (2020): 101185, doi:10.1016/j. arr.2020.101185.

52. Anne Marie W. Petersen and Bente Klarlund Pedersen, "The Anti-Inflammatory Effect of Exercise," *Journal of Applied Physiology* 98, no. 4 (2005): 1154–62, doi:10.1152/japplphysiol.00164.2004.

53. Petersen and Pedersen, "Anti-Inflammatory Effect of Exercise," 1154–62.

54. Emily Yi-Chih Ting, Albert C. Yang, and Shih-Jen Tsai, "Role of Interleukin-6 in Depressive Disorder," *International Journal of Molecular Sciences* 21, no. 6 (2020): 2194, doi:10.3390/ijms21062194.

55. Frederic Derbré, Mari Carmen Gomez-Cabrera, Ana Lucia Nascimento, Fabian Sanchis-Gomar, Vladimir Essau Martinez-Bello, Jesus A. F. Tresguerres, Teresa Fuentes, Arlette Gratas-Delamarche, Maria Monsalve, and Jose Viña, "Age Associated Low Mitochondrial Biogenesis May Be Explained by Lack of Response of PGC-1α to Exercise Training," *AGE* 34, no. 3 (2012): 669–79, doi:10.1007/s11357-011-9264-y.

56. Nada Sallam and Ismail Laher, "Exercise Modulates Oxidative Stress and Inflammation in Aging and Cardiovascular Diseases," *Oxidative Medicine and Cellular Longevity* (2016): 7239639, doi:10.1155/2016/7239639.

57. Pierre-Eric Lutz, Philippe Courtet, and Raffaella Calati, "The Opioid System and the Social Brain: Implications for Depression and Suicide," *Journal of Neuroscience Research* 98, no. 4 (2020): 588–600, doi:10.1002/jnr.24269.

58. Nevena Jeremic, Pankaj Chaturvedi, and Suresh C. Tyagi, "Browning of White Fat: Novel Insight into Factors, Mechanisms, and Therapeutics," *Journal of Cellular Physiology* 232, no. 1 (2017): 61–68, doi:10.1002/jcp.25450.

59. Sogol Javaheri and Susan Redline, "Insomnia and Risk of Cardiovascular Disease," *Chest* 152, no. 2 (2017): 435–44, doi:10.1016/j.chest.2017.01.026.

60. Michael R. Irwin, Richard Olmstead, and Judith E. Carroll, "Sleep Disturbance, Sleep Duration, and Inflammation: A Systematic Review and Meta-Analysis of Cohort Studies and Experimental Sleep Deprivation," *Biological Psychiatry* 80, no. 1 (2016): 40–52, doi:10.1016/j.biopsych.2015.05.014.

61. Franzen and Buysse, "Sleep Disturbances and Depression," 473–81.

Chapter 11

1. D. E. Nichols, M. W. Johnson, and C. D. Nichols, "Psychedelics as Medicines: An Emerging New Paradigm," *Clinical Pharmacology & Therapeutics* 101, no. 2 (2017): 209–19, doi:10.1002/cpt.557.

2. M. W. Johnson, W. A. Richards, and R. R. Griffiths, "Human Hallucinogen Research: Guidelines for Safety," *Journal of Psychopharmacology* 22, no. 6 (2008): 603–20, doi:10.1177/0269881108093587.

3. Sean J. Belouin and Jack E. Henningfield, "Psychedelics: Where We Are Now, Why We Got Here, What We Must Do," *Neuropharmacology* 142 (2018): 7–19, doi:10.1016/j.neuropharm.2018.02.018; James J. H. Rucker, Jonathan Iliff, and David J. Nutt, "Psychiatry & the Psychedelic Drugs: Past, Present & Future," *Neuropharmacology* 142 (2018): 200–18, doi:10.1016/j.neuropharm.2017.12.040.

4. Michael Pollan, *How to Change Your Mind: What the New Science of Psychedelics Teaches Us About Consciousness, Dying, Addiction, Depression, and Transcendence* (New York: Penguin Random House, 2018).

5. Rucker, Iliff, and Nutt, "Psychiatry & the Psychedelic Drugs," 200–18.

6. Johnson, Richards, and Griffiths, "Human Hallucinogen Research," 603–20.

7. Andrew Jack, "GSK Shifts Away from Antidepressants," *Financial Times*, February 4, 2010, https://www.ft.com/content/103e87d2-11c4-11df-9d45-00144feab49a.

8. Pollan, *How to Change Your Mind*.

9. David E. Nichols, "Psychedelics," *Pharmacological Reviews* 68, no. 2 (2016): 264–355, doi:10.1124/pr.115.011478.

10. Franz X. Vollenweider, "Brain Mechanisms of Hallucinogens and Entactogens," *Dialogues in Clinical Neuroscience* 3, no. 4 (2001): 265–79, doi:10.31887/dcns.2001.3.4/fxvollenweider.

11. Nichols, "Psychedelics," 264–355; Robin Carhart-Harris, Bruna Giribaldi, Rosalind Watts, Michelle Baker-Jones, Ashleigh Murphy-Beiner, Roberta Murphy, Jonny Martell, Allan Blemings, David Erritzoe, and David J. Nutt, "Trial of Psilocybin versus Escitalopram for Depression," *New England Journal of Medicine* 384, no. 15 (2021): 1402–11, doi:10.1056/nejmoa2032994.

12. Rafael de la Torre, Magí Farré, Pere N. Roset, Neus Pizarro, Sergio Abanades, Mireia Segura, Jordi Segura, and Jordi Camí, "Human Pharmacology of MDMA," *Therapeutic Drug Monitoring* 26, no. 2 (2004): 137–44, doi:10.1097/00007691-200404000-00009; Susan Schenk and David Newcombe, "Methylenedioxymethamphetamine (MDMA) in Psychiatry," *Journal of Clinical Psychopharmacology* 38, no. 6 (2018): 632–38, doi:10.1097/jcp.0000000000000962.

13. Pollan, *How to Change Your Mind*.

14. David Nutt, "Psychedelic Drugs—A New Era in Psychiatry?," *Dialogues in Clinical Neuroscience* 21, no. 2 (2019): 139–47, doi:10.31887/dcns.2019.21.2/dnutt.

15. Michael C. Mithoefer, Charles S. Grob, and Timothy D. Brewerton, "Novel Psycho-pharmacological Therapies for Psychiatric Disorders: Psilocybin and MDMA," *Lancet Psychiatry* 3, no. 5 (2016): 481–88, doi:10.1016/s2215-0366(15)00576-3.

16. Pollan, *How to Change Your Mind*.

17. Ira Byock, "Taking Psychedelics Seriously," *Journal of Palliative Medicine* 21, no. 4 (2018): 417–21, doi:10.1089/jpm.2017.0684.

18. Roland R. Griffiths, Matthew W. Johnson, Michael A. Carducci, Annie Umbricht, William A. Richards, Brian D. Richards, Mary P. Cosimano, and Margaret A. Klinedinst, "Psilocybin Produces Substantial and Sustained Decreases in Depression and Anxiety in Patients with Life-Threatening Cancer: A Randomized Double-Blind Trial," *Journal of Psychopharmacology (Oxford, England)* 30, no. 12 (2016): 1181–97, doi:10.1177/0269881116675513.

19. Rucker, Iliff, and Nutt, "Psychiatry & the Psychedelic Drugs."

20. Carhart-Harris et al., "Trial of Psilocybin versus Escitalopram for Depression," 1402–11.

21. Carhart-Harris et al., "Trial of Psilocybin versus Escitalopram for Depression," 1402–11.

22. Alexander V. Lebedev, Martin Lövdén, Gidon Rosenthal, Amanda Feilding, David J. Nutt, and Robin L. Carhart-Harris, "Finding the Self by Losing the Self: Neural Correlates of Ego-Dissolution under Psilocybin," *Human Brain Mapping* 36, no. 8 (2015): 3137–53, doi:10.1002/hbm.22833.

23. Lisa Jerome, Allison A. Feduccia, Julie B. Wang, Scott Hamilton, Berra Yazar-Klosinski, Amy Emerson, Michael C. Mithoefer, and Rick Doblin, "Long-Term Follow-Up Outcomes of MDMA-Assisted Psychotherapy for Treatment of PTSD: A Longitudinal Pooled Analysis of Six Phase 2 Trials," *Psychopharmacology* 237, no. 8 (2020): 2485–97, doi:10.1007/s00213-020-05548-2.

24. Johnson, Richards, and Griffiths, "Human Hallucinogen Research," 603–20; Genís Ona and José Carlos Bouso, "Potential Safety, Benefits, and Influence of the Placebo Effect in Microdosing Psychedelic Drugs: A Systematic Review," *Neuroscience & Biobehavioral Reviews* 119 (2020): 194–203, doi:10.1016/j.neubiorev.2020.09.035.

25. National Institute on Drug Abuse, "Hallucinogens," https://nida.nih.gov/drug-topics /hallucinogens; Hartej Gill, Barjot Gill, David Chen-Li, Sabine El-Halabi, Nelson B. Rodrigues, Danielle S. Cha, Orly Lipsitz, et al., "The Emerging Role of Psilocybin and MDMA in the Treatment of Mental Illness," *Expert Review of Neurotherapeutics* 20, no. 12 (2020): 1–11, doi: 10.1080/14737175.2020.1826931.

26. Jerome et al., "Long-Term Follow-Up Outcomes of MDMA-Assisted Psychotherapy for Treatment of PTSD," 2485–97.

27. Daniel Rosenbaum, Cory Weissman, Thomas Anderson, Rotem Petranker, Le-Anh Dinh-Williams, Katrina Hui, and Emma Hapke, "Microdosing Psychedelics: Demographics, Practices, and Psychiatric Comorbidities," *Journal of Psychopharmacology* 34, no. 6 (2020): 612–22, doi:10.1177/0269881120908004.

28. Ona and Bouso, "Potential Safety, Benefits, and Influence of the Placebo Effect in Microdosing Psychedelic Drugs."

29. Ziad Nahas, Lauren B. Marangell, Mustafa M. Husain, A. John Rush, Harold A. Sackeim, Sarah H. Lisanby, James M. Martinez, and Mark S. George, "Two-Year Outcome of Vagus Nerve Stimulation (VNS) for Treatment of Major Depressive Episodes," *Journal of Clinical Psychiatry* 66, no. 9 (2005): 1097–104, doi:10.4088/jcp.v66n0902; Jiliang Fang, Peijing Rong, Yang Hong, Yangyang Fan, Jun Liu, Honghong Wang, Guolei Zhang, et al., "Transcutaneous Vagus Nerve Stimulation Modulates Default Mode Network in Major Depressive Disorder," *Biological Psychiatry* 79, no. 4 (2016): 266–73, doi:10.1016/j.biopsych.2015.03.025.

30. Harold A. Sackeim, A. John Rush, Mark S. George, Lauren B. Marangell, Mustafa M. Husain, Ziad Nahas, Christopher R. Johnson, et al., "Vagus Nerve Stimulation (VNS™) for Treatment-Resistant Depression: Efficacy, Side Effects, and Predictors of Outcome," *Neuropsychopharmacology* 25, no. 5 (2001): 713–28, doi:10.1016/s0893-133x(01)00271-8.

31. Nahas et al., "Two-Year Outcome of Vagus Nerve Stimulation (VNS) for Treatment of Major Depressive Episodes," 1097–104; Sackeim et al., "Vagus Nerve Stimulation (VNS™) for Treatment-Resistant Depression," 713–28; A. John Rush, Lauren B. Marangell,

Harold A. Sackeim, Mark S. George, Stephen K. Brannan, Sonia M. Davis, Robert Howland, et al., "Vagus Nerve Stimulation for Treatment-Resistant Depression: A Randomized, Controlled Acute Phase Trial," *Biological Psychiatry* 58, no. 5 (2005): 347–54, doi:10.1016/j. biopsych.2005.05.025.

32. Fang et al., "Transcutaneous Vagus Nerve Stimulation Modulates Default Mode Network in Major Depressive Disorder," 266–73.

33. Wiktionary, s.v., "vagus," https://en.wiktionary.org/wiki/vagus.

34. Paul E. Holtzheimer, Mustafa M. Husain, Sarah H. Lisanby, Stephan F. Taylor, Louis A. Whitworth, Shawn McClintock, Konstantin V. Slavin, et al., "Subcallosal Cingulate Deep Brain Stimulation for Treatment-Resistant Depression: A Multisite, Randomised, Sham-Controlled Trial," *Lancet Psychiatry* 4, no. 11 (2017): 839–49, doi:10.1016/s2215-0366(17)30371-1.

35. Nicole C. Swann, Coralie de Hemptinne, Margaret C. Thompson, Svjetlana Miocinovic, Andrew M. Miller, Ro'ee Gilron, Jill L. Ostrem, Howard J. Chizeck, and Philip A. Starr, "Adaptive Deep Brain Stimulation for Parkinson's Disease Using Motor Cortex Sensing," *Journal of Neural Engineering* 15, no. 4 (2018): 046006, doi:10.1088/1741-2552/aabc9b.

36. Auvelty package insert, prescribing information, 2022. Axsome Therapeutics, Inc., New York, NY, accessed September 2, 2022, https://www.axsome.com/auvelity-prescribing -information.pdf.

Index

Page numbers with *t* indicate tables.